THE home zone

THE home zone

MAKING THE
MOST OF YOUR
LIVING SPACE

RYLAND
PETERS
& SMALL

London New York

SENIOR DESIGNER **Paul Tilby**
SENIOR EDITOR **Clare Double**
LOCATION AND PICTURE RESEARCH
 MANAGER **Kate Brunt**
PICTURE RESEARCHER **Emily Westlake**
PRODUCTION **Patricia Harrington**

ART DIRECTOR **Gabriella Le Grazie**
PUBLISHING DIRECTOR **Alison Starling**

First published in the United States
in 2002 by Ryland Peters & Small, Inc.
519 Broadway
5th Floor
New York NY 10012
www.rylandpeters.com

10 9 8 7 6 5 4 3 2 1

Text by Ros Byam Shaw, Caroline Clifton-Mogg,
Leslie Geddes-Brown, Vinny Lee, Fay Sweet, and Judith Wilson.

Library of Congress Cataloging-in-Publication Data

The home zone : making the most of your living space / by Judith Wilson ... [et al.].
    p. cm.
  ISBN 1-84172-267-7
  1. Living rooms. 2. Interior decoration. I Wilson, Judith, 1962-

NK2117.L5 H66 2002
747.7'5--dc21   2001048833

contents

INTRODUCTION

It is a natural instinct to want to live in a home that is comfortable, well appointed, and finished with decorative pieces and colors that add beauty and please us. But, instinctive as this desire may be, getting our home to be more dream and less disaster does not necessarily come easily. It can seem a daunting task.

As with most things in life, the best place to start is at the beginning, but one person's beginning can quite easily be another's finishing line. That is why a book like *The Home Zone* is so useful, combining as it does both the aspirational and the functional side of decorating and designing life. It is a rare individual, other than a professional designer, who understands the practical and the aesthetic in equal measure. For most of us, one element is easier than the other: lighting plans—easy; which lights to have—difficult, and so on. In *The Home Zone*, the first section illustrates some inspirational styles—ideas to give you ideas; the second part takes you through each room in a more concentrated manner; and the third section gets right down to the domestic nitty-gritty, with information on everything from lighting and flooring to window treatments and fabric furnishings. You can tackle large and small projects with equal confidence.

The Home Zone will give you a clarity of purpose that will help to define your design aspirations. I am a great list maker, particularly where anything to do with the house is concerned, and before reading this book it might be useful to note down absolutely all the projects you would like to undertake in your home—large or small, practical or decorative, urgent or still a

daydream. You may not do them all, but you are bound to do some of them and anyway, everything appears less daunting when written down. The further beauty of making a list—or even lists—is that, when ideas are set out on paper, relationships between seemingly unrelated tasks become apparent: repainting the walls in one room, for example, could coincide with rewiring and introducing a new lighting system there; installing a new shower in a previously unused small bedroom might be combined with a new or revamped storage system for linens, clothes, and related objects.

It is important to think laterally about how you want your home to work. Some of us live in spaces that were designed in another time for people who lived very differently to the way we live now, both in terms of how they passed their days, and what sort of decoration they favored. Priorities are different today: try to think of the space in which you live in a broad, total sense, rather than compartmentalized into separate rooms with specific uses; think about how you really want to use the space in terms of how you spend your time when there.

When faced with an empty, unprepossessing room, bear in mind that every room has a

personality—it is up to you to find it. And every room, no matter how uninspiring initially, will have something in it that pleases you—even if it is something very small. Think positive—the room may be narrow, but perhaps it is flooded with morning light; conversely, it may be very dark, but beautifully proportioned.

Another way to make the right decisions is to try to think about a project, and the space available, in the way that an interior decorator would: take nothing for granted, and be flexible about both the layout of the rooms and the furniture within them; decide what you really want and how you want it to work. Most of what you own is movable. Just because it has stood for a length of time in one room or against one wall doesn't mean that it always has to. It might look better in another place in the room; it might even—revolutionary thought here—look better in another room altogether, or with a completely different function; a cabinet that has always been used to hold china and glass, for example, might make a pretty and unusual linen cupboard. Furniture—particularly, of course, old furniture—does not merely have one life or even one use. Your eyes may have got used to its fulfilling a certain role, but that doesn't mean to say that there is not a different life or role waiting for it, and you could be pleasantly surprised with the change. On a more familiar scale, thinking of alternative functions for familiar pieces of furniture is perhaps like rooting around in your wardrobe and producing a new, successful outfit from familiar, sometimes forgotten, pieces of clothing, used in a different way or in different combinations.

Although it is certainly not necessary that every room in a house be decorated in the same style—indeed, it is usually preferable that they should not be—there should always be a visual link between rooms and between any connecting areas. It may be of color or texture, but aim for flow throughout the space rather than staccato movements.

If you are buying new things for a room, large or small, do not automatically reject something on the grounds of its high cost. Very often, the expensive purchase—the beautiful pillow, the handmade door handles—will be the thing that lifts the whole room and gives it a signature. Better by far, in my view, to save money on the utilitarian than forfeit the unique and rare, for they are the things you will always remember— and if you do not buy them, you may always remember them with regret.

If you are by now raring to get down to work, I must inject a word of warning. Working on a house can become addictive. Like those cosmetic surgery junkies we read about, you will often find that when you have tackled one home project successfully, however small it might have been, there wells within you an unstoppable urge to go on to the next. It might be something as small as getting around to clearing out the junk-filled cupboards in the living room, or finally organizing some bedroom curtains that are the right length and keep out the morning light. But beware—if it works, it will be catching. Flushed with success, you will find yourself looking around you with an eager eye for new challenges, and before you know where you are the whole place will be being revamped, recolored, and rearranged.

I have done a few houses myself in my time— sometimes in their roofless entirety, sometimes just a bit of decorative tweaking. Actually, there is no such thing as just a bit of decorative tweaking—once you start, you find more and more things that you are itching to change. Something that I would never do now would be to buy a home that is described as "needing no work": taste is so individual that anyone with even the mildest of opinions on decoration is bound to want to change the status quo. When I first worked on a house, it was done out of necessity, but I realize that it has now developed into a habit—a mild addiction; I say that I could stop at any time, but I wonder. It is a bit like having a baby—wonderful idea before it happens, not much fun while it's going on, but a thrilling and completely satisfying end result—at least, until one starts to see where improvements could be made (in childhood terms, this part is rather like those sweet cuddly babies becoming teenagers). This means that over a period of time—several years usually— I begin to think "Well, perhaps what we really need is this," or "Next time wouldn't it be nice to have one of those," and before I know where I am—and certainly before the other people living in the house know where they are—we are off again, either in the same house or, more often than not, starting again somewhere new. And each time that I do it, I think it will be the never-to-be-repeated best—the perfect home, a machine for living and so on. The house that we have now, for instance, is all I could want— it is pretty, suits us very well, everything works, and it is a pleasure to come home to; and yet, and yet, perhaps the living room could be a bit wider, and the kitchen has always been a little dark... As I say, when you're hooked, you're hooked. But it could be worse—you could be hooked on stripping down vintage motorbikes, or making models of cathedrals from matchsticks.

With a book like *The Home Zone*—indeed, with any source of advice or suggestions on how to renovate and decorate a house or apartment—it is important not to feel daunted by the quantity of advice and suggestions offered. Rather than feeling that all ideas are essential and that in some way your schemes are inadequate if not every part of them has been carried through, think of the ideas more as one of the large banquet menus of the nineteenth century—but service *à la française* rather than service *à la russe*, the former being the occasions on which many different dishes were laid out on the table at the same time and guests helped themselves only to those dishes which tempted them, rather than being offered each dish in succession, as in the service *à la russe*. And, as it is inspiration that is offered here, not commandments, remember that when you study the different inspirational styles shown, although each one is perfect in its entirety, style is in the end a completely personal thing. Many a good room is created using a little of this and a little of that, mixing periods, styles, and color. The important thing is to make sure each room is harmonious, and that everything within it is in proportion with everything else, and, of course, that you are completely happy with it. Hominess is often a rather derided virtue these days, but what it conveys—a home in which you and your family are happy to live and in which you feel comfortable and relaxed—must surely be the most important consideration of all when planning any changes or improvements in your home. So read on and enjoy the experience!

Caroline Clifton-Mogg

inspirational
interiors

SIMPLE & NATURAL

A neutral palette, spanning ice to taupe, and natural textures, from crunchy linen to rough wood, makes this relaxed look easy to achieve. Work with clear-cut furniture silhouettes, choose solids over patterns, and leave ample room for the play of space and light.

The relaxed mood so characteristic of simple, natural rooms has catapulted the look into our design consciousness in recent years. Soothing to the spirit, tranquil to the eye, it's hard to resist the charm of a white-toned interior, unlined curtains diffusing sunlight, pale garden roses in a jar. Yet, while those components are crucial—the crisp white fabrics, textured wood, and stone surfaces—there's scope to personalize. This is a look to dress up or down, according to whim, season, or color preference.

Don't disregard pure simplicity because you have a home jammed with children and pets. It can be immensely practical. White-painted walls are easy to touch up, cotton slipcovers can be washed, and natural surfaces are simple to clean and maintain. This is also a cost-effective look. Precisely because colors are neutral, they won't go out of fashion, so your initial financial outlay will last longer. "Utility" fabrics like duck or muslin are inexpensive, as is basic white paint, and the "distressed" thrift-store or auction furniture essential to the style may be bought cheaply, then repainted or slipcovered.

Opposite below:
Concentrate on pared-down architectural features that contribute to a tranquil mood. This unadorned grate allows the eye to go straight to the beauty of the fire, and the pleasing mix of natural textures, from brickwork to wood.

Main picture:
White walls, cotton slipcovers, and painted boards are essential basics. Enhance the whites' purity by adding minute color splashes. Fresh flowers provide an instant fix; so, too, does one item in a dark contrasting neutral.

Above left: **In a sparse white room, the play of sunlight and shadow has valuable decorative potential. Leave windows unadorned, or choose unlined window treatments, to allow sun to cast graphic patterns on walls and floors.**

Below left: **The natural look is easy to transfer to a modern interior. Stick to the characteristic whites and natural surfaces—slate, wicker, and wood—but choose furniture in boxy shapes.**

When a room is sparingly furnished and decorative details pared down to a minimum, visual emphasis inevitably falls on its bare bones. Take time to evaluate what you have to work with. Of course, elegant sash windows and paneled shutters will give a head start. But it's not a disaster if the room lacks architectural distinction. Adding Swedish-style composite paneling to one wall or laying a reclaimed wood floor can make a huge difference. Replacing a faux period fireplace with a boxy style also sets the right tone.

While a white-on-white color scheme is the basis for the look, consider the natural light in your room before finalizing decisions. Pure brilliant whites may be uncomfortably dazzling in a sunny area, or look too blue in the cooler light of a north-facing aspect. It's also worth remembering that bright white is not the antidote to a naturally dark room: soft-toned grays are a better choice. Whites can range from blue-white to lavender-white,

through to grays, putty, and creams. Not all whites will look good together. For this reason, combine all potential paints, fabrics, and flooring samples in the room to be decorated, to see how they look in varying lights. This will also mean that brighter whites won't make varying tones look dirty.

Walls should be plain, yet that needn't mean flat paint. Vinyl silk paints give off an attractive light-reflecting sheen; then there are subtle white-on-white self-patterned wallpapers. If you want to add texture to a basic white wall, consider painting over tongue-and-groove paneling or bare brickwork; or paint different walls in varying off-whites to highlight natural shadows. For extra contrast, white walls may be combined with one wall in pale pink polished plaster, or concrete. And remember that an all-white room may actually lose its architectural definition. By using several gray-whites for details such as molding, you will enhance the details.

Flooring needs to be natural-textured and pale-toned. If you have good floorboards, use them; even if they're in a slight state of disrepair, it is still worth taking time to sand and repair them. Boards may be waxed, stained, pickled, or treated with Swedish oil and soap to give a pretty bleached effect. Alternatively, paint them in white or gray-blue. If you want a wood floor and the existing boards are past redemption, replace them with reclaimed boards, which are naturally worn in, rather than laying a shiny laminate wood floor, which will look uncharacteristically new. Go for paler woods, such as oak and maple.

In a kitchen, hall, or bathroom, the neutral tones and hard-wearing surfaces of stone floors are practical, from the creamy notes of limestone to gray slate. Consider underfloor heating to take away the chill of stone underfoot. Try to combine a mix of hard and soft floors if you use the natural look throughout your home, but keep to the same tones. Instead of carpet, try knobbly seagrass, coir, or sisal, or, for a bedroom, a softer wool–sisal mix. These days there's a huge choice of colors, from pale honey to gray-green, as well as weaves, from herringbone to giant crunchy knots. Look out for unusual natural options, such as bamboo, which is ideal for a bathroom.

Fabrics should be predominantly solids, in appropriate shades across the white spectrum, from whites and off-whites to natural linen tones or pigeon gray. Look for those with loose weaves and matt finishes, and try to mix a number of different textures, an essential tip for giving interest and lift to lots of solids. Look at cottons, linen, denim, and utility materials like muslin or canvas, from drill to cotton duck. Fabrics for window treatments should be fluid enough to hang in a relaxed way; textiles for slipcovers should look crisp. Although the basis of the simple and natural look is white-on-white, choose a few fabrics that will introduce accent colors. Consider darker grays, biscuit, or soft flesh pinks and Swedish gray-blue.

Fabric furnishings must be well made, and the simpler the style, the more important this is. For windows, if you are not overlooked and have the right architectural features, go for white-painted paneled shutters and eschew curtains. Most of us have more need for privacy, however. Plain blinds, from a white blackout window shade to linen or cotton Roman shades or thin cotton roll-up Swedish styles are all options. Always line Roman shades—in bright light, everything (from rods to

Opposite left: **If there isn't a suitable pale wood table and chairs for the natural look, a dining room is easily transformed with snowy white linen, white china, and glass. The less fussy the tableware shapes, the better.**

Main picture: **Kitchens should be simply designed, with flat panel doors and minimal handles, so the emphasis is on the surfaces. Choose natural stone countertops and floors, and wood or painted wood. Too much white and the kitchen looks clinical. Look out for unusual veneers, such as burl walnut, which looks good with stainless steel.**

Right: **Pale wood units are a versatile option for the natural look. Teamed with stainless-steel surfaces, they look contemporary, or paved with creamy stone counters they appear more rustic.**

Below right: **If a dining room sits between an open-plan kitchen and a living room, choose sophisticated furniture, but in pale, bleached woods. This choice will sit as well with a white sofa as in a white and steel kitchen.**

rings) will show. Curtains need to hang simply: go for tie, tab, gathered, or ring headings, on an unpretentious iron, thin wood, or brass pole. Unlined drapes look great, but for warmth and privacy, add white window shades.

Other fabric furnishings need to be equally informal, and slipcovers, not tight upholstery, are a key element to the look. Have slipcovers cut on the baggy side; the finish is more relaxed, and allows room for shrinkage after cleaning. And give due thought to cleaning, because white covers must be washable or at least drycleanable. Utility fabrics, while cheap and robust, do shrink substantially, and should be preshrunk before being made. Keep slipcover detailing understated, with minimal piping, easy ruffles, and

Opposite above left: **For a truly plain and simple look, dress up the bed in crisp, almost monastic fashion. Regular pillows, and a flat white sheet or bedspread are the only true essentials. Keep clutter to a minimum.**

Opposite above right: **A serene mood is paramount in the bedroom. Go as bare and plain as you dare, using natural light to provide decoration. Here, plexiglass shutters filter light; translucent shades or unlined curtains will also do the trick.**

Opposite below: **A fast-track way to the simple look is to concentrate on symmetry. Positively Zenlike in its pairing of identical pillows, rugs, and bedside tables, this white and taupe bedroom exudes calm.**

This page, clockwise from top left: **The pure and simple bathroom relies on natural surfaces, from limestone and marble to wood and glass, designed along chunky yet sleek lines. Allow for good storage to minimize clutter: pick giant wicker baskets or leather or wooden boxes to introduce more natural textures. Contrast surfaces with contemporary plain white sanitaryware and modern chrome fixtures. The ultimate in simplicity is a wet room, with walls and floor in identical stone. It's easy to get carried away with the monastic mood and forget about comfort. But bedrooms and bathrooms need fluffy towels, plump cushions, and tactile fabrics.**

buttons or simple ties for fastenings. A set of identical white linen or cotton slipcovers is a great way to unify a mismatched set of furniture, or a set of dining chairs. For headboards or the odd armchair, contrast the slipcovers with tight upholstery in burlap, jute, or natural linen.

Furniture should be in natural materials, especially wood and stone. Go for distressed or raw-looking surfaces rather than anything over-polished. Metals, too, make a wonderful contrast to an all-white background: aged finishes like rusty wrought iron, or the faded gilding of a mirror. Yet not everything has to be antique. Contrast the curvier shapes of period pieces with boxy, modern silhouettes and smooth, utility surfaces: a rectangular slate-topped coffee table, perhaps, or the dull sheen of a zinc kitchen table.

When arranging a simple and natural room, the aim is to maintain an air of space and light, without furnishing it so sparsely that the look becomes unwelcoming. So take time to play around with the furniture, until the balance is right. Employ as many tricks as you can to encourage natural light into the room to enhance the white-on-white theme. A big mirror propped against one wall, white-painted floors, and curtains that push right away from the window all help. Precisely because of its simplicity, this is the perfect style to consider in a small room.

If you're worried that the room looks too sparse, concentrate on the subtle details that help it to look lived in. A real log fire, the play of sunlight on a bare white wall, casually placed garden flowers on a table will all bring it to life, as will sensual comforts such as plump feather-filled cushions and a warming mohair throw. And, while decorative accessories should be kept to a minimum, they should work hard to earn their places in the room. Choose personal items that people will want to examine and pick up, anything from a few well-chosen black-and-white family photos, simply framed, to knobbly beach pebbles or giant creamy altar candles. Scale them up, choosing one large bowl over several small ones, but leave plenty of space for the room to breathe —don't stuff every surface. The essence of the simple and natural look is peace and tranquility. It's also the perfect example of less is more.

Top: **Loft apartments are** ideal backgrounds for a sleek and modern look, but their inevitably big industrial windows and high ceilings need a practiced eye to furnish. Work on a large scale, and use the typically long, lean outline of contemporary sofas and tables to balance the space. A curved lampshade or squashy beanbag will soften the straight lines.

Above and right: **You can** create a softer or more masculine take on the modern look using different fabrics and colors on the same basic furniture and surfaces. Above, brown matt wool upholstery and black leather seats are perfect for a bachelor pad; right, a similar sofa, upholstered in white, and teamed with tub chairs, takes on a more feminine note.

Opposite main picture:
Vast expanses of plain wall, teamed with equally plain upholstery, risk looking sterile. This is where contrast of texture helps. Here reflective glass mixes with soft fabric, and polished concrete floors with flat white walls. The play of light can replace pattern, but flashes of bright accent color, either as vases or painted directly onto the wall, will also lift a neutral interior.

Left: **Take care with a gray-on-gray scheme, so it doesn't look either too harsh or too clinical. Experiment with shades from gull white to charcoal, then lift the tones using metallics, warm woods, and glass. If you don't want to add color, black-and-white photography can look stunning with graphites.**

SLEEK & MODERN

Cutting-edge rooms demand boxy furniture, streamlined surfaces, and moody tones from graphite to gunmetal, biscuit to beige. Texture is key. Capture the gleam of glass and smooth stone, touchy-feely leathers, and the confident gloss of lacquer and stainless steel.

Spawned by the cool, empty interiors of late Nineties minimalism, the sleek and modern look isn't one to be undertaken lightly. It's also a consciously urban fashion. Taken to extremes, it offers no midway path; there's no mixing of furniture types, no compromise on styles. This makes it perfect for decorating addicts wanting an excuse to sell their last decade's furniture and start afresh. Yet, if you prefer a more comfortable take on the modern look, there are still plenty of style elements to adopt. And who knows—the mantra of functionalism and order might just rub off a little, and make your home a serene place.

In practical terms, what first appears to be a high-maintenance and expensive look has plenty of benefits for today's time-pressed home owners. With the style's emphasis on hard surfaces, from limestone floors to stainless-steel walls, cleaning is relatively easy, provided you're armed with the correct products and a penchant for buffing. Equally, the top-quality wools, leather, and faux skins for upholstery are robust and less likely to stain. Of course, you can spend a small fortune on solid wood floors and polished plaster walls. But you don't have to. There are plenty of good-looking equivalents like concrete,

This page and opposite above left: **With their flat-fronted cupboards, cubed or rectangular outlines, and pared-down style, modern kitchens need subtle detailing to stop them from looking clinical. Vary cupboard fronts with frosted glass or colored laminate, or by mixing pale wood with white. Under-cabinet lighting can give interest to a plain steel or glass splashback.**

Opposite: **If dining tables and chairs are part of an open-plan living area, they must look good with a sleek kitchen or stylish sofas. Choose modern tabletops which won't need a cloth: laminate, stone, cement, wood, or glass all look stylish and are robust as well. Try no-nonsense seating in modern materials like polypropylene—so you can introduce flashes of color—or aluminum.**

or wood veneers laid over composites, which look similar and cost half the price. You may need to invest in some new pieces of furniture to get the right silhouette, but the sleek look, taken literally, needs only a few key pieces.

As the look is visually dramatic, consider the style of your home before starting off. It's great for lofts, new-built houses, and open-plan urban apartments; less easy to carry off in suburban houses with a warren of small rooms. It's also perfect if all the architectural detailing has been removed from your home because the simpler the background, the better. If you are about to embark on building work, certain details enhance the look. A cavity fireplace, with stainless-steel surround and contemporary fixtures, shadow gaps instead of baseboards, and a run of flush, built-in cupboards are great basics. If you do have ornate moldings or a marble fireplace, it's a crime to rip them out. The clash of ultramodern with period details can be stunning.

Get the surfaces right, and the other details will fall into place. As fabric furnishings play such a small part, you can afford to concentrate on unusual surfaces. Eschew flat surfaces for a sheen or gloss. Essential materials to consider are stone, from marble and limestone to granite; metals, from stainless to waxed mild steel; glass, from toughened clear to sandblasted; and solid wood or wood veneers. Rather than dividing your surfaces into separate floor, counter, and wall categories, think radical. Toughened glass looks as good for a bathroom worktop as, more conventionally, for a shower screen; and stainless steel is as dramatic on the kitchen floor as for the splashbacks. The key is that the surfaces look expensive, even if they aren't.

For walls, you might choose that classic minimalist staple of brilliant-white paint, but there are plenty of other options. For example, glossy lacquer paints are newly available in dark moody colors, or experiment with a

Right: **Stainless steel doesn't have to look masculine or utilitarian in a bathroom. Here, wrapped around the softer lines of an oval tub, it provides a sleek and pretty take on contemporary surfaces. Also look out for oval all-stainless-steel tubs.**

Center right: **Modern bathrooms are designed to be super-efficient rooms for washing, rather than places in which to linger. Keep things functional by wall-mounting your sanitaryware—even the toilet—a particularly useful space-saver for a small bathroom. Pick surfaces that can be used on floors and walls, to give a visually cohesive look, also a useful trick for small rooms.**

Above far right: **The ultimate minimalist bathroom combines glass, stainless steel, and very contemporary fixtures. There should be no clutter, so plan bathroom cupboards behind glass doors.**

Right: **If a connecting bathroom is visible from the bedroom, take care to marry the two looks. Take tips from modern hotel design, and sink the basin into a stone counter, with glass shelves for cosmetics.**

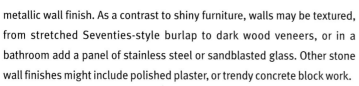

metallic wall finish. As a contrast to shiny furniture, walls may be textured, from stretched Seventies-style burlap to dark wood veneers, or in a bathroom add a panel of stainless steel or sandblasted glass. Other stone wall finishes might include polished plaster, or trendy concrete block work.

Floors and countertops will probably constitute your greatest investment, particularly in a kitchen or bathroom. In recent years, the choice of stone has increased hugely. Limestone comes in every color from soft gray to beige and almost white. Then there's granite, in shiny or honed forms, slate, and marble. For a budget stone look, consider concrete (for floors and counters), or for a matt, city-slicker look, there are rubber floors, from plain to patterned, or linoleum. Wood is also ideal, but go for rich, dark tones, from wenge to iroko, and the wider and glossier the floorboards, the better.

With the emphasis on natural stone and metal surfaces, it's inevitable that the classic sleek and modern color schemes are variations on the monochrome. You can pick from cool white-on-white, mixed with natural tones or with silvery metallics. Or there is the quite masculine palette of gray-on-gray, from graphite and gunmetal to pale blue-grays and off-whites. Soften the monochrome tones by adding in sharp accent colors, from lilac and scarlet, through to burnt orange, deep purple, or citrus yellow, either in a piece of contemporary furniture or used on walls or scatter cushions.

Many a rigorously designed modern interior has been ruined by a sloppy choice of furniture. You simply can't put a leather chesterfield into a modern stone and glass room. Far better to store inappropriate pieces, and budget

for an inexpensive sofa that looks right. The malls are full of good copies of designer pieces. The essential silhouette to choose is boxy and slim; a sofa may be long and low to the ground, or Seventies-style L-shaped, armchairs square, bedheads slick and rectangular. To team with your upholstered pieces, choose glass- or stone-topped coffee tables, the amazingly useful and lean sideboard, and contemporary dining chairs, from plastic to steel. Furniture surfaces may be dark wood, brilliant gloss paint, lacquer, or glass, all with stainless-steel detailing.

Fabrics need to be matt and slick, appropriate for the tight, figure-hugging silhouettes of sofas and chairs. Sleek isn't uncomfortable, however. Think about wool, from flannel to bouclé, and alcantara, leathers, and Seventies-inspired vinyls. Solids are most effective, but the odd graphic, geometric print can look good. The pared-down silhouette extends to windows, too. Choose treatments that are streamlined and allow for light-play: Venetian blinds with metallic or wood slats, perforated cotton shades and sliding Japanese panels. Increasingly, contemporary blinds companies are offering exciting trim options, from crystal beads to leather detailing. Curtains should be sculptural in firm folds of white linen or contemporary metallic or synthetic fibers.

Stick to the basic principles of form and functionalism to accessorize this most urban of looks. If you have cherished accessories, store them in built-in cabinets, and choose instead one or two large-scale pieces: a giant cylindrical glass vase, or a burnished Vietnamese platter. You don't have to spend a fortune on abstract art. Ask an art supplier to stretch a giant canvas, and paint it in muted shades to match your scheme.

Top left: **Look for pared-down furniture in the bedroom. Experiment with low platform beds on steel legs, futon wood styles, or contemporary steel frames. A plain, upholstered divan, pushed up against the wall without a headboard, gives a similarly sleek look. Dress the bed in minimal vein, with tightly tucked-in sheets.**

Top right: **The more clinical the bedroom, the better, so clothes and accessories need to be well hidden in a row of flush, flat-fronted closets.**

Paint them to match the walls, or experiment with sandblasted glass, stainless-steel, or laminate fronts.

Above: **This dividing wall acts as a headboard, an important design feature. Choose either a panel of wood laminate, used on top of composite, solid wood, or a plain upholstered rectangular headboard in a matt fabric. Overscale it to extend high above the bed, and a good foot on either side. For a really functional bedroom, build in wall lights as well.**

Opposite top left: **Let the period appeal of a rustic architectural feature shine, by dressing the rest of the room in plain, simple colors and fabrics. Comfortable details such as a thick padded mattress, cushions, or deep-pile wool rug are crucial, too.**

Opposite center, left and right: **Pick unfussy antique furniture that has a lovely shape, and set interesting pieces against a plain wall to show off a pretty outline. Classic chair and table styles will endure forever, so they are an investment.**

Opposite below: **Mix and match patterns freely. Classic stripes may include ticking, antique or new, deckchair canvas, wovens, or printed designs. For florals, consider embroidered textiles, prints, upholstery weaves, and traditional chintz.**

Left, above and below: **The most successful country interiors combine warmth, comfort, and a relaxed mood. Fresh flowers, books, and candles all add to the ambience.**

COUNTRY & RUSTIC

Relaxed in spirit, naturally tactile, the country look combines warm and faded colors, homespun textiles, and the patina of antique woods. For the classic mix of antique chintz and tapestry, or the cleaner lines of modern rustic, keep things simple and informal.

The traditional country look has been cleaned up of late. Gone are the ruffles and groaning pine hutches, the shiny chintz and the china ornaments. In their places have arrived rustic textiles, hard-working surfaces, and a faded color palette, making the perfect backdrop for the new stars of the country look: pretty antique pieces, from furniture to textiles. No matter if they are distressed or worn; what counts is that they are unique, decorative, and functional. The new look has its roots half in the Shaker ethos, with its clean lines and pale colors, and half in "modern country," the latest preoccupation with sparse furniture and raw, honest textures. The key is that nothing should look too new: instead, the rooms in your home should seem to be naturally evolved and well loved. An informal mood counts most of all. At the heart of any successful country interior is the clarion call to find a sofa, pick up a book, and settle down.

As a decorative style, the country look is guaranteed to be low maintenance and family friendly. If you live in the country, you will already know that an outdoor lifestyle dictates the need for washable floors, upholstery that withstands pet hairs and kids, and warm, cozy window dressings to keep out the chills of inclement weather. If you live in the city, you can still capitalize on that practicality. Country style is also inexpensive to carry off, and its classic looks will endure. Because it relies on a mixture of furniture styles, it's the ideal way to deal with hand-me-down family furniture, thrift-store buys, and possessions collected over the years. You won't need to buy new furniture, just sort through what you already have. And rigorous sorting is crucial. For country style, don't read jumble or clutter.

While the classic country cottage has low ceilings, small rooms, and even smaller windows, making the perfect background for antique rustic pieces, you can still adapt the look for a different property. It will work successfully, in plainer vein, against the taller ceilings and sash windows of a standard row house. Certain elements can even work successfully in an urban loft apartment: an overstuffed, ticking upholstered wing chair or cherrywood farmhouse table provides a marvelous conflict of styles. If you don't have rustic architectural features, it's better to work with a plain room than to attempt to add obvious fake beams or leaded windows. And, if your country property does boast outstanding details, such as a stone fireplace, use them as the visual inspiration for your scheme.

When choosing everything from wall surfaces to furniture, remember that things must look slightly battered or distressed; there's no place for spanking new upholstery or garish gilding. So conserve rather than restore. Look at what you have to play with. There's a definite charm to a nineteenth-century sofa with its stuffing peeking out, to mirrors whose glass is gently foxed, and broad floorboards worn to a slope from generations of passing feet. And if you don't have the real thing, you can always fake it. Many a new pine chest of drawers or door can be given the country look with watered-down vinyl flat-finish paint, some steel wool, and finishing wax.

On walls, you can achieve the worn-out look by using flat latex paint, broken stenciled patterns (large abstracts only, no flowers or leaves) in faded shades, or by stripping off all wallpaper and creating pretty patterns with plaster. If plaster is bumpy, so be it: the contours are part of the country charm. Consider, too, the appeal of painted or unpainted brickwork. Wallpaper certainly fits in with the rustic look, but go for faded

shades and avoid small patterns. There's potential here to use florals, but go for rambling large-scale blooms and use sparingly in a bedroom or bathroom, as the only pattern in the room. Woodwork should always be painted with eggshell, as it has minimal sheen, or dead-flat oil paints, now available from specialized period paint suppliers.

In terms of color, it's not so much the exact shade you pick that matters, but the tone. Fresh pastels or any colors with too much white should be avoided in favor of washed-out or muddy tones. Adding a little black pigment to ready-mixed paints is one way to take the edge off their brightness. Instead of fresh white paintwork, experiment with woodwork in the same tone as the wall color, or choose one of the "old" whites available from specialized paint lines. Historical paint lines are also brilliant sources of muddied colors, ranging from pale stone and lichen shades to salmon pink, moss, and terracotta. And if you're stuck for inspiration, you can't lose if you look out the window. Nature's tones, whatever the season, are guaranteed to provide a suitably earthy palette.

Flooring should be robust, easy to clean, and naturally textured. But it should also be cozy underfoot. The ideal combination of function and comfort is to expose good wood boards or flagstones if you have them, then (for warmth) add faded kilims, sisal mats, or traditional wool herringbone runners on top. Wool carpet is perfectly acceptable in a country home, but save it for the upper floors, where muddy boots are well out of the way. If you pick a neutral gray or beige, then more interesting antique rugs can be

Opposite above: **For the ultimate rustic kitchen, ignore purpose-made cupboards entirely, and store everything from pans to food on an eclectic mix of mismatched, distressed furniture. Look for open shelves, long serving tables to be used as a sideboard, and a mix of chairs. To match the look, the stove should be a freestanding range, and the sink a ceramic one on a stand.**

Opposite below:
The range is an essential part of the country look, so build a relaxed freestanding kitchen around it. Wall cabinets may have wood or painted-wood doors in plain, paneled, or glazed styles. Base cupboards for pans and pots can be combined with a hutch for china and glass. No country kitchen is complete without a central table, either in plain scrubbed pine, or with an oilcloth or cotton cloth on top. Stick to muted colors: soft blues, greens, pinks, and cream, and matt, easily maintained surfaces like tiles, paint, and wood.

This page: **Adopt the habit of eating in the kitchen, and table and chair choices can become more informal. If you have chosen a particular rustic look for the kitchen—Shaker, perhaps—then pick simple furniture that fits the theme. Ladder backs, antique wood benches, old school stools, and French country chairs are all excellent choices. If chairs are mix-and-** match second-hand, paint them in different colors for fun. Tables will most likely be wood, from pine to cherry, or more unusual fruitwoods through to mahogany. With simple, classic styles, the dining room can easily be accessorized with basic chunky plates and glasses for everyday use, or dressed up with a linen cloth and antique ceramics and crystal for dinner parties.

Left and below: **To create a pared-down rustic look, keep to very simple bed and window treatments. Some pattern is nice; stripes give a fresh, crisp finish, or use strips of fabric in a contrast shade to trim a Roman shade, tablecloth, or the leading edge of plain linen curtains.**

Below left: **In the country bedroom, you can layer textiles and use fabrics to dress up the bed. Think about quilts, cushions, bolsters, eiderdowns, and dust ruffles. Layer them on an iron or simple wood bed frame, not a padded headboard.**

placed on top. In a kitchen or bathroom, natural linoleum is an appropriate choice, or terracotta, slate, or limestone. Underfloor heating is definitely worth the investment if you go for stone.

A tantalizing mix of textiles is a crucial part of country style. This is the one place where you can afford to experiment with pattern, and there is a huge choice. At the really traditional end, there are overblown faded chintzes, needlepoints, tapestries, and paisleys, in classic patterns and textures. For a simpler look, choose ginghams, madras cottons, and stripes, from ticking to deckchair canvas. Think about contrasting different textures, from the deep pile of velvet to tight-woven cottons. And mix your patterns with plenty of solid fabrics, which is the key to keeping the country look simple. While floral chintzes look overpowering *en masse*, a single pillow on a muslin-covered armchair has enormous charm. This is a great opportunity to experiment with antique textiles, and don't worry if they have a few holes. Good places to hunt for remnants, from mattress tickings to linen sheets, are antiques fairs and yard sales.

When planning fabric furnishings, comfort counts as much as style. Thick, heavy curtains are a must, whether cozily interlined, or assembled from a tapestry or blanket flipped at the top to create a valance. Hang drapes from heavy wood or brass poles and rings. Keep to plain and simple cotton or linen Roman shades, or traditional cream window shades to team with curtains. Use wooden shutters if you have them, and if the look seems too

Left: **You can create a very pretty country bedroom without masses of florals. A decorative metal bed, sophisticated painted furniture, and voile curtains are the essentials.**

Above: **The paneling and fresh blue and white of American country style are perennially popular. Patchwork quilts, bordered pillowcases, and crisp white linens are basics.**

Right: **A practical bathroom floor could be lino, vinyl, sisal, or carpet. Walls may be painted or tongue-and-groove. A rolltop bathtub is a must, but sanitaryware doesn't have to match. Restored period pieces (and faucets) have more character.**

sparse, hang gauze or voile panels in front for softness. Steer a course between a mix of tight upholstery—upholstery nails can look very decorative teamed with simple fabrics like cotton duck or ticking—and baggy slipcovers. If a sofa has seen better days, gently drape a quilt or needlepoint panel over the back of it. Battered leather chairs are increasingly popular as part of the modern country look, and look especially fetching with faded floral cushions.

When arranging furniture, aim for an unusual mix of different periods of furniture, and styles, from Louis XV gilt to Victorian buttonback chairs. Combine country fruitwoods with painted, distressed pine, cast iron with upholstered pieces, or marble tops with scrubbed pine. Don't overstuff rooms; instead, allow enough space to enjoy the contours and textures of each piece. Once you're confident creating that casual mix, extend it to the kitchen and bathroom. For the rustic look, it's much more fun to abandon the idea of an off-the-peg design, and treat these functional rooms as any other: a freestanding bathtub, kitchen range, or cupboard is infinitely more appropriate and welcoming than a built-in design.

Employ restraint when it comes to filling rooms with possessions. Of course the country look is all about bookshelves stuffed with books, kitchen shelves piled with plates, and family photographs in the foyer. But try to pick out just the prettiest things, and keep the rest for a rainy day. Remember that "country" has widened its brief, so that in among the flower-sprigged china and botanical prints there should be some surprises: chunky creamy ceramics, distressed terracotta pots, and twigs from the backyard, plopped into the milk pitcher.

Right: **Choosing the right furniture silhouette is vital. Look for sofas with curved backs and deep, sweeping seats, boxy little Thirties-style armchairs, round and oval stools, and elongated, slim tables. For cushions, slim rectangles and round and bolster shapes are all appropriate.**

Below left: **Gilded metal furniture featuring knot or looped details, curlicues, or squiggles suggests salon chic. Such details might be found on lamp bases, mirror frames, glass-topped tables, or dressing tables. Stick to burnished effects rather than vulgar bright gilding.**

Below right: **The truly elegant drawing room has more than its fair share of symmetry. Twin sofas, a pair of chairs each side of a fireplace, or artwork arranged symmetrically are all possibilities.**

Left: **Daybeds are vital pieces in the contemporary elegant living room. Reminiscent of Thirties boudoirs and salon style, they may be boxy and modern, or sinuous and curvy; what matters most is that cushions and bolsters are plump. Use one as the focus of a chic drawing room.**

Above: **Shapes and colors needn't all be curvy and pale to make the mood elegant. As long as natural light is soothing and well controlled, and fabrics tactile, boxier outlines will work. Expensive-looking leathers, suedes, and lacquer do the trick here.**

For this combination of salon chic and fresh modernity, team luxurious textiles with curvaceous furniture, decked out in pale tones from shell to pistachio and ice blue. Think elegance, symmetry, and subtle glamour.

CONTEMPORARY ELEGANCE

Above: **In among proper sofas and armchairs, add smaller salon-style chairs, from Louis XV armchairs to velvet-covered pouffes and lyre-backed gilded chairs with satin seats. Chosen not so much for comfort as for the way they set a mood, they can be decoratively covered in anything from a remnant of hand-painted silk to plain linen with an embroidered monogram.**

Hovering between the sophisticated textiles and tailored shapes of the twenty-first century, and the signature glamour of the Thirties, this style is elegant yet accessible. Not to be confused with its younger sister, boudoir style, this may be a look consciously adopted by anyone "growing into" a second or third home, and perfect for pied-à-terre city life or singletons minus pets or kids. Even in a family home, grown-ups could adopt the look for the adults' bedroom. While it's not exactly style on a budget, and is distinctly high maintenance, it has its compensations. Whether you view it as couture home style, or the interiors version of immaculate grooming, it's set to keep us on our toes, vacuum and duster firmly in hand.

With its signature pastel colors and silky fabrics, this look gives the impression of being expensive, yet there are cost-effective ways to recreate a similar luxury feel. Quite apart from the ruinous cost of real silks and animal skins, it's worth investigating sophisticated, synthetic equivalents because they look just as good and are drycleanable to boot. These days, you can even find washable suedes. If you don't want to bypass at least a dash of real silk—on cushions, perhaps, or to upholster an occasional chair—then invest in stain-guarding. You can also conjure up an extremely elegant look by adding one or two key luxury pieces to an essentially bare, restrained room.

We all know the film-star charm of a high-ceilinged upstairs drawing room, sweeping staircase, or pairs of tall French windows, and if you have them, they may inspire you to try contemporary elegance. Some studios, for example, boast such features because they are part of a remodeled house. If your rooms are more modest, you might take a marble fireplace, parquet floor, or simpler French windows

Left, right and below right: **Kitchens can also match the style. Sleek, expensive-looking surfaces include glossy granite, marble and slate worktops, unusual wood veneers from maple to walnut, and plenty of sophisticated black. Keep appliances and taps functional yet smart in stainless steel.**

Below: **Dining chairs can also feature sophisticated, curvy outlines. For a smarter look, choose upholstered, waisted chairs in moleskin, suede, or linen (but think first about how they will be cleaned). Everyday, yet supremely elegant kitchen-dining chairs include the classic Arne Jacobsen 3107 chair (below), whether in bleached wood or its many pastel varieties.**

as a starting point. And even if you are beginning with four basic white walls, remember that salon chic is determined as much by textiles and furniture shape as by architectural distinction.

The quality factor is crucial. Finishes must be immaculate, and plumbing first rate. Doors should snap shut with a satisfying thud, and carpets should feel soft underfoot. If you're on a tight budget, you might invest in a few quality fixtures—a giant antique mirror, for example—and keep everything else simple. As a tranquil mood is essential to the look, invest in great lighting so that ambience is easy to control. Plan for a selection of uplighters, downlighters, and table lamps, controlled from a single switch and with a dimmer. Pretty lamps with cone or waisted silk shades, ornate metal wall lights, or angled downlighters, to highlight art, are all options.

Surfaces should be either very matt or reflective, and the best look has a good mix. For the reflective style, consider fondant-colored walls overpainted with opalescent washes, a ceiling stuck with silver handmade paper, or metallic wallpapers. For matt, choose wallpaper with sophisticated stripes, pale damask patterns, or abtract designs such as bamboo. Fabric, from padded and battened linen to silk, may be used on walls. Then there are wood veneers in exotic woods like burl oak or walnut, or mirrored paneling.

For floors, pale wooden boards or traditional oak parquet are highly appropriate. Although this is a style with its roots in plains, a wood floor can be successfully dressed up with a pure wool rug in a graphic design. Or buck current trends and lay a pale neutral carpet. Sisal–wool mixes are another option, as are the more expensive but very chic linen and Brussels weaves. For sophisticated bathrooms, pale limestone, marble, or ceramic tiles in a traditional black-and-white checkerboard are good choices.

The strongest theme for color is neutrals, especially shades of ivory, bone, and pearl combined with darker chocolate and mocha. But look too at "neutral colors," which are paler than true sherbet shades, and range from pinkish beige and shell, through to eau-de-Nil, lilac, and celadon green. Good accent colors might be plum, graphite, or metallics. When picking fabrics, don't restrict color to cushions: there's something unashamedly luxurious about a prettily colored sofa or occasional chair in palest silk.

Top left and right:
To create the right mood in a bathroom, at least a sliver of marble, polished granite, or limestone will help, if only for a bathtub or basin surround. It may seem a large investment, but you can buy inexpensive plain white sanitaryware to go with it. Consider elegant options for faucets. Either choose state-of-the-art chrome fixtures or period-style faucets and shower mixers—and avoid gold-effect versions.

Center left: **Read luxury for contemporary elegance, and create a bathroom that looks and is indulgent. Details such as choosing a bigger-than-normal bathtub, placing it in the center of the room, or adding two basins, will make all the difference. Great lighting in a bathroom feels luxurious, too. Instead of overhead downlighters, install uplighters or lights on each side of the mirror for the most flattering makeup illumination.**

Center right and right:
A bathroom-dressing room is a popular trend. Consider sinking bowl-style basins into a continuous countertop, either marble, glass, limestone, or solid wood. Drawers and cupboards beneath the counter can hold everything from towels to bathroom essentials. If a counter isn't an option, pretty and glamorous basin styles include bowl-effect basins, from glass to stone, on simple stands.

Opposite, clockwise from top right: **Inevitably, the bed is center stage in the elegant bedroom. It needs to look very luxurious, crisp, and well-proportioned. First consider the headboard. Leave rounded, padded types for clear-cut rectangular styles; the taller, the better. Upholstery can be anything from neutral linen to moleskin or suede; choose these in preference to harder-edged wood styles. A tailored dust ruffle is also essential on a divan, with neat knife pleats at each corner. Either match the dust ruffle to the bed, or choose a contrasting fabric. Create a truly indulgent bed with plenty of pillows, including square continental ones, and make sure linen is pin-neat in crisp cotton, linen, or with hemstitch details. Eschew fat, bumpy quilts in favor of a flat bedspread, and add a tactile throw, perhaps in mohair or cashmere, neatly folded. Keep bedroom colors to a cool, neutral palette, with touches of pale pink, lilac, or chocolate for extra sophistication. A long, low bedroom stool at the end of the bed, upholstered in animal skin, creates a final glamorous touch.**

Fabric texture is key. In addition to silks and satins, consider linen, velvet, and moleskin; suede, leather, and faux animal skins are also excellent. Experiment with a good mix of textures—cashmere curtains teamed with organza inner curtains, perhaps, or a zebra faux-fur throw lined with pink satin. Let yourself be indulgent when choosing textiles. Curtains may go in two directions: either tailored, sculptural folds, perhaps with pin-tucking or contrast edging at the hem, or hanging full and loose. If you're using silk, check if it will fade (many of the cheaper silks do). Hang drapes from narrow metallic poles, perhaps with curlicue finials, or from fabric-covered valances, Thirties style. Shades should be sheer; shade-makers now have a good selection of sophisticated synthetic fabrics, or find a specialized company that makes shades from delicate fabrics without needing lining.

The whole point about contemporary elegance is that furniture should have beautiful sweeping silhouettes and plenty of curves, so plan fabric furnishings to give a mix of figure-hugging tight upholstery, and tailored slipcovers featuring corner pleated skirts, and minimal detailing. Think

Above: **A four-poster bed is the last word in elegance, but you need to choose the right style. Steer clear of very ornate designs or overpowering fabric hangings, and choose instead painted wood, decorative metal frames, or a contemporary, Shaker-style four-poster in pretty, warm woods such as cherry. This white bed is tranquil.**

Center: **The right mix of lighting is particularly important in bedrooms. Try a number of wall lights and bedside lights, operated from a central switch with a dimmer, rather than overhead lighting. Reading lights should be at the correct height to give a powerful beam. Choose metal, fabric, or parchment shades in simple cone or waisted shapes.**

Right: **Clutter is out in the contemporary elegant bedroom, so make sure you have enough storage for clothes and personal items. If necessary, think about banishing closets to a spare bedroom, to keep the master bedroom clear. In addition to the bed, another essential is a comfortably plump, well-upholstered daybed, armchair, or small sofa.**

about cushions: long, bolster styles and pilule shapes are particularly appropriate. Try to get a contrast of furniture shapes, from the more contemporary long, lean silhouette to the elegant curves of antique pieces. No living room or bedroom, for example, is complete without a contemporary daybed, a couple of Louis XV salon-style chairs, and squishy, upholstered stools. A glass-fronted drinks cabinet is also fun. Other furniture needs glossy finishes—lacquer or highly polished wood—or curly metal detailing, whether on a decorative floor lamp or a mirror frame. Glass and mirrors, with their glamorous reflections, are also essential, from an overmantle mirror with gilded frame to glass chandeliers or a mirrored dressing table in Thirties vein.

Accessorize contemporary elegance with a confident hand, but keep it simple. A large sculpture or collection of period glass will look more arresting than many smaller objects. Give thought to what hangs on the walls. Contemporary art or symmetrically arranged paintings, in soft colors, will mix well with the elegant furniture. Don't restrict yourself to the living room; great art looks good in a sophisticated bathroom, too. Try to lose the clutter. If at all possible, place technology, from TV to CD, in a cabinet and books behind closed doors. And pick flowers carefully—go for tall stems and luscious scents, from glamorous lilies to roses.

Left: **You can achieve striking decorative effects simply by juxtaposing the clean, simple lines of one piece of furniture, perhaps a sofa, with the more romantic curves of an older, eclectic find.**

Below: **Mixing old and new doesn't have to mean blowing your budget on precious antiques or expensive designer buys. With the increasing interest in twentieth-century classics, just as enjoyable a mix may be achieved by gathering together an Eames classic, Sixties bubble chair, and assorted other styles.**

OLD & NEW

There's fun to be had in the mixing of old and new, creating idiosyncratic looks that can't be bought off the peg. Highlight the clash of antique and modern with quirky decorative touches, or throw it into sharp relief by contrasting with a simple, pure interior.

We all recognize the appeal of a home in which the owner has mixed old and new with a confident eye and daring spirit. Because the result is unique, we are by turns intrigued and inspired by it: each room offers a visual surprise. This form of decorating also allows for a highly personal interpretation of style. The freedom to mix across historical periods and decorative categories, without feeling bound to follow any rules, is guaranteed to provoke exciting new looks. Even better, you can mix and match as little or as much as you like. Combining old and new can be done modestly, by juxtaposing one or two quirky antique accessories in a room, or on a grand scale, taking over a whole house. Aim for a fun, experimental mood, but to avoid the Miss Havisham cliché keep a tight rein on clutter. Mixing old and new is all about constant change, so when you bring the next great discovery home put something else away.

Provided you have a well-developed sense of what you like, or the enthusiasm to experiment, mixing old and new is one of the easiest and most relaxed looks to achieve. As it is all about trial and error, you won't make mistakes, just discoveries. Many a well-respected decorator and antique dealer will admit to constantly rearranging furniture in a room to achieve the right mood, or to delivering a crazy piece of furniture to a home, just to "look and see." This is also one

of the most user-friendly styles to fit in with a busy or family lifestyle, since nothing is too precious. What matters is its decorative appeal. "Old" doesn't have to mean antique—instead, it can be defined as junk or secondhand—and "new" doesn't necessarily mean expensive designer acquisitions; it can just as easily mean a furniture-sale bargain from a chain store, or an interesting hardware purchase from around the corner.

When planning decorations to go with eclectic furniture and accessories, first decide if you want to create a blank canvas for the blend of your possessions. Of course, the most gallerylike choice will be white walls, wood or sisal flooring, and natural upholstery. But you can make changes here. Walls might be painted a vivid color; flooring could be textured stone or rubber in a strong shade, because a funky backdrop will still throw possessions into sharp relief, and make them fun to live with. What counts is that the decorations don't tie the interior to particular pieces; you're aiming

Above: **Mixing old and new decorative styles and periods can look truly original. It often helps to keep a theme in mind. Here the room takes an ethnic motif— for furniture, decorative accessories, and rugs.**

Right: **An all-white background, and neutral flooring and upholstery, throw the emphasis onto an elegant mix of antique and modern pieces. This is a very natural, relaxed look.**

Above: **Highly functional kitchens often lack character. Just by choosing a theme—here, old weighing and measuring equipment—the most frequented room in the house is transformed into the most interesting. This combination of catering-style stainless steel and antique wood promotes a relaxed and fun mood.**

Left: **Sometimes, the architecture of your home will provide decorative cues or links. Here, the giant industrial-style light fixtures cross the divide between minimal white kitchen and spacious loft apartment.**

to create a classic backdrop for an ever-changing selection of things. And pieces don't need to "match" the architectural vocabulary of the house, either. There might be an exciting contrast in an elaborately carved eighteenth-century door panel, propped in a contemporary interior, or a giant beanbag placed against Colonial wood paneling.

In direct contrast to the gallery effect, you might choose an exotic mix of furnishings, and use the decorations themselves to create a clash between old and new. Consider twenty-first-century finishes—a metallic wallpaper or polished plasterwork—contrasted with a Gustavian-style armchair or a marble-topped washstand. Or reverse the process using traditional patterns and fabrics. You might choose a *toile de Jouy* wallpaper, combined with Sixties plastic dining chairs, or a lounge-lizard modern sofa, complete with built-in computer terminal, set next to antique chintz curtains. If you don't want such a direct juxtaposition, choose unusual, textural wall and floor treatments that will add just a touch of exoticism to each room. A leather-

Below right and left: **Choosing classic white bathroom fixtures, and neutral surfaces, from white tiles to wood boards, frees you to add old or new touches. Great with classic white are gilded distressed mirrors, muslin-covered armchairs, or mirrored retro side tables; or try a bright polypropylene or metal bathroom cabinet or a funky set of scales.**

Above: **The ultimate freestanding kitchen follows no style guidelines, yet it helps to pick a theme. In this kitchen, disparate fixtures, from the retro refrigerator to the work table and ceramic sink, work because of a strong utility theme and the continuity of the pure white color scheme.**

Left: **A classic, very simple kitchen can be accessorized with contemporary fixtures or antique accessories according to fashion. This mix of white-painted units, tiled floor, and marble top will endure for a decade.**

tiled or colorful Moroccan-tiled floor, burnished metal wall, or *trompe l'oeils* on cabinet doors would all do the trick.

If you prefer to restrict matters to mixing old and new furniture, then you can do so in many different ways. Choose all pieces in one color and finish; for example, all white or all cast iron. With upholstered chairs, unify many styles from contemporary to antique using a single fabric: Schiaparelli pink cotton will look as exciting on a Victorian slipper chair as on a modern seating cube. You can also categorize by shape—square pieces, curvy ones—or by a theme. In this way, for example, a kitchen might be personalized with a huge collection of kitchenalia through the ages. And don't forget to rethink your definitions of "old." Instead of going for real antiques, you might want to stick within the twentieth century, searching out modern classics to set against this decade's trends.

Sometimes the inclusion of just one or two items from a very different decorative period can be enough to turn an ordinary interior into something spectacular. This can work either way. An ultramodern white and stainless-steel kitchen might benefit from the addition of a scrubbed wooden table, teamed with contemporary chairs, to take the sterility off the design. More conventionally, interior designers frequently add the clean lines of a modern plexiglass table to a room full of traditional antiques. Similar results may be achieved with accessories. The surprise of a hi-tech lamp silhouetted against an oil painting, or a stone bust as the only decoration in a sleek and functional limestone bathroom, can have extraordinary appeal.

However consciously you mix old and new together, the resulting look will, by definition, be the most personal and comfortable style to live with. It's the natural progression of every home, however carefully tended and revamped, to gather pieces from different periods. In turn, such a style allows you to be constantly on the search for new finds, and—because the look is so eclectic—you won't need to abandon one style and start afresh with another. For the interiors fan, that's surely the best excuse ever to shop.

Above: **Although a bold mix of styles is always arresting, it takes time and effort to get right. Picking one or two large objects to draw together disparate pieces is a good starting point. This might be a great piece of art or an unusual furniture piece. In this bedroom, the artwork is the central focus for an eclectic mix of glass table, wooden bed, and retro leather chair. It's a great style if you like to gather favorite things in your bedroom.**

Above left: **Sometimes, it's not so much the mix of old and new styles that creates an impact, as the surprise of placing a beautiful antique piece into a simple white interior. Here, the dark wood and pretty outline of the bed look fresh and distinctly contemporary.**

Above right: **The decorative frame of an antique bed can be "dressed" to create different moods. Hung with antique textiles and decked with lace-edged pillows, this bed might look over the top. But accessorized with classic, fresh white linen and crisper textiles, it takes on a fresh, modern look.**

Left: **Don't be afraid to experiment with an antique bed in a contemporary interior. Using an old design is often the way to engineer a truly romantic mood. The process works in reverse, too. A steel-framed four-poster, set against Colonial paneling, will have a similarly stunning effect.**

room
by
room

kitchens & eating areas

The kitchen is the engine room of a home. It is where the practical business of storing and preparing food takes place, but in recent years it has also diversified to become a dining and family room as well. This important space should be carefully planned so that it is an efficient yet enjoyable and welcoming place to be.

Far left:
Most standard units come in a limited choice of sizes. Mix these regular units with specially made ones, freestanding furniture, or features such as shelves or wine racks to achieve a neat fit in your space. If your kitchen is open-plan or doubles as a dining area, a display of decorative items will play down its practical side.

Left: **A galley-style kitchen, with cabinets either side, focuses attention on the dining area beyond, but also allows the kitchen to gain natural light from the window. Glazed ceramic floor tiles also help to reflect daylight.**

Opposite main picture: **Practical work surfaces need not be dull: this industrial corrugated steel is attractive but also hard-wearing.**

Planning your kitchen

Before planning a kitchen, it is important to identify what sort of space you really need: family-friendly, for example, or designed for cordon bleu cooking? Analyze the area available and your lifestyle. Start by thinking about what type of kitchen will suit your home and your needs. How many people will use the space? How will they use it? Are you a working, single person who mainly eats out, or does the kitchen need to double as a playroom and dining area? How many people would you like to be able to seat? Then, take a piece of paper and a pencil, and map the outline of the room, marking in the solid features such as windows and doors, and also the utility outlets. Next sketch in the machines and equipment you need to install, keeping in mind whether or not they need to be near water pipes and electrical sockets.

The basic guideline to planning a kitchen is to achieve a "work triangle." The points of this imaginary triangle are where the sink, stove, and refrigerator are positioned. These features should be separate, but within easy reach of each other. The triangle gives you easy access between the main work areas in the kitchen, enabling you to cook in comfort. In most cases, the triangle will need to give a little, depending on the length and configuration of your walls. The triangle may also have to bend to work around the main thoroughfare or traffic route in the kitchen. Ideally, the main route of access and exit to and from the kitchen should not intercept the work triangle because this will interrupt the flow of activity—and may lead to accidents if people are crossing the path of a cook with a hot pan in their hand.

Opposite, top to bottom:
Good storage planning will pay off, and in small kitchens every nook and cranny will be needed. Pivoting shelves reach the back of a corner unit; useful but attractive lengths of link chain provide storage for frequently used tools without blocking the window; niche storage for dry goods and books.

Opposite: **Color is a practical, effective way of taking the hard edge off a steel or industrial-style kitchen, and is useful for giving a dual-purpose room a more relaxed feel. Here hot orange warms the cool blue of the metal facades and accessories.**

If the room is large, a central island or work station will help break down the distances between each point. In a family room, you may find that a sturdy dining table can double as additional work surface. Another alternative is to have tall stools around an elevated work surface so it can also be used as a breakfast bar or casual dining area.

At the planning stage, aim to position appliances with similar functions together: for example, dishwasher, sink, and washing machine are best kept near each other so all the plumbing and wet work can be conveniently grouped. It's useful to have the fridge and freezer together, too. Not only are their functions compatible, but it will also make unpacking shopping easier.

Where possible, these chilling and freezing machines should be positioned away from hot machines such as stoves, and tumble dryers, which might affect their cooling functions. If a fridge does have to be placed next to a wall-mounted oven or a stove, place an insulating panel between the two. Most modern machines should be adequately insulated within their casing, but an extra panel is a worthwhile precaution.

When looking at machines and appliances, take into consideration not only the space that you have available in the kitchen, but also the way you cook. Do you honestly need six burners, an oven, and a broiler, or do most of your meals go in a microwave? Are a double sink and drainers necessary if you have a dishwasher? Try to achieve a sensible balance of space, machine size, and capacity.

Storage is also important, but again consider how much you really need. You'll need more shelf space if you are a once-a-month supermarket shopper, less (but more fridge space) if you buy fresh food two or three times a week.

Safety and hygiene are priorities in a kitchen, with its hot pots and pans and sharp blades, and mix of raw and cooked foodstuffs. Make sure the area is uncluttered and easy to move around in, and that there are plenty of suitable surfaces for resting hot pots and preparing food with sharp knives, as well as a nonslip floor surface and work surfaces that are easy to clean thoroughly.

Top: **Solid cabinet doors make small kitchens look smaller. Clear or opaque glass, mesh, or reflective surfaces such as polished steel or punched panels can have the opposite effect. If you choose glass, make sure it is laminated safety glass for kitchen use.** Pale wood surrounds and white walls also add to the feeling of space and light.

Above: **In this long, narrow kitchen, a trolley is useful for transporting ingredients and taking flatware and china from the sink or dishwasher** to its home or the table. Simple door and drawer handles provide a good, easy grip and suit a streamlined galley style like this one. Avoid ornate styles: they can be difficult to grab with greasy hands, and will also be troublesome to clean.

Above: **In this kitchen there are two dining options—a snack or breakfast facility at the edge of the island unit, well away from the heat of the stove, and a more traditional table and chairs in the center of the room.**

Right: **There are two distinct eating areas here: the long table and bench for family dining, and a small pull-out table for a single diner. The pull-out table can also be used as an additional serving station or a place to prepare vegetables. It is designed to roll neatly back into a niche in the unit, and the front is edged with a matching drawer facade so it is camouflaged when not in use. The bench and table will push back against the wall to save space, too.**

Kitchen-diners

Kitchens that double as dining spaces have to be versatile and therefore well planned. They need to accommodate the practical kitchen functions as well as the more relaxing and sociable process of dining, and be adaptable so they function for both family meals and, if there is no separate dining room, for more formal entertaining.

The main rule is to make sure the dining table you choose is a suitable size for the space. Diners need to be able to push their chairs back and move comfortably around the table without knocking against surrounding cabinets and machines. Remember to site the table far enough away from heat sources such as stoves and ovens, so that diners do not become overheated (or even burned). And, ideally, guests should face away from the pile of pots waiting to be washed.

If your kitchen is a modest size, use a small table or a foldaway style with flaps that can be set up when required,

so that it won't dominate the kitchen when it is not being used. If possible, extend a countertop to make a breakfast bar, with stools tucked underneath. For more generously sized rooms, larger tables, with removable leaves or insets, can also be useful since they will provide plenty of working space for the room's kitchen role, but can be reduced in size for smaller or intimate meals.

If the surface of your table is wood, or other material vulnerable to scratches or marks, cover it with plasticized cloth or a similar protective, easy-to-clean surface for cooking, preparing food, or feeding young children. Otherwise, choose a practical melamine or laminated tabletop. This can always be covered with a linen or cotton tablecloth to give a less utilitarian feel when you entertain.

Lighting plays a very important role in changing the mood of a room like this. For example, task lights directed over work areas can be dimmed or turned off for dining and

Main picture: **The stylish mid-twentieth-century chairs, with their curving backs, become a decorative feature in these simple surroundings. A freestanding cabinet, displaying glassware, gives a more homey aspect to the room.**

Above: **Pale wood chairs and table complement this white kitchen. White is the perfect shade to make a kitchen feel crisp, fresh, and clean, while dishes and utensils displayed on open shelves keep the room from looking too clinical.**

Left: **A round table makes a welcome change from the straight lines and angles of most kitchen units, and in theory you can seat more people around a round table than a square one. Although the kitchen scheme is simple, the blue chairs with their rattan seats inject a spot of color and soften the overall appearance.**

a softer ambient light with a decorative lighting feature, such as candles, centered on the table. For family mealtimes or busy breakfasts, lighting needs to be stronger and more targeted, so an adjustable hanging light (with a dimmer switch) can be a useful option positioned directly over the table.

Decoration also plays a vital role in accommodating the two activities. Above all the decor should be practical, and surfaces durable and easy to wipe clean. Storage should be plentiful so the bulk of kitchen gadgets and utensils can be stowed away out of sight when dining is the primary function of the room.

Simple decorating schemes generally work best in a kitchen-diner. Aim to plan decoration to make a functional and hygienic base for the kitchen, then add extra flourishes when you lay the table for dining. A bright cloth, glittering glasses, and china and flatware can all be used to build up decorative interest on the table. In smaller spaces, aim for a sympathetic decorative scheme that will link the dining and kitchen functions rather than exaggerate their different uses. For example, if you have a hi-tech steel-clad kitchen, the dining furniture should be contemporary and in a similar style or finish. In a traditional scheme—for example, a painted and wood kitchen—the furniture should be complementary in style, with perhaps country-style wood chairs with rattan seats and a classic sealed wood table as the focus of the room.

Good ventilation and an extractor fan are necessary to make a kitchen comfortable for eating (and, of course, cooking) in. The buildup of steam from boiling water and pots, the heat from broilers, stoves, and burners, and the aromas of cooking food can make a room overheated and stuffy. If the room is not adequately ventilated, the heat and smells will linger. A good hood and extractor fan over the burners are a great asset, and louvered windows or window vents will also help reduce steam and heat.

Above and above right: **In a small kitchen without space for a freestanding table, this folding, pull-out surface, which has a matching drawer facade, is an ideal snack bar. The surface is made in two sections, that double back neatly, and slides back on steel runners. The variety of tones in the natural slate flooring, laid in a diamond pattern, brings together the colors used in this scheme— the cool silver of the stove and storage jars, the soft blue of the cabinets above, and the pale brown tone of the wood.**

Left: **This island unit doubles as a breakfast bar, and the stools provide a comfy perch. The island has been picked out in pale yellow-cream that contrasts with and separates it from the green units behind. It also forms a barrier between the working kitchen and the rest of the room, so the kitchen is visually self-contained in this open-plan space. To prevent the strong color from becoming overpowering, there are areas of plain white wall and ceiling, and the floor is covered with light, speckled polished granite.**

In many homes the kitchen's role has expanded to incorporate a number of other functions. It is no longer just for food preparation and dining, but also accommodates children's play, TV watching, and general relaxation. In new homes the kitchen is generally built larger than it was thirty years ago, and in many older homes owners have extended their kitchen, often with a light-filled conservatory-style room, or knocked down an internal wall to create a larger all-purpose living space. In loft developments—perfect for open-plan living—people make the most of the openness, using temporary dividers, such as folding or movable walls, to define or enclose areas.

As with kitchen-diners, good ventilation is vital in these larger rooms. Although steam and water vapor will generally disperse, smells and moisture may linger; and if you have upholstered furniture, curtains, or other fabric furnishings near your cooking area, they may absorb moisture and smells, as well as grease, which can cause damage and staining.

Storage in multipurpose spaces should be generous. It can also double as display, so groups of glasses or matching plates become part of the overall appearance of the room. Try to allocate storage so it is specific to the function of that part of the room. This reduces muddle and will also cut down on journeys from one area to another. Kitchen storage should cope with foodstuffs and washing equipment; the dining area needs cabinets to hold dishes, glass, table linen, and flatware; and the living area requires a section for books, magazines, and home entertainment items.

In an open-plan kitchen, different functions will need different lighting: task lights for food preparation and cooking, perhaps under wall-hung cabinets and over the stove, and softer background lighting for the table. Areas can also be defined by rugs, mats, or flooring finishes. For example, the cooking area could have a utilitarian tiled or slate floor,

Open-plan kitchens

Opposite far left: **A wall of open shelving, painted bright yellow, contrasts with the neutral tones in the rest of the room. The shelves have been constructed around narrow windows to provide a view and also to allow natural light in at counter level.**

Opposite center: **Color has been used here to play down the industrial look of this steel kitchen and make it compatible with the multi-purpose room.**

Left: **Here an island unit doubles as a breakfast bar and casual dining table, to be used with adjustable wooden stools. It also forms a useful barrier between the working part of the room, with the sink and oven, and the entertaining area.**

with the dining and living sections based on a softer, warmer wooden floor. Rugs can also bring a softer feel to a dining or sitting area. (If laid over a polished wood or similarly shiny surface, they should be placed on nonslip backing.)

Open-plan and multipurpose kitchens are popular with families because an adult can prepare a meal while still being able to see and talk to other family members or guests, while small children can be kept out of danger—but still easily visible by an adult—in a play area separated from the kitchen by a child gate or screen.

Above: **In this converted factory, an industrial-style steel-clad kitchen is softened by a leather daybed and simple, classic furniture in the living and dining area. Although there are three distinct functions housed here, each has its own defined space.**

Left: **In this L-shaped room, the main dining and living section occupies the longer leg, while the kitchen and casual eating areas are in the more compact end. This configuration contains the kitchen neatly, although it is still part of the same room. Color has been used to link areas and define their uses: the red leather seats of the Fifties chrome stools link with the more formal skirted covers on the dining chairs.**

Island kitchens

A kitchen "island" is a freestanding, usually central, block of countertop. Island kitchens revolve around this station and are usually spacious rooms where the island acts as a central point between the three points of the work triangle.

The shape of the island varies—it can be square, rectangular, or even curved. It may be decorated so it stands out as a feature from the rest of the units and scheme, or it may be finished to match the overall scheme. Well-finished edges are important; they should be smooth and rounded so they do not catch on clothing or hurt passersby.

The island itself is a very flexible piece of furniture. The simplest model may be a food preparation and storage

Opposite above:
The rounded end of an island unit is extended beyond its base to create a simple breakfast bar deep enough for informal meals. This kitchen's built-in storage with sliding, rolltop panels keeps the majority of the kitchen machines and gadgets out of sight but still easily accessible.

Opposite below: **In this large kitchen, the island unit contains a sink and forms part of the work triangle between the large refrigerator and the stove. It is also a good way of reducing the distances between one side of this spacious room and the other; it provides a central point and work surface, cutting down on walking around while cooking. The gleaming copper pans give the room a decorative focus.**

block on wheels. A static plumbed and wired version offers other options. The area beneath the counter can be left empty, fitted for storage such as drawers and cupboards, or house machines, perhaps a dishwasher or even a second fridge. The top can be inset with burners or a griddle. With sockets the island can be a work station for anything from food processing to coffeemaking.

Another advantage is that an island can be raised to provide an area that is comfortable for you to work at standing; taller and smaller people are therefore not restricted by standard-height kitchen units. Alternatively, some standard units can be raised on adjustable legs, and to add extra height a butcher's block or thick chopping board can be set into a recess or surround (to stop it from slipping) on the surface.

The true working area of an island unit, especially a large or square design, is around its edges. The central part may not be readily accessible, but it is an ideal point over which to hang pots and pans—the area will not be in direct contact with or at head height of a person working at the unit, but it and any hanging utensils are still accessible by an outstretched arm. But remember that pots and pans left on display in a central area like this will be a feature—so they should be good quality and perfectly clean.

Top: **This unit has a flush facade with recessed handles so a person can work close to it in comfort. The work surface overhangs on the other side; a stool could be stored underneath here, to pull out when needed. The below-surface storage contains herbs and** spices used for cooking on the burners above. Storing them in the unit makes seasoning easy. Pans hang overhead within reach.

Above: **This island creates a corridor on one side while providing a work area for the kitchen on the other.**

Freestanding & country-style kitchens

When installing a kitchen, one of the first questions you have to ask yourself is whether you want it to be fully built-in, freestanding, or a combination of both. Built-in kitchens are often the best option in small rooms because they can be tailored to fit into every available inch, so maximizing your counter and storage areas.

Freestanding kitchens give you the flexibility to add and subtract pieces of furniture as you go along or as your budget permits. In addition, you can take the furniture with you when you move, whereas built-in units stay in place. You may opt for a bit of both, built-in units containing appliances such as the sink, which has to be plumbed in, and wall-mounted stoves that need to be wired and vented, with freestanding furniture in between.

The mix-and-match option is also a cheaper way of redoing an existing kitchen. Instead of ripping everything out and starting from scratch, you can leave a number of the existing units, such as those containing appliances, in place. You can then choose to replace other units, or fill in any spaces, with freestanding furniture. The latter two configurations create very personal kitchens because they are individually devised. Built-in kitchens are

Below: **A Scandinavian-inspired setting has a modern double oven and burners, but both are vented through a traditional-style chimney.**

Top right: **Hutches can be created by hanging a row of shelves on a wall over cupboards. You could use standard cabinets below and** custom-made shelves above. The unit doors may be painted *trompe l'oeil*-style to give the impression of paneling, or gain a decorative border, nailed to the door and painted.

Above: **A light curtain makes a softer option than solid doors.**

Above right: **Cream is a good background color for displaying china against. It is also warmer and less stark than pure white.**

Opposite above left: **Checkerboard patterned floors are classic and work well with many styles. The old enamel stove adds a rustic touch to this setting. All vintage equipment should be reconditioned and checked before use.**

Opposite above right: **This modern kitchen is designed to look old. The paintwork has been rubbed to give a worn look, and the units echo traditional country style.**

Opposite below: **This kitchen has been constructed from a variety of furniture, most of which is finished with matching handles.**

generally bought from a manufacturer's stock selection and are configured in a uniform way, although you can customize standard units with decorative details or by adding different door handles.

Freestanding kitchens are generally associated with the country look because the rustic kitchens of times gone by were essentially that, made up of a couple of cupboards, sometimes a hutch, and a good, solid wood table. Function was the order of the day, although hutch shelves were sometimes arranged with a display of best china or other decorative tableware.

As a rule, the country look remains loyal to natural materials. Wood plays a key role, as do stone and terracotta flooring and plain, glazed ceramic tiles. But this particular

decorative style is wide-ranging because it comes from many countries. If you want to play up Mediterranean influences, introduce stronger hues and a primary color—red, blue, or yellow—mixed with liberal amounts of white. For Scandinavian overtones, try a palette that has a gray tint, elegant lavender blues, and soft mossy green.

American country style is most widely associated with the beautifully simple Shaker look: well-made, practical paneled cupboards with round wooden knobs, peg rails, and walls painted white or off-white. Cupboards are usually painted cheerful colors such as cranberry red, medium blue, and yellow-green.

Neutral country style means cream, or warmer tones with more yellow, and natural wood. This background is warm but not overpowering, so you can add decorative accessories, pretty fabric, or china. The kitchen will be a perfect, uncomplicated backdrop for these items.

Country furniture is usually wood—painted, stained, or waxed. The pristine fresh look of painted furniture is ideal for some styles, but others need a little more character and age. Painted surfaces can be rubbed with sandpaper or steel wool, giving the corners a worn appearance as the wood peeks through the upper layer of paint. Bear in mind that wood needs to be waxed or sealed to protect it from wear, and always use a chopping board on your wood table. This is protective and easy to remove for washing.

Another aspect of the freestanding and country-style kitchen is that you can find great pieces of furniture if you employ a little lateral thinking. A ceramic sink can be countersunk into a small wooden table, which will also double as a sink surround. An old chest of drawers, perhaps with a couple of damaged drawers, can be adapted to form the base of an island work station, and a section of a broken marble tabletop or a butcher's shop countertop can be adapted to form a perfect meat-chopping or pastry-rolling surface in a household kitchen.

Opposite above left:
The flue of this stove has been vented out through an existing chimney, but the opening has been sculpted in an unusual shape.

Opposite above right:
A selection of furniture has been assembled to form this kitchen. The sink, resting on top of a set of shelves, is plumbed in beneath wall-mounted faucets. Blue paint makes the scheme coherent.

Opposite below left:
Vintage patterned tiles mix with plain contemporary ones to form a splash protector.

Opposite below right:
Existing features such as an old painted cupboard and stone floor provide a source of inspiration for this decidedly rural look.

Top right: **A reclaimed stone sink resting on brick pillars is easily incorporated into an arrangement of freestanding units.**

Center right: **An old wood table is positioned to form an island unit. The style and color of the table complements the existing antique fireplace.**

Right: **Ceramic tiles can be beautiful as well as useful. Their easy-to-clean surface has made them a long-standing kitchen favorite. Here they soften a kitchen in modern traditional country style.**

Left: **This central beam shelf is a useful and decorative storage feature.**

A room to relax, read, or party in, the living room must
be all things to all people—flexibility and beauty are just
the start. The smaller it is, the harder it has to work,
so plan it minutely and it will pay you dividends. Add
soothing colors and all your favorite things.

living rooms

Planning your living room

For the lucky few, the living room is a dedicated sitting room, a tranquil space for winding down in, even a cool style statement in terms of the objects and furniture on display. But for the greater majority, it is the nerve center of the home, where family life, TV-watching, computer-shopping, and socializing coexist, day in, day out. The living room is a harder working room than most of us realize. So give it due attention. Plan it as carefully as the kitchen or bathroom, and the whole family will reap the rewards.

Before you do anything else, take a mental trawl through your lifestyle and ask some salient questions. How much time will be spent in the room, and what activities will go on there? What favorite possessions do you want to show off? What needs to be stored? Where is technology to go, from TV to CD? If you entertain frequently, can space be rearranged

easily? Finally, pay attention to mood. If this is the one room where you can relax, be sure there is excellent control over natural and artificial light, sound, and comfort levels.

Correct furniture arrangement is paramount. Good planning means you can watch TV in comfort (because there's a coffee table nearby), and chat easily with friends (because the chairs are close enough). Careful space management may even squeeze in enough room for a separate seating area for quiet reading or card games. See whether there is a natural focal point in the room, be it a fireplace or a great view, because incorporating that into a scheme can be a useful decorative starting point. It sounds like a cliché, but drawing a scale plan of the room and cutting out scale shapes of existing furniture really will help. In terms of human traffic flow, remember that space between

furniture always seems less once it is translated into three dimensions, so err on the generous side.

Plan where to house the technology at the outset, and the room will look slick. It's not an issue whether or not the TV is on show, but do try to conceal trailing wires. On-show options include purpose-built trolleys (often on contemporary castors), plastic cubes (so the TV seems to "float"), and a wall-mounted folding arm (useful in tiny spaces). Alternatively, conceal "the box" within a built-in cupboard, low sideboard, or in a purpose-built alcove, so only the screen is on show. The video player doesn't have to sit directly below the TV and is more practically stored in a cabinet next to the stereo, near the videos and CDs. If you

Opposite: **A real or real-effect fire is a natural focal point, and always worth the investment. Match mantelpiece styles to the rest of the room. Don't be sentimental about keeping a period fire surround if your look is contemporary; replace it with a modern hole-in-the-wall style.**

Below: **When different living areas coexist, simply facing seating away from the dining table can be just as effective as a physical division.**

Left: **When planning furniture layout, think through every possible living-room activity. Is there a light and low table by a reading chair and an armchair by the phone? For entertaining, is there room for extra seats, and places to put drinks?**

Below left: **For the ultimate contemplative living room, devoted to music, books, and conversation, pare everything to the minimum. Let the visual focus fall on a great view and stylish furniture.**

must have a computer in the living room, screen it carefully from the main sitting area. And save rewiring the house with built-in speakers for the next move. Instead, paint existing speakers to match the walls, or disguise them in a wicker basket on top of a shelf unit.

Good lighting can make or break a living room. If possible, replace central hanging lighting overhead—it casts ugly shadows—but don't do away with overhead lighting altogether. Every living room needs the option of bright light sometimes. Strategically placed downlighters not only provide ambient illumination (add a dimmer, so you can control the level), but may be angled to cast specific beams over paintings. Plan for more side lights than you think you'll need, and put all lights on a central switch with a dimmer. Don't forget task lighting, for reading, and a smattering of styles to add decorative interest.

Controlling natural light is equally important. Everyone longs for a sunny living room, but if sunlight is too dazzling, consider screening it with translucent shades, Venetian blinds, or plantation shutters, alone or in addition to curtains. If the room is naturally shady, place at least one chair and table next to a window to capitalize on daylight.

Choosing a style and refurbishing is the exciting part, but give great thought to your budget. A living room demands investment pieces of furniture, from sofas to bookshelves, not to mention yards of fabric and the almost ruinous cost of having fabric furnishings made. It can be an expensive business. So try to compose a classic scheme that will endure over at least a decade—thus helping to spread the cost—which can be updated with trendier accessories.

First look at what you have. A couch can be reupholstered in a new fabric, or a battered table given a new, distressed paint finish. If buying a new sofa, try to pick an enduring style—antique ones are often the best—that can be given contemporary upholstery. And if you need new curtains, consider ready-mades. There are some great, inexpensive styles in chain stores. Remember, it's always better to invest in a good curtain or slipcover maker and use a budget fabric, than the other way around.

Go classic, too, when choosing the colors and surfaces of the room. A neutral color scheme, wood or sisal flooring, and hard-wearing fabrics, from linens to wool, are the order of the day. A neutral background provides the best backdrop for pretty possessions and art, and is easily updated with fresh splashes of color. Don't be afraid to make the living room the most sophisticated room in the house, particularly if you like to entertain. A gilded mirror or precious painting will set the right "public" tone and be enjoyed by everyone.

Main picture: **Plan good storage for a hard-working living room, so that books, magazines, and videos can be cleared away quickly. Anything dual-purpose, from a coffee table with drawers to floor-level cabinets that support the TV and a dining-work table, will help the room work harder still.**

Opposite above: **Zone a small living space correctly, and it becomes dual-functional. Create two separate living-work areas with back-to-back storage units or a desk butted up to a sofa. Squeeze bookshelves into every corner.**

Opposite below and below: **There are various devices for separating areas without compromising the spirit of open-plan living. A change of floor levels, simple wall divisions, or a subtle shift in furniture style or color—plastics versus leather, primaries contrasted with neutrals —also creates changes.**

Zoning your living space

Above: **A neutral color scheme helps to unify, rather than demarcate, zones within an open-plan apartment. This means the space looks bigger, and it's a flexible arrangement as furniture moved from one zone to another will suit either setting.**

In a small home, where rooms must be dual-functional, or in a loft or open-plan apartment, in which a seating or dining area will be just one of several activity zones, it's essential to define "living space" boundaries. Everyone needs to know there's a specific area for relaxing. The demarcation may be anchored physically, using partitions or by the placement of furniture, or visually, using color to define areas.

Either way, think first about the flow of human traffic. In a small home, locate the living area in a quiet spot, away from busy access routes from front door to kitchen, or the playroom to the staircase. In an open-plan space, locate sofas well away from central kitchen and play areas, and nearest to the bedrooms, for guaranteed peace. When kids are around, this also cuts down on stray sticky fingers.

If construction work is an option, there are myriad ways to divide zones. Mezzanine floors and raised platforms are particularly suited to lofts or radical remodeling. If you are knocking down walls to create an open-plan space, leave some sections, to create natural divisions between spaces. Or replace walls with a glass brick or sandblasted glass wall. More flexible options include traditional double doors, pivoting or fold-back panels, or sliding canvas "walls."

A carefully placed U- or L-shaped seating configuration is the simplest way to define a living space; alternatively, try two identical sofas, facing each other, with a central coffee table. These arrangements mean you are sitting looking inward, so they feel instantly cozy. Contemporary sofas lend themselves particularly well to specific groupings, as many are available as modular units to rearrange.

Do remember that while furniture can, and will, define a space, silhouettes shouldn't be so bulky as to destroy the view through an open-plan area, or fill up too much space in a small room. Choosing low sofas, substituting a daybed for a sofa, or swapping a boxy armchair for a slimmer one can all help. One of the most common problems in an urban row house is how to unify two halves of a knocked-through living room. By putting sofas back to back in the center of the room, you will create two well-defined seating areas.

Color is a powerful tool. In a white-painted loft with wooden floorboards throughout, the living zone might be highlighted by painting the wall nearest to it in a bright or pastel shade. Alternatively, matching colorful upholstery for chairs and sofa will set the zone apart, perhaps in direct contrast to monochrome natural materials and furniture used elsewhere. Bold accessories can also be a defining influence. Think about cheerful abstract rugs in blocks of color, a painted wall canvas, or bright metallic bookcases.

If you prefer not to have striking contrasts, then keep all furniture, from sofas to dining chairs, firmly within a monochrome palette, so the eye travels easily across an open-plan space. This also allows more freedom for moving furniture as the mood takes you. In a small house, a strict, muted color scheme also avoids jarring contrasts.

Tailored lighting also helps "zone" a space. In an open-plan apartment, try to have downlighters on a different circuit to, say, the kitchen area; otherwise, the sitting area will look too brightly lit. At the very least, put in a dimmer switch. You can have fun choosing lighting for specific areas. Centrally arranged downlighters will pool light onto a specific seating spot. Inset floor lights can lead the way to a sitting or dining area, or a string of tree lights can encircle it. Within the zone, play around with options of glowing side lamps, wall lights, floor lamps, or bright task lighting.

Opposite: **If space permits, provide two separate seating areas: one for conversation or television, the other a quiet space for reading or listening to music. Unify both using an identical color scheme. In a large room, several clusters of seating help the room seem intimate.**

Below left and right: **If sitting and dining areas are squeezed into a smaller area, arrange furniture so it doesn't impede the view across a room. Low furniture, glass or clear plastic tables, and woven or wire chairs all create the impression of space and light.**

Below: **Conversions of industrial buildings into homes call for the creation of ingenious multipurpose living spaces. Experiment with mezzanine levels, platform rooms, and internal "pod" rooms within a large space. When dealing with a totally open-plan environment, always try to sandwich the dining area between kitchen and sitting area; no one, however neat, wants to relax right next to dirty pots and pans. Here, a cohesive color scheme, boxy silhouettes repeated throughout kitchen, dining room, and sitting room, and cleverly concealed TV area all create a simple, streamlined living space.**

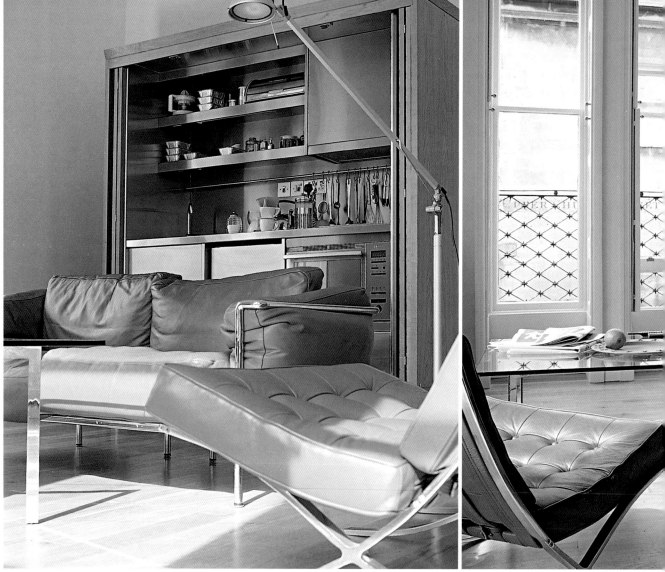

Compact living

Most of us have less living space than we would like, and some, from row-house owners to studio dwellers, are especially space-challenged. Yet squeezing a relaxing living area into a one-space home often provokes creative solutions. Accept that your living space needs to be flexible, practical, and utterly neat, and you've won half the battle. Also remember that in a small space everything, from the kitchen to the front door, is on display. So either decide that's acceptable, or figure out ways to hide certain features.

In open-plan homes, choose a unifying decorative theme in terms of color and surfaces. In a small space, there's little point in zoning; the emphasis should be on cohesion. This not only simplifies the look, but also helps blur boundaries between different activity areas. Adaptable surfaces, which are as appropriate in a kitchen as in a living area, include wood, glass, stainless steel, and leather. With these, pick a neutral scheme: classic all-white or—if you want color—no more than three specific shades, to avoid visual confusion.

Think about choosing dual-purpose and flexible furniture. A daybed can double as a sofa, a coffee table with drawers becomes a storage unit, a fashionable seating cube acts a side table. Stacking dining chairs are also a boon. Rather than one huge sofa, consider two mini sofas—a design much beloved by contemporary furniture designers —or a number of armchairs teamed with a daybed. Stick to similar furniture styles throughout. You need to be able to mix and match different pieces across the whole area, so aim to choose chair styles, for example, that look as good tucked under the dining table as positioned next to the sofa.

If you're not comfortable having everything out on show, investigate ways to separate living and work areas. Kitchens are difficult to disguise, but—provided you stick to a minimal galley—may be hidden behind purpose-built folding glass or composite doors, sliding painted or wallpapered panels, or pivoting metal or glass doors. Avoiding structural changes, freestanding bookshelves and mobile screens can create a suitable barrier. Face living-room furniture away from the kitchen, preferably toward a pretty window or fireplace, and each area will take on a well-defined mood.

Above left and opposite:
It is often better to put up with an open-plan kitchen as part of one large room than ruin its proportions with a solid dividing wall. Galley kitchens are easily disguised behind sliding screens or folding doors. If you adopt the minimalist look, match cabinet fronts to those in the living area—blurring the boundaries between work and relaxation zones.

Above top and bottom:
Not all divisions need to be solid. In this relaxed interior with eclectic furnishings, plain white cotton and voile drapes are an enticing alternative, and can be tied back or let down to create impromptu screens between bathroom and sitting area.

Opposite: **Allow for the possibility of changing displays according to the season or your mood. Paintings propped on shelves or on a mantelpiece have more flexibility than wall-hung versions; set aside a few simple frames that may take fresh images or photos from time to time.**

Below: **Open shelves running the breadth of fireplace alcoves and chimney breast provide a fresh take on the conventional cupboard and shelf option. If you are storing papers or photos on open shelves, give a cohesive look by choosing attractive files or storage baskets: cardboard and wicker are good choices.**

Left: **Plain walls create the best background for displays of contemporary art. Work out the best picture arrangement on the floor first, and measure appropriate gaps before you hang them on the walls.**

Bottom: **Create "invisible" storage by building a fake wall 20in (50cm) or so from the original wall. Then use the space to build a series of different-sized cabinets with flush doors, or inset storage alcoves.**

Storage & display

However busy it becomes in reality, the living room should have the potential to look and be tranquil and neat. That's why great storage is crucial. Long before deciding on storage styles, think long and hard about what really needs to be stored in the living room. Depending on the size of your home, it may be possible to relocate certain items—old photos, perhaps, or out-of-favor CDs—to the attic or basement. If space is tight, have regular clearouts. Things you keep in the living room should be items for enjoyment only—music and books, treasures and mementoes.

Built-in storage has the advantage of being tailormade to suit your possessions, from book heights to TV size, and can match your chosen decorative style. Try to think beyond the conventional option of a bookshelf and cupboard in each fireplace alcove, which makes a room smaller. Closed storage options include a whole wall of paneling, with individual doors that pop open to reveal cupboards, small alcoves inset into the wall — which hold everything from the TV to a vase — or shallow cupboards, wall-mounted or built into an alcove, with frosted glass or plexiglass doors.

The advantage of freestanding storage is that it goes with you when you move. Don't just think of bookshelves: other options include mix-and-match units offering shelves and cupboards, traditional chests or storage ottomans, or, less conventionally, a sideboard or map chest. Inside each item, provide easy access to items like CDs and videos by placing them in cheap plastic racks, and keep bulky things such as photo albums low down so they are easy to lift out.

Above and left: **You can build bookshelves into many alcoves—under the stairs, around a door, in a redundant fireplace or, conventionally, flanking a chimney breast. They needn't be painted white:** match the colour to the walls for a more integrated look.

Opposite: **For a contemporary look, arrange books vertically and horizontally on simple open-ended shelves.**

Opinions differ as to whether books should, or shouldn't, be included in a living room. In a very elegant room, many colorful spines may spoil a decorative scheme. In general, however, books add a lived-in, comfortable air. Don't just fit bookshelves into an alcove. Shelves can be fitted around a door, open shelves mounted just below the ceiling, or spanning a bare wall. Spend time arranging shelves neatly; otherwise, books quickly look messy. And they don't have to be book-filled. Several modern shelves, with a broad front edge, look fabulous propped with framed family portraits.

The best living rooms bear the personality of their owner. So collect favorite things in here, from serious art to stones gathered on the beach. Less is more in terms of display. A mantelpiece may need only a cluster of ceramic vases to look good. (Don't rely on flowers to enliven a room, as they are not always available in winter.) Pay attention to picture display, too. Instead of dotting paintings around the room, hang a cluster on a single wall — infinitely more arresting.

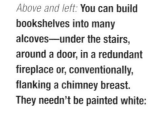

Creating the comfort zone

A peaceful and cozy ambience is the prime objective in any living room. In pursuit of this, choose comfortable furniture that helps everyone relax. Look for deep seats, high arms that will support the head if lounging, and well-stuffed seat cushions. A daybed is great for listening to music, a wing chair ideal for reading. If choosing new upholstered pieces, never be embarrassed to stretch out in the store: everyone has their own comfort priorities. Look for a mix of scatter cushions. Fat, feather-filled ones are great, but a sturdy bolster or neck-roll shape is helpful for reading support.

Color, more than any single object, will affect the room's mood. Try to think beyond fashionable shades, and pick a scheme that is soothing, relaxing, and will endure. A neutral base is safest, but go for the warmest neutrals you can, favoring pink or yellow tones of taupe rather than gray, creams and flax shades rather than pure white. If having color is a priority, it is cheaper to put it on walls rather than on upholstery; walls are easier to repaint or repaper. Go for tranquil soft pastels, from putty pink to Swedish gray-blue, or really deep tones of terracotta, ocher, or olive.

And give due attention to flooring. Despite the lack of softness underfoot, many people still prefer the stylish look of floorboards, rather than picking carpet. Think about your lifestyle. If you're the type to sprawl on the floor, or you have young children, then laying a wool rug over the boards in the central sitting, TV-watching area is ideal. There's a huge

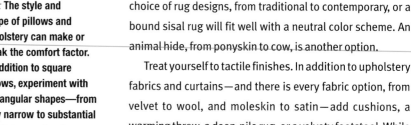

Left: **The style and shape of pillows and upholstery can make or break the comfort factor. In addition to square pillows, experiment with rectangular shapes—from very narrow to substantial versions—and go for squashy feather-filled ones. The same rules apply to upholstered furniture. Avoid over-zealous upholstery that's straining at the seams.**

choice of rug designs, from traditional to contemporary, or a bound sisal rug will fit well with a neutral color scheme. An animal hide, from ponyskin to cow, is another option.

Treat yourself to tactile finishes. In addition to upholstery fabrics and curtains—and there is every fabric option, from velvet to wool, and moleskin to satin—add cushions, a warming throw, a deep-pile rug, or a velvety footstool. While a daybed with fabric hangings, or a curvy deep sofa with lots of cushions, provide obviously romantic-looking living-room options, even hard-edged contemporary furniture will seem cosseting when teamed with the right textiles.

In pursuit of that all-important ambience, gather together as many tools as you can to create a tranquil mood. Low lighting, the flicker of firelight, deliciously scented fresh flowers, and plenty of candles are just some essentials.

Opposite above and below: **Warm, rich wall colors impart an instantly cozy atmosphere to a living room. Experiment with shades from terracotta to scarlet and warm ocher to chocolate brown. Balance the vivid walls with neutral upholstery, flooring, and window treatments.**

Above: **Combine a variety of light sources to create ambience. Firelight, candlelight, and mood lighting from table lamps provide the basic mix.**

Above right: **The living room should contain your favorite things, and the more exotic and personal the mix, the better. Experiment by mixing original art, hand-painted textiles or lampshades, and antique textiles.**

Right: **All the best living rooms have a quiet corner for contemplation, be it a luxurious daybed or an armchair close to the fire. Include a table for books and a coffee cup, decent task lighting, and plenty of pillows for comfort.**

From childhood we dream of a room of our own—a private place, an escape from the noise and demands of other people. As adults, we may choose to share this intimate space with the one we love, but our bedroom remains a personal retreat and a place to feel safe.

bedrooms

Opposite: **In this studio, a single spacious room is bedroom and living room, united with a subdued palette and clever choice of spare, multifunctional furnishings. The bedroom area, partially hidden by a flexible wooden screen, is lined with a discreet floor-to-ceiling closet. The bed can be folded up into the wall during the day, to maximize living space.**

Right: **Japanese-style screens pull across one end of this loft to make a private, wood-lined sleeping area. The bed is raised on a wide platform to emphasize its status as a special and separate place within the expanse of wooden flooring.**

Below right: **An antique sleigh bed is dressed in ruffle-edged cotton with a canopy of gauze, for pure romance in an intimate small bedroom.**

Small bedrooms

When we are sleeping, we are vulnerable, and our instincts still dictate we sleep most soundly when feeling most secure. Far from being a disadvantage, a small bedroom can increase that sense of security, cocooning us within its walls as if safe in a nest.

A small bedroom, well organized, can be as satisfying aesthetically as it is practical. Bedroom necessities are few: a bed large enough for sprawling, with a mattress relatively hard or soft according to taste; a table or shelf on either side of the bed; lights designed for bedtime reading; closets and chests for clothes; a couple of hooks on the back of the door for robes. These are the essentials and, with clever planning, they can be fitted into a space not much bigger than the bed itself.

The most efficient way to utilize space is with built-in furniture. Most small bedrooms have at least one wall that can be filled from floor to ceiling with a closet. To maximize every bit of wall space, it is usually worth commissioning made-to-measure woodwork if at all possible. In an old house, for example, closets may fit best on either side of a fireplace. When planning hanging space, always make sure it is deep enough for a wooden clothes hanger, plus the bulk of the garment hanging on it, to move freely without scraping against the back of the closet or the door. Trying to give yourself a few more inches of floor space at the expense of the closet is a false economy that will irritate ever after.

Beds can also be built in and designed to incorporate invaluable storage in that dead space underneath, which is otherwise the preserve of fluff and children playing hide-and-seek. A simple wood plinth, extended at the top to provide bedside shelf space and with a mattress laid on top, makes a stylish bed for a modern room. Wall lights, as opposed to table lamps, leave more space for books, alarm clocks, and water glasses.

There are two decorative routes for a small room: one works to create the illusion of space; the other makes a virtue of necessity by emphasizing its inherently cozy, enclosing qualities. The first demands coherence, plain pale colors, and a lack of clutter only possible with ample closet, shelf, and drawer space. A color scheme of neutrals and naturals is soothing and not quite as demanding, or potentially dazzling first thing, as brilliant white. Don't forget the power of mirrors—unrivaled for magnifying light and volume, as well as being invaluable for checking whether your slacks are the right length. Sliding mirrored doors can look sleek and contemporary while giving the illusion that a room is twice its real size. Using mirrors to panel small areas of wall and alcoves can make even the most cramped space feel bright and airy.

Fabrics, whether bed linen, curtains, or rugs, provide the softness and texture that are essential to the feeling of comfort in a bedroom. Blackout roll-up or Roman shades take up less floor and wall space than curtains, and are good for a pared-down look. If, however, you are going for all-out coziness, there is no better way to promote it than with acres of drapery, be it wafting voile or heavy folds of linen. Fabric can even be used to line the walls, stretched on strips of wood like a soft, slightly textured wallpaper. A patterned fabric will draw the walls in around you, making you feel thoroughly cocooned and insulated from the outside world. Using the same fabric for walls, curtains, and bed hangings helps to give decorative coherence to a small bedroom which might otherwise be overwhelmed by too much pattern.

Far left: **Foldaway beds used to be ugly, uncomfortable, and needed two people to raise and lower them. Modern versions are elegant in looks and operation.**

Above left: **One solution to sharing living and sleeping space is the bed that can simply be rolled and folded out of the way, like this combination of tatami mats and futons.**

Above center: **This apartment has been divided into zones by a combination of shelving, storage, and screen walls, that partially enclose the sleeping area. A cool chain-link curtain provides a hazy view through windows beyond and a modicum of privacy.**

Opposite above right: **A big bed, tucked under the eaves, makes a bedroom both snug and welcoming.**

Right: **Skillful use of mirrors, here in the closet and a wall panel to its right, create the illusion of space.**

Above left: **Extra space in a bedroom means you can afford to have pieces of furniture that are more beautiful than useful, like this sculptural and decorative stepladder.**

Left: **Space also means you can accommodate oversized furnishings like this theatrical bed, with its elongated posts, flanked by generous side tables and large lamps to match.**

Spacious bedrooms

Space is always a luxury, and bedrooms should be luxurious spaces. The joy of a large bedroom can be the opportunity to use it for activities other than just sleeping and dressing. If your rooms are large, but few, you may be tempted to devote a corner of your bedroom to work space. But sharing the place where you sleep with a computer and an in-tray is far from ideal. Most of us prefer to escape from work for the night, even if only from the physical reminders of it. A bedroom should be reserved for quiet, private relaxation— writing letters at a small desk, reclining on a chaise longue to watch television, or reading in a comfortable armchair.

Empty floor space gives you the freedom to play with the arrangement of furniture. Placing a bed in the middle of a room can look very dramatic, for example. Armoires are freestanding, and you can indulge in the old-fashioned convenience of a spacious dresser with three-sided mirror. You could even create a walk-in dressing area with screens or partitions. And, if there is still room to swing a handbag, you can add purely decorative pieces, a screen or a pretty stool, or you could even install a beautiful bathtub.

The idea of making use of your bedroom during the day is far from new. In the eighteenth century, it was polite for society women to entertain friends in their bedrooms. Modern notions of privacy tend to preclude such intimate hospitality, but a large bedroom can still have the feel of a boudoir—a room you can retire to at any time of the day. Your spacious bedroom can become private study, salon, or even living room, if you choose.

Above: **Space in this airy, modern bedroom just seems to go on and on, through the wall of windows, onto the balcony, and into the distance beyond the trees. The pair of chairs, placed to make the most of the view, are an invitation to indulge in leisurely conversation.**

Top far left: **White-painted walls and floorboards maximize the light and volume of a huge bedroom** in a warehouse conversion where you would be tempted to put on your rollerskates to go to the bathroom.

Top center left: **A handsome antique copper bathtub on a raised platform at one end of this bright room looks like a particularly inviting place for a long soak. Placing a bathtub within a bedroom can be an elegant solution if you don't have enough space for a connecting bathroom.**

Top center right: **The unconventional positioning of the bed between two windows, instead of pushed against a wall, gives this room drama and focus.**

Top far right: **High ceilings are a license to go to town with light fixtures, whether your taste is for traditional chandeliers or something more unusual, like this futuristic spiky ball.**

Right: **This exotic, oriental-style four-poster with its high mattress has something of the feel of an old-fashioned box bed. However cavernous the surrounding space, lying inside its wooden frame you would feel as snug as a child in a den.**

Opposite above left:
The extra-large bed in this spare, modern interior is raised off the ground on hidden legs so it appears to hover, inviting you to float to sleep as if on a magic carpet.

Opposite above right:
A four-poster bed without canopy or curtains has instead a mosquito net suspended above. It could be draped over the posts as a diaphanous tent.

Opposite below left:
A folding wooden screen and a sizeable bedside table help to mark out the territory occupied by the bed in this loft conversion. Table lamps providing low pools of light contribute to the feeling of intimacy.

Opposite below right:
Although placed against a window, this bed offers a sense of protection, thanks to its curved headboard carved from a massive piece of wood.

Creating intimate spaces

Nowadays a sense of intimacy and privacy is particularly important to us in our bedrooms, and as much as we may value the aesthetics of large, open-plan, multifunctional rooms, the territory occupied by our bed demands special attention. The person who can sleep soundly on a mattress in the middle of a ballroom is a rarity. Such exposure makes the rest of us feel a little insecure.

Creating a cozy bedroom space within a larger room need not entail curtains and posts. An ample headboard, a soft rug on floorboards, or a piece of furniture, protectively

placed, can be enough to provide that sense of safety and enclosure that encourages total relaxation. Movable screens, whether freestanding or incorporated in the design of a larger room, act as flexible walls. Even something as physically insubstantial as a mosquito net can be a sufficient barrier between a sleeper and the outside world.

If there is enough ceiling height, a sleeping platform is both an efficient use of space and a way of carving out separate territory within a larger room. Climbing a ladder to bed, like clambering into the top bunk as a child, feels like retreating to a treehouse. And there is the added advantage that no one will notice if you haven't made the bed.

Whatever means you choose to make your bedroom area feel suitably snug, lighting can make or break the effect. Wall lights or table lamps that cast a warm, low pool of light next to your bed can be enough to create an intimate feel.

Bedroom furniture & storage

The bed remains the central feature of any bedroom, its style dictating the feel of the whole room, whether a plain, modern divan or an antique extravaganza. As has always been the case, it is likely to be the most expensive single item of furniture in the room. And, while its looks will dominate the decor, its comfort is equally important. Choosing the right mattress is not simply a question of ensuring a good night's sleep; it can also minimize the problems of back pain. If you prefer a softer mattress, you should choose a bed with a sprung divan base. Mattresses suitable for laying on wooden slats tend to be much firmer.

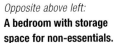

Opposite above left:
A bedroom with storage space for non-essentials.

Opposite above right:
Bedside shelf space is cleverly incorporated into this rustic bedhead. Twiggy branches support both tables and shelf in this wood-lined room.

Opposite below left:
Slick built-in bedroom storage flanking the bed is linked by a high wooden shelf that frames and shelters it.

Opposite below right:
A fake-fur throw and stacked pillows make this bed inviting. A padded headboard, plenty of shelf space, and the movable bedside table make for convenience and comfort.

Top right: **Sharp lines combine with soft fabrics.**

Above left and left:
Stylish modern storage in a bedroom lined with storage and, left, the more old-fashioned solution, a beautiful Arts and Crafts oak linen press.

Antique bedsteads can be very beautiful but apparently impractical, as they are rarely a standard size; Victorian double beds, for example, are often far too narrow to accord with modern ideas of kingsized comfort. However, a Victorian double can make a pleasantly generous twenty-first-century single and, even if you cannot find a comforter exactly the right size, there are companies that will tailor-make a mattress to fit an old bed frame for a price that compares favorably with a good-quality standard mattress.

As discussed at the beginning of this section, the essentials of bedroom furniture are few. Whether or not you choose to expand beyond them is as much a matter of space as personal taste. A small bedroom tends to dictate its layout and contents, which may consist of nothing more than the bed itself and built-in storage, plus that crucial shelf space to put the things you need to reach once you are comfortably ensconced under the covers.

Unless you enjoy the luxury of a separate dressing room or walk-in closet, storage for clothes, shoes, and all the paraphernalia of getting ready to greet the world is the most important bedroom requirement after the bed itself.

Never before have so many people owned so many clothes. Where once a few hooks and a wooden chest would have sufficed, we now require ranks of drawers, tiers of shoe racks, and yards of hanging rods. Built-in closets that reach right up to the ceiling, and drawers that slide out from under the bed (good for infrequently used items, like ski gear), are ways to maximize limited storage space. Some companies specialize in storage alone and offer an array of ideas on how to make the most efficient use of available space, from hanging shoe pockets to stacking transparent boxes for shirts and sweaters. Inevitably, some items will be more easily accessible than others. Again, unless you are blessed with a surfeit of closet space, you will probably find that a certain amount of reorganization is a biannual necessity— moving summer clothes to the back in winter and folding away bulky sweaters on top shelves in the summer. Labeling boxes in which you keep things for infrequent use can save a lot of time rifling and rummaging.

Unlike a kitchen or bathroom, where hard, wipe-clean surfaces are desirable and practical, a bedroom needs the

softness offered by fabrics to make it feel comfortable and welcoming. Apart from the obvious indispensable bed linen, you may want cushions as well as pillows to encourage lounging on, as well as in, the bed. Flooring should feel warm to bare feet in winter, especially that little patch where you first touch down on getting out of bed. This may be the only room in your home where you decide to have wall-to-wall carpet. Otherwise, a bedside rug can suffice.

As in all rooms, lighting and the control of light is important. If you like to sleep in perfect darkness, you will require blackout blinds or curtains lined with blackout material. As for artificial lights, remember that bright overhead lighting is unflattering to you and to the room. Side lights are far more conducive to relaxation, and you can use a dimmer to control their intensity. Bedside reading lights should be strong enough to avoid eye strain.

Opposite far left: **A collection of magazines stacked on these bedside shelves leaves just enough room for the alarm clock. The problem of where to position a bedside light has been solved by attaching an adjustable lamp to the side of the shelves.**

Opposite above left and right: **This compact single bedroom makes good use of the space under the built-in bed to provide deep storage drawers for clothes and bed linen. A tiny wall light is placed at the right height for perfectly comfortable reading in bed.**

Opposite center: **In this room, a long shelf takes the place of a headboard, making a good opportunity for display and book space combined.**

Opposite below: **Alcoves built into the wall support a grouping of favorite pictures for an unusual, changeable bedhead display. Again, ample extra storage is provided in drawers underneath the bed.**

Below left: **An antique chest of drawers with a pick-and-mix selection of handles doubles as a dressing table in this pretty attic bedroom.**

Right: **The curves of an old wrought-metal bedstead are matched by the shapely lines of an antique armchair in this charming old-fashioned room, complete with its original fireplace. The yellow-gold of the bedstead warms the room's neutral color scheme.**

Below right: **A double-ended antique bedstead makes a comfortable couch by day with pillows propped at each end. The table lamps have cloths draped over their shades, a lo-tech answer to the dimmer switch for a softer, diffused light.**

Although the bathroom has a practical function, it should also be a place to unwind and relax. In recent years, bathrooms have been given sculpted units and hi-tech faucets, but the classic rolltop bath is still a perennial favorite, so anything goes. Most sanitaryware is produced in white, in ceramic, enameled metal, or preformed acrylic, so add color and pattern to your bathroom with accessories and decoration.

bathrooms

Opposite main picture:
A wall-mounted shower over a tub is an easy way of doubling facilities in a small bathroom. The hand-held shower on the bath is useful for washing hair (and ideal if you don't use a shower often).

Above: **Internal windows allow natural light to penetrate through to the center of this bathroom. These porthole-shaped windows are an attractive and useful feature of the room. Here the tub has been boxed in and faced with** tiles that match the wall finish, to create a contained bathing space with privacy from the main door.

Above left: **Custom-made shower enclosures can be built to fit most spaces.**

Below left: **Spare, simple design schemes are easier to keep looking chic than fussy and frilly finishes. The recessed shelf and stone sink vanity provide practical storage and are easy to clean, but still look utterly stylish.**

Planning your bathroom

When planning your bathroom, take it in four stages. First identify your needs and examine the room available. Do you only have space for one bathroom, or could you divide up its functions, thereby taking the pressure off the main bathroom? For example, could you plumb an additional toilet under a staircase or in a deep cupboard in a hall or foyer? Is there an area in a bedroom for a self-contained shower unit and a basin, or have you a spare bedroom that you want to transform from scratch into a spacious and indulgent bathing room?

Second, make a list of your bathroom priorities and think about how you use the bathroom. Is the shower more frequently used than the bathtub? If you are part of a couple, both getting up and washing at the same time, would it be easier if there were two hand basins? Do you have young children, and if so would a bathtub with an integral shelf or seat make bathtime easier for everyone?

From this information you should be able to identify and select your bathroom fixtures, the size and shape of bathtub you want, and the type of material it is made from. Other considerations are the shape and finish of the faucets and spouts, and whether you want a wall-hung or pedestal hand basin or basins.

Finally, the decoration of a bathroom, large or small, needs to be carefully considered. Surfaces must be water-resistant, as well as steam and moisture tolerant. Avoid sharp corners and angles, and cover any hot pipes. Floors must be nonslip, especially when wet, and where rugs or mats are used, they must have a nonslip backing.

Although the bathroom is primarily a place for cleansing, it also needs to be regularly and thoroughly cleansed itself. To make this easy, use smooth, wipeable finishes and keep clutter to a minimum. Good ventilation to expel steam quickly and keep the room fresh should also be a priority.

Spacious bathrooms

The spacious bathroom gives good scope for decoration and furnishing. You might want to sacrifice a spare bedroom for the luxury of a larger or adjoining bathroom. Sizeable rooms may also incorporate additional functions such as exercise room, dressing room, linen storage, or laundry space.

A big bathroom can be divided into sections so that one area caters for speedy washing and showering first thing in the morning, with another for calmer, more relaxing bathing. In a bathroom divided like this, or where you want to have a change of mood, choose lighting that is adjustable, either by a dimmer switch or separated on two or three circuits. With different circuits it is possible to switch off bright central lights and leave on only the lower-voltage, peripheral lights, creating an intimate and more low-key atmosphere which can be augmented by scented candles.

The toilet in a large bathroom can be concealed or boxed in so that it is private and can even be used separately while someone else is in the main bathroom, but if you do this the enclosure must have an efficient extractor fan. If a large bathroom is so spacious it lacks intimacy, you can create rooms within the room by putting up glass panels or

Above left: **Tongue-and-groove paneling can be used to help divide up a large wall and bring interest to a plain surface.**

Top center: **This tub has a broad surround of polished granite, wide enough to make an attractive shelf for bath oils, books, or other requirements.**

Above right: **A raised dais has been created and the bathtub sunk into it, creating a luxurious focal point to this simple room.**

Opposite above left: **This contemporary style of boxy bathtub can be made from precast concrete, specially sealed granite, or polished stone panels. The large mirrors are strategically placed for making up and grooming. Natural light is best for this—if you don't have a window in the bathroom, you can buy special lightbulbs that replicate daylight.**

Opposite above right: **Vintage baths, reconditioned or even re-enameled, make unusual bathtubs.**

Opposite below left: **The rolltop bathtub is a classic. Old cast-iron designs can be heavy when they are filled with water, so check floor structures and beams before installing one. A good supply of natural light is useful in a bathroom, so leave windows clear if you are not overlooked.**

Opposite below right: **A freestanding frame with waterproof curtains makes a mobile shower enclosure that can be folded up and moved away when you want to use just the tub.**

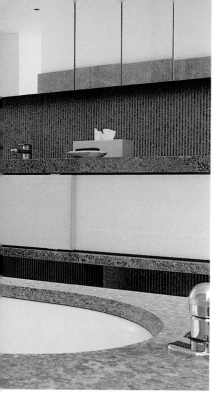

partitions, or using wood or bamboo screens. These will define specific areas of the room and make them appear cozier and more personal.

Freestanding furniture (including a bathtub with space all around) is another way of occupying space and making the room feel more comfortable. An easy chair, a padded stool, and a small table to hold magazines and towels are all possibilities, but be careful if you use upholstery or cushions. They should be aired frequently so they do not become damp and eventually moldy. Also plan carefully what other accessories you bring into the room—books and paintings may suffer in a damp atmosphere. Pictures should be sealed in a frame for protection; if you have a painted feature on a wall, give it a coat of sealant or varnish.

Opposite: **This wall-hung hand basin takes up the minimum of space and leaves the maximum area of wall on show, making the small room feel less cramped. The choice of a flexible fabric shower curtain, rather than a rigid shower panel, also allows the full extent of the room to be seen. The sliding door in the foreground is a great space-saver, too, as it does not require room for access—it simply slides back over the existing wall area.**

Left: **A linear floor plan is always an effective and space-saving small-bathroom arrangement. Here the tub is plumbed in at the far end of the room, where headroom is restricted, and the basin, toilet, and shower have been installed in a line along the same outer wall. The facilities used most often—the toilet and hand basin—are best positioned nearest the door, whereas the bathtub, which is used least, can be farthest away.**

Small bathrooms

Advances in technology mean that shower and toilet plumbing can be installed in locations that would previously have been too difficult or expensive to tackle. These developments have been instrumental in the growing trend for dispersing elements from the main bathroom and creating useful, additional compact washing spaces in other rooms or areas of the home.

Above: **Folding panels contain the bathroom in this open-plan living and sleeping space. They can be folded back so the bathroom becomes an integral part of the space. The classic white and off-white scheme is plain, but helps to make the overall ambience light and airy.**

Left: **Tall windows and a stunning view reflected in a long mirror exaggerate the size of this small bathroom. Restricting clutter also makes the room seem larger.**

Save space by doubling up facilities, such as installing a shower in a bathtub, or opt for a specialized unit like a self-contained corner shower that will slot neatly into a niche or area of wasted space. Macerator toilets can be plumbed in away from the main drain pipe, but should be regarded as an occasional-use facility rather than a main one. There are also reduced-size hand basins and bathtubs that give adequate washing space without taking up too much room.

Decoration can be used to make a small space feel more spacious. A mirror, which is always useful over a hand basin, can be extended so it covers a whole wall and reflects the available daylight, view, or the opposite wall. Small does not have to mean dull—since there is less space, you could choose more expensive decoration. For example, mosaic is costly, but on a modest scale it could be affordable.

Wet rooms & showers

Showers are energizing and refreshing, and showering is usually quicker and more economical of water than bathing. Traditionally showers were installed over the bathtub, but increasingly they are becoming a separate facility. In a wet room—a tiled and completely watertight space with a sloping floor and a central drain—the shower is the primary water source. The great advantage of a wet room is that there are no damp, clinging shower curtains or rigid glazed panels to restrict the bather, and you don't have to climb precariously out of the tub when you have finished.

Modern shower cabinets or cubicles may not only supply a flow of water, but also offer steam or saunalike facilities. Custom-built shower units can be tailored to fit into most corners or niches; they don't have to be constructed around two parallel walls. You need a single wall into which the plumbing and electrical components can be safely installed; then the other walls or panels can be erected from that.

Preformed shower cubicles come in a complete, sealed unit so the base, roof, and walls are joined, but they are generally available only in standard sizes. This type of product is ideal for steam and sauna options because there is no fear of leakage or seepage, but must be well ventilated in order to prevent mold from forming. These cabinets may also have integral lighting and a preformed seat or bench.

The traditional shower has a single head, either on a rigid pipe or a flexible hose, but some contemporary designs have a variety of nozzles and sprays at different levels that can be directed at all parts of the body. The heads may also be adjusted to give various strengths and pulses of water, from strong massage to a soft, aerated flow.

There are several options for shower doors. In addition to standard hinged doors that open out from the unit, there are bifold doors that fold like pleats in the middle. These are useful for showers in restricted spaces. Sliding doors are another space-saving option, as is a pivot door that swings around a stationary central column.

With wet rooms and custom-built shower cubicles, it is vital to make sure the space is thoroughly sealed with a polyurethane membrane before any tiles, stone, or plaster are applied. Since the water is not contained, it will spray in all directions and seep through any unfilled cracks or gaps, and may cause wooden floorboards or beams to rot.

Glass is a useful material for shower screens and surrounds because it is waterproof and contains the spray

while allowing light to penetrate, but only use glass that is specially finished for the task — in other words, laminated and reinforced safety glass. Another safety feature of modern showers is a preset temperature lever, which maintains the water temperature at body heat and can only be adjusted when the lever or button on the dial has been specifically pressed down and moved.

To prevent a windowless wet room from feeling claustrophobic, you can create "windows" with mirrors or opaque glass. Set an opaque-glass panel or mirror into the wall with a fine strip light sealed in behind, to create the illusion of space and light beyond. A mirror may also be useful for grooming in the shower. Look for one with an enclosed heating element that won't fog up.

Left: **These two separate tubular modules, below right and left, contain a shower and a hand basin and toilet. Their opaque surrounds provide privacy, but are not so dense that they obstruct the flow of light or form an obstacle in this open-plan living space, above. The round shape is also soft and less obtrusive than a square, pillarlike block.**

Opposite above left: **Subtle lighting behind this opaque glass screen creates a change in mood and makes this enclosure a relaxing and restful environment for a shower.**

Opposite above center and right: **A custom-built, curving, nautilus-shell-like construction allows the bather to shower in a self-contained niche, with natural light coming in from both sides, while still providing ample space for a hand basin and toilet in the room. Inside, the blue and white mosaic tiles look fresh and light.**

Opposite below left: **In this wet-room arrangement, the window gives ample ventilation while the tiled floor and wall keep spray from damaging the surfaces beneath.**

Opposite below right: **This bath- and shower room is contained within an opaque glass cube. The recessed floor area with a central drainage point makes a generous shower tray, and the shower head set in the ceiling is high enough to give ample pressure for a good flow of water.**

Above left: **This rounded bathtub has a contemporary linear hose and lever faucet. In this neutral scheme the black fixtures are a feature.**

Above: **A sheet of metal provides protection for this unusual glass sink and round mirror. The wall-mounted spout and lever faucets are plumbed through the panel.**

Left and right: **Jacuzzi and spa baths must be cleaned regularly to keep stale water from accumulating in the pipes. If the bathtub has a surround, fixtures can be plumbed in at any point around it.**

Fixtures

When choosing your sanitaryware—the basin, toilet, and bathtub—aim to keep all pieces in a similar style, for example, all angular or all rounded, which will help give a cohesive appearance to the scheme. If you choose to mix styles, for example, by making a special feature of a glass hand basin or a steel bathtub, it's best to keep the rest of the sanitaryware plain and simple.

Traditional styles can be successfully mixed with new; for instance, a modern monoblock arrangement of a long spout and lever faucet can be installed over a rolltop bathtub, and Victorian-style crossbar faucets may be used over a simple modern basin, but the general rule, especially with faucets and spouts, is to keep the style and finish the same. If you have chrome accessories for the hand basin, then have the same finish for the bathtub, shower, and toilet fixtures.

Most modern bathroom suites are made from manmade materials such as acrylic resin mixes and plastics. These synthetic materials can be cut, carved, routed, sandblasted, and inlaid to form an almost limitless array of shapes. They can also be colored and textured to look like marble or other stone finishes, and have the advantage of being substantially lighter and warmer and softer to the touch than traditional ceramic ware.

Cast-iron bathtubs have been around since the Victorian hip bath, filled from the kettle and used in front of the stove.

Above: **Wall-mounted fixtures make cleaning thoroughly around the sink easier, but be careful not to plumb them in too high above the basin or the water will splash as it hits the surface. This angular sink looks similar to a shower tray. It has been set on top of a table-like surface, as a shallow but ample hand basin.**

Below: **Lever faucets are not just stylish, but can also be useful for people with impaired grip or hand movement. Some designers search out the sort of faucets used in hospitals and laboratories.**

Above right: **A rolltop tub can be boxed in or left to stand on raised metal feet. If you choose the second option, the exposed outer surface of the tub can be painted to match or contrast with the overall scheme of the room.**

Below right: **This hand basin has been countersunk into the top of an old console table. The depth of the sink may preclude the use of the drawer beneath, but there is generous space on each side for toiletries and cosmetics.**

Copper is another metal that can be formed into a bathtub. It conducts heat well, so it warms quickly. Modern tubs are also made from steel, either polished or with a flat finish. These are often double-skinned, creating an inner vacuum that has an insulating effect. Wood has long been popular in Eastern countries for constructing plunge and hip baths, and has become increasingly popular in other parts of the world. Wooden bathtubs need careful maintenance; indeed, most manufacturers advise against using standard shampoos and highly scented bath products in them, as they will damage the surface. Some wood baths also have to be kept damp in order to avoid drying out, shrinking, and cracking.

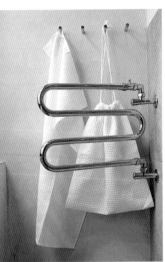

Left above, center, and below:
A heated towel rod will air and dry towels after use, and make them warm and cozy to wrap around you when you step out of a shower or bathtub. Wall-mounted towel rods take up a minimal amount of space, and some

of the more interesting designs can create a feature on an otherwise bare wall.

Bottom right: **This narrow metal-covered recess above the bathtub provides just enough storage space for toiletries in regular daily use.**

Below: **Contemporary mirrors may have useful integral lights or a light panel built into their surround. A wall light on an adjustable bracket is another option, as is an adjustable mirror that can be brought to the light source— particularly good if your**

bathroom benefits from natural light. A traditional problem of bathroom mirrors has been the obliterating effect of condensation and steam, but modern heated mirrors, backed with a small integral heating element, overcome this.

When installing the larger bathroom fixtures, especially the tub, check that the floor beneath is solid and firm before you apply sealer or stick tiles to the wall above a rim. This is because, when it is full of water, a tub or basin may move slightly. This action will be exaggerated on an unstable floor surface and may cause the gap to widen and so allow water seepage, but the movement may be accommodated with the use of a flexible filler or sealant.

Plugs and drains for bathtubs and basins come in various styles. The traditional option is a metal or rubber disk on the end of a chain with a grid overflow on the wall of the bathtub. More modern versions are operated by a lever that lowers a round disk over the drain outlet, forming a seal that is almost flush with the bathtub base. In modern hand basins, the pivotal metal disk is popular. The disk simply swings from the open to closed position with a gentle push.

Sinks, toilets, and bidets come in a variety of shapes and sizes. Wall-hung units—some of the most contemporary designs—create a clean, spacious look, as well as making it easy for the area around each item to be thoroughly mopped and wiped. The second option is a pedestal fixture that is secured to the floor with the unit resting on top. The third choice is a box base: this is a unit, premade or tailored to fit, into or onto which the fixture can be placed. With the first and last systems, the fixtures can be raised or lowered to a height that is most comfortable for the user, but pedestals usually come in a standard size.

Although underfloor heating was invented by the Romans, a people who also enjoyed the pleasures of bathing, it has recently undergone a renaissance. It is an ideal way to heat a bathroom because there are no exposed pipes to accidentally knock against, and the warm air rises from the floor, creating an equally ambient temperature. With solid floors such as concrete and stone, it also makes the surface more pleasant under bare feet.

All bathroom lighting should be sealed and specifically designed for use in this room, where the combination of water and electricity can be lethal. For areas where close examination takes place, such as dental-flossing or make-up application, a mirror and adjacent light are useful.

Above left: With wall-mounted fixtures such as these, pipes are set directly into the wall—no need to drill holes in the surround of the bathtub. Here the only openings in the tub are for the overflow and drain.

Left: Some shower fixtures have a pivoting single lever that operates the temperature, by moving from left to right, and also the water pressure, which is operated by moving the lever up and down.

Right: Traditional fixtures such as these Victorian-style metal and ceramic ones can be bought secondhand and refurbished, although it is wise to check that the old openings are compatible with modern pipework. If they have a brass finish, they will need regular cleaning, as the water and temperature variation will cause marks. You can also buy modern reproductions with a nontarnish sealant, designed to work with modern plumbing.

Above: For putting on make-up and grooming, a main, general-purpose mirror plus a magnifying one for closer inspection are useful.

Bathroom storage

Large bathrooms may double as dressing rooms or linen closets, so well-designed and adequate storage is important. Conversely, in a small bathroom you need plenty of storage to keep things neat and contained, so that the appearance of the room is spacious rather than cluttered.

Bathroom storage needs to be tailored to different requirements. Baskets are fine for dry items such as hairbrushes, make-up brushes, and cosmetics, but for wet or dripping things—shower gels, shampoos, and soaps—containers should be waterproof and made of mesh or some other open-work construction. This prevents water from puddling in the base and eventually becoming stale.

If you keep clothes or linens in the bathroom, good ventilation is essential; otherwise, steam and moisture will make the fabrics damp and liable to musty aromas or mold.

A mix of concealed and display storage means that less attractive items such as spare toilet paper can be kept out of sight, while attractive elements such as perfume bottles or shells can be grouped and left on show.

Don't forget those useful accessories which are, in effect, storage items, too. Most bathrooms need a towel rod, toilet-paper holder, soap dish, glasses, and laundry basket.

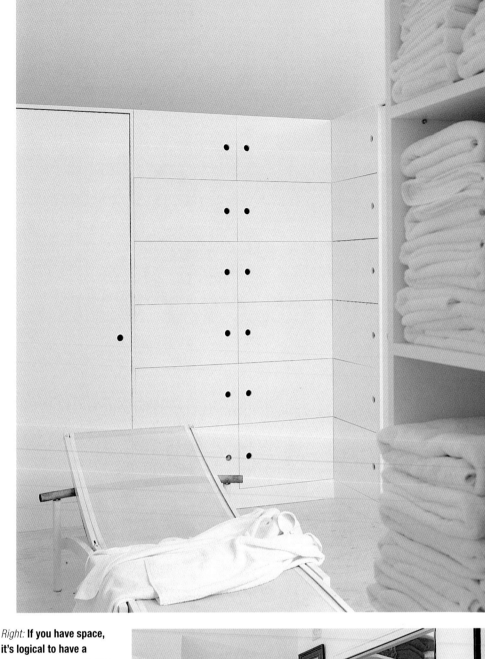

Right: **If you have space, it's logical to have a dressing room next to the bathroom, as washing is usually followed or preceded by dressing or undressing. They have practical advantages: dirty clothes can be placed straight in a laundry basket, collected for washing, and delivered back to the same place.**

Left: **A mix of storage styles: a traditional bath rack complements the rolltop bathtub, while open glass shelves go with the stylish modern basin.**

Opposite top: **Open shelves** provide generous storage for stacks of white towels. Mismatched and old towels are best stored behind doors or in covered shelves like those at the back of the room. Items on display should be attractive to look at, or they will detract from the overall appearance.

Left: **Mirrored panels, flush with the wall, create a smooth finish. Recessed cupboards faced with mirrored panels will have the same effect.**

Right: **These individual compartments, just large enough to accommodate a pair of shoes, form a frame to a dressing table-hand basin area in this multipurpose bathroom scheme. Towels are neatly stored in a deep basket below the bottom shelf, and cosmetics live in colorful baskets that can easily be lifted to the upper level. The drawers under the basin are ideal for holding smaller items such as jewelry, in trays or individual boxes.**

Left: **This shelf provides dual storage space: bottles and jars can line up on the top surface, while brushes, towels, and cloths hang on hooks beneath. Because the products on top are liable to drip or become wet, the upper surface and the front edge need to be covered in a water-resistant finish. It is also advisable to pipe a line of flexible sealant along the edge that butts up to the wall. Facecloths or small terrycloth mats are useful for resting damp bottles on, since they absorb drips of shampoo or soapy water and can easily be washed and replaced.**

Above center: **A narrow shelf below a mirror-fronted cabinet provides a useful area for soaps and shampoos that have been decanted into matching chrome dispensers. Using compatible containers removes the jarring mix of colors and contents of standard packaging.**

Above left: **A grid of plastic cubes, here used to display a fossil collection, is visually pleasing, but can also be a practical way to store items away from water vapor but still in sight. Keep regularly used items on the lower levels and seldom-used ones above.**

Until the Industrial Revolution turned us into commuters, most people worked at home, living above the store or workshop, making and mending, buying and selling. Two centuries on, the hi-tech revolution is sending us back home again. Thanks to the microchip, making space in the house for a desk and computer has become a priority.

work spaces

Above left: **The presence of a generous sofa and coffee table suggests that this home office, designed for two, is also a place for conversation and debate.**

Left: **Comfort and good looks meet in a spacious office that has a living-room feel. Combining elegantly stored reference books and files with well-chosen ornaments adds to the sense that this is a room for pleasure as much as for toil.**

Above: **In addition to the functional—chair, desk, computer, filing cabinet, and bookshelves —there is space in this bright, light room for the visually appealing.**

Opposite above right: **Separated from the living room by a wall, this essentially open-plan home office can be screened by pulling across the voile curtain to create a symbolic rather than physical barrier. The white walls and white desk continue the decorative theme of the room beyond.**

Opposite above far right: **The only clue that this richly decorated room (with its painted, throne-like chairs) is also a work space is the computer. Even the shelving is unusual in shape.**

Opposite below left: **An airy workshop full of visual inspiration—ideal for encouraging creativity.**

Opposite below center: **Compact, neat, organized, and with a place for everything, plus the bonus of a view. Box files stacked on simple shelves provide convenient, accessible storage, and the built-in desk that spans one wall of this small, sunny room makes the most of limited space.**

Opposite below right: **Looking through the dining area to an office that has been separated by a screen wall in the vast volume of this New York conversion.**

Dedicated work spaces

The long list of advantages of working from home is balanced for most people by a shorter list of disadvantages. Top of this list is likely to be the lack of a clear boundary between work and home, between your public self and your private one, between pressure and relaxation. If your house is also your office, you may miss the sense of arriving back home after a long day, shutting the front door behind you, and heaving a sigh of relief and release.

When your commute consists of a trip down the stairs and across the hall (or upstairs into what used to be a spare bedroom), having a room in your home that you use only for work is one way to achieve that distinction. Commuting down the path to an office in the backyard is even better, especially if it has a phone line and modem. Apart from the psychological benefits of being able to close the door on a dedicated work space, there are obvious practical advantages, too: privacy, peace, and freedom from distraction; the opportunity to be as messy or as organized as you please; the freedom to create a selfish environment best suited to your own working practices.

Combining working from home with bringing up a family can be a very satisfying compromise between the conflicting demands of career and childcare. However, convincing a child that your deadline is more important than their dead snail can take considerable powers of persuasion. Demarcating your dedicated work territory within the house is crucial here—sticking a large "Do not disturb" sign on the door of your office is one way out.

Work spaces in other rooms

A shortage of rooms may mean that the only possible place to create work space is within another room that has another use, or you may not need a full-time, dedicated work area. In these cases, the choice is usually between sharing your living areas with working space, or sleeping with working space. Parents with children at home may prefer to work in the relative quiet of their bedroom, often the only room in a busy house, apart from the bathroom, where you can escape from the activity and bustle of television, homework, and play. Single people and those without children may prefer to reserve the bedroom for pure relaxation and, instead, find a corner of the living room where they can install themselves to work. In this case, you might consider a "galley" office that can disappear behind closed doors at the end of the working day.

In either case, there are issues to resolve, both of decorative aesthetics and of practical organization. Office furniture can be ugly and ungainly, and its machinery—the bland beige plastic of computers with accompanying scanners, printers, speakers, and bird's nest of cabling—is far from good-looking and can be difficult to accommodate on and under even the most generously proportioned desk. Only recently have computer designers caught on to the

Right: **Working, eating, and relaxing are accommodated elegantly in a single, stylish room. The desk, lamp, and chair (below) all share an unusual delicacy of design.**

Below: **Custom-made built-in furniture makes the most of space in a bedroom where closets, shelving, desk, and drawers are all of a piece. Take away the computer and box files, and the desk would work equally well as a dressing table.**

Opposite above left:
One way of creating a sense of separation in an open-plan space is to build another floor on a platform—here used as an office. Not acoustically, or even visually, separated from the other areas, the different level marks this area as new territory.

Opposite above right:
A wall of this bedroom has been devoted to desk and office storage, to create a compact work station.

Opposite below: **A raised platform and change of flooring mark this office within a much larger room. The desk is placed to make the most of natural light, and ample shelf space keeps it neat.**

importance of looks as well as performance. The resulting trend for smaller and more stylish hardware is a bonus for anyone attempting to work from home and unable to hide away their assortment of electronic office trappings.

The issue of organization is also an aesthetic one. While a separate office allows you to shut the door on a desk piled with files and a floor spread with assorted papers, this level of chaos—however essential to your mental processes—is less acceptable in a bedroom or living room. Clearing away at the end of a working day is an essential discipline in a room that you also use for relaxing and escaping from work.

Right: **A wall of shelving provides ample space for reference books, but also incorporates drawers of different sizes for storing small items and stationery. This is a convenient and efficient way of combining different types of storage within a single unit.**

Far right: **These simple metal shelves, often used for retail display, are fully adjustable. Here they are used to store labeled boxes of different sizes.**

Below left: **Here antiques, including a metal-framed garden chair and an old document chest, are commandeered to make a bright, attractive office. Wicker baskets store files, and even the laptop is unobtrusive in pale gray.**

Below right: **This curved, two-tier desk makes particularly good use of available space, with everything within arm's reach of the chair.**

Work space furniture & storage

One of the less obvious, but significant, advantages of working from home is the opportunity to choose your own furnishings and design your own surroundings exactly to suit yourself. For example, there is no one design of office chair, however adjustable in all dimensions, that suits every size, shape, and personal preference. Some people like armrests, some like a footrest. Others feel horribly stuck in a chair without castors.

For any sedentary work, the comfort of chair and desk combined is important: the chair must be supportive and should encourage a good working posture; the desk should be the right height so your legs can move freely underneath it and your arms are not straining unnecessarily to reach a keyboard. It should be big enough to leave room for more than the minimum equipment of telephone, computer, keyboard, and lamp. It should be solid enough not to wobble. These issues are more important than looks or style, and are worth spending time and effort getting right.

Lighting is equally important for comfort. Siting a desk beneath or next to a window makes the most of natural light, with the added benefit of a view, somewhere to rest the gaze and something to interest tired eyes. However, bright

sunlight can be hot, glaring, and cause distracting reflections on a computer screen. Ideally, your computer screen should be at a ninety-degree angle to the source of light. Blinds to control the intensity of light are usually necessary. Likewise, artificial light should be strong enough to avoid eye strain without dazzling, and its source should be adjustable. The classic gooseneck remains an excellent design of desk lamp.

Just as you can never have too much closet space, you can never have too much shelf, drawer, and filing space in an office; better to have empty shelving (it will eventually fill up) than nowhere to put things other than in piles on your desk or on the floor. Tools and the sources of information you use most frequently should ideally be easy to reach from your chair. How you choose to store the remainder of documents, computer disks, and loose papers associated with your work will, again, be a matter of personal preference. The more you can enclose in drawers, filing cabinets, and boxes, the less dust your work space will gather. Providing a place for everything, even if you don't always put it there, makes an office look and feel organized, a quality that you hope will be reflected in the work itself.

Above right: **Aesthetics and efficiency can go hand in hand, as this slightly eccentric desk arrangement shows. The tower of white plastic drawers is like a small piece of table sculpture, its round finger holes echoed by the lamp and mirror. Even the roller address file has curves in all the right places.**

Right: **An interesting use of materials makes this slim desk stand out from the crowd, its one wooden drawer balanced by a wrap of punched metal. The chair matches its marriage of wood and metal, but uses them in a more conventional way. This stylish "office" would not look out of place in a modern bedroom.**

children's rooms

Plan the children's spaces with practicality and a sense of fun. Designs should be flexible, because kids' needs and tastes change even faster than our own. It's perfectly possible to integrate a cool play space into a design-conscious home—plenty of good-looking storage is the key.

Above: **Children appreciate scaled-down furniture. Search thrift stores for quirky period styles or investigate mini versions of classic chairs. Painted Swedish styles, bright plastics, and wipe-clean laminates are all options.**

Above right and center: **The vast floor spaces of lofts and open-plan homes are a boon to active kids, who can race around in any weather. A structure like a mini maze contains mess and is great fun. Relish the planes of color and hard surfaces found in contemporary interiors —they provide the perfect backdrop for children's bright art and playthings.**

Right: **A comprehensive storage system is the key to kids and adults happily sharing a space. Built-in cabinets are neater than open shelves. Experiment with unusual doors such as plexiglass, painted board with fretted patterns, or stainless steel.**

Main picture: **At one end of the house, a sunroom play space affords good noise control and means kids benefit from natural light all through the year.**

Play spaces

The best play zones boast enough space to run around, a quiet lounging area, and tables for concentrated activities. Few of us can devote a separate room to the kids, and with the trend toward open-plan living, it makes sense to integrate play space. There's no need to compromise your style. Adapt what furniture and surfaces you have to cater for the children's safety and freedom, and your own sanity!

Consider the available space—along with human traffic through it—then exploit it for the kids' needs. Can dining furniture be moved to one side, allowing a free run from kitchen to back door, or a sofa swapped for a window seat to free up floor space? Think about safety. Is the runabout zone away from the kitchen? Are trailing cords or rugs securely in place? A play space with direct outdoor access is a boon; so, too, is proximity to a downstairs bathroom.

Practical surfaces are essential. Plain painted walls touch up well, and laminate or wood kitchen cabinet doors wipe down easily. Children spend lots of time on the floor, so choose hard-wearing, comfortable flooring. Laminate or real wood floorboards, colorful rubber or linoleum, or limestone (with underfloor heating) are great options. Add a soft rug if possible. If the dining table is precious, protect it with a vinyl tablecloth. If you buy a new table, bright laminate, zinc, stainless steel, or painted board all scrub up well. Rethink upholstery: a set of slipcovers will protect a chic sofa, which would otherwise be ruined by sticky fingers. Strong, washable fabrics include cotton duck, denim, and ticking.

Storage is paramount, not just for toys, but for bulkier items like musical instruments. Plan it minutely, with a home for everything. Fill open shelves with identical containers—wicker baskets or plastic crates are good— which looks more stylish and makes categorizing toys easier. Locate favorite toys and books on the bottom shelves so kids can help themselves. Within wall cabinets—always a neat option—provide different-sized boxes, from small containers for tiny toys to lidded crates for craft activities. Tailormade alcoves, for videos or books, are also helpful. Storage needn't be built in. Freestanding options include traditional map chests, a sideboard, or school-style lockers.

Don't forget a chill-out zone for watching videos or taking a nap. If there's no space for a sofa, children will find beanbags, seating cubes, or floor cushions just as much fun. Put the video player and videos low down, so kids can get to them, and wall-mount the TV to save space.

Babies' & toddlers' rooms

In the early years, babies and toddlers need little in their rooms. Concentrate on buying the basic furniture—a crib, clothes storage, changing table, and feeding chair—and choose surfaces that are practical and comfortable. The prime aim is to create a tranquil environment for you and your child, so that feeding, sleeping, and diaper changing—at whatever time of day or night—is reasonably stressfree.

The crib is the most important buy, and these days there's a good choice of models in white-painted and colorful finishes, retro metal styles, as well as the traditional cherry or pine. Consider if it's a better investment to buy a crib-bed, which will grow with the child until he or she is four or five. Don't waste money on a changing table, which you won't need within two years. Provided there is diaper storage close by, a padded changing mat on top of a low chest of drawers will suffice. Babies and small children don't need a designated closet. Store clothes instead in wicker baskets on shelves, hanging from hooks, or in a conventional chest of drawers that will grow up with the child.

Try to steer clear of traditional "baby" motifs on wallpapers or fabrics: within a couple of years, your child will have outgrown them. A fresher, more contemporary approach is to pick plain, painted walls in soft pastels or clear primaries, teamed with lots of white. Contrast the plains with funky abstracts little ones will appreciate—freehand painted stripes on one wall, perhaps, or a spotty dotted fabric on a window shade. Flooring should be neutral and easy-care. Carpet is softest, but a jolly rug laid over floorboards or linoleum is equally good.

Instead of buying coordinating bed linen, go for a mix-and-match selection. Basics include cotton sheets, blankets, a bumper, and a quilt; after one year, you can add a pillow and baby comforter. These days, there's a huge selection in the mall, from sheets in hot colors and pastels to contemporary fleece blankets and appliqué quilts.

Control of natural and artificial lighting is essential. Simple curtains—choose solids, checks, or an abstract nursery design—should be teamed with a white blackout

Top and above left:
Bright primaries and acid shades stimulate children and fit well into a modern home. Either team one painted wall with white, or contrast blocks of color using a mix of modern furniture. Polypropylene drawer units, plastic chairs, and contemporary blinds all offer splashes of brights, yet are supremely child-friendly.

Above: **If the dominating style at home dictates a softer color scheme, choose knocked-back pastels in preference to fondant pinks and blues, which run the risk of looking syrupy in a child's room. Muted shades also create a better background for the inevitable primary-colored toys.**

Above left and right:
Little eyes need bright colors for stimulation. Consider bold stripes, bunting, a hand-painted frieze, or giant dots on the ceiling. Babies spend a great deal of time on their backs, so give them something to focus on.

Left and right:
Storage should be practical and simple. Neatly stacked purpose-built shelves make for easy access, as do hooks, small alcoves, or a row of baskets.

blind to cut out the sun for daytime naps. Other simple window options include plantation shutters, Roman shades, or Venetian blinds. Install a dimmer switch to an overhead light, and add an entertaining plug-in nightlight. A string of twinkling tree lights is also fun.

Don't go overboard with nursery decorations in a baby's room. It's much nicer to start a personal collection of treasures—christening presents, perhaps, or family snapshots—that can be added to over the years. Yet every baby needs stimulating things to look at. Twirling mobiles, a string of bunting, an older sibling's paintings, or a shelf full of favorite stuffed animals have great visual appeal.

Girls' rooms

Most girls have a finely tuned sense of what they like. Ask your daughter about her color preferences, then steer a tactful course between hers and yours. Children's tastes change fast, so avoid frilly fads and provide neutral decor with lots of scope for change. White walls may be teamed with a single wall of color—repainted lime one year, scarlet the next. A curtain pole with clips allows unusual drapes to be swapped, from sparkly saris to floral cottons.

Make the bed the focus of the room. The bed is a child's relaxation zone, so make it cozy. While little girls will enjoy

Opposite and left:
Children love theme rooms, but don't restrict girls to a fairy grotto. Boat, castle, or treehouse murals are much more exciting, but keep painting simple with bold shapes and bright colors.

Above right: **Treat older girls to the grown-up options of a double bed, four-poster, or a romantic hanging such as a flower-studded mosquito net. All will cross the boundaries between girlhood and the teenage years.**

Clockwise, from above:
Little girls love pretty colors, but that doesn't have to mean pink. Soft gray-blues, lilac, pale sherbet yellow, or grass green are all equally good alternatives. Give a girl's room a fresher, more contemporary edge by substituting traditional floral prints for leaves or butterflies, and mix with checks, whitewashed wooden floors, or tongue-and-groove boards.

high-sided Goldilocks-style or alcove beds, older children find bunk or platform beds more fun. A divan with another bed underneath is handy for sleepovers. For the boudoir look, consider a four-poster, from which everything from curtains to tree lights may be hung. Let little girls create their own looks with bed linen. Floral or gingham styles, embroidery, and blocks of plain color create a good mix.

If space permits, add a low table for quiet activities such as drawing, and a display shelf. All little girls have special treasures to show—make the display area accessible so they can add to their collections. A giant pinboard will also delight them. Cover cork with a bright fabric, or try powder-coated steel and magnets for a contemporary look.

Boys' rooms

Given their natural energy levels, boys need ample play space, furniture they can climb on, and robust surfaces that improve with wear. Those are the basics, yet boys are also sensitive to style, so ask about their favorite colors, too.

The bed is the mainstay of any boy's room, but try to make it as exciting as possible. For a little boy, commission a creative carpenter to turn a plain divan into a spaceship or car made from composite panels (spray-painting gives a more robust finish). Even better, choose a bunk bed or platform bed with desk and computer area beneath. Ladders, ropes or mini slides all add play opportunities. Older boys may prefer a classic bed style from a wooden sleigh bed to an iron school-style bedstead, or an army canvas camp bed.

Keep remaining furniture to a minimum, so even a small room has play space. Wall-mounted shelves and hooks for clothes will take the place of a closet, or add castors to chests of drawers so furniture can be pushed back for play. While a hard floor, from wood to rubber, makes a better surface than carpet for toy cars, it's also useful to provide a low table on which complex Lego structures can be kept. Robust surfaces include zinc, stainless steel, and composite.

Boys need decent storage to make clothes and toy-clearing easy. Help them sort myriad tiny toys by compartmentalizing storage first. Choices might include: open shelves, furnished with mini crates; apothecary-style chests of drawers, with many little drawers; or—for older boys—stainless-steel office drawer units on castors. Wicker baskets on the floor make great instant storage for bulkier

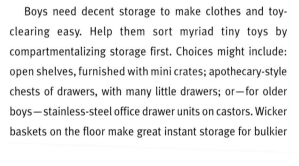

Above and right: **Try to avoid busy-patterned wallpapers that kids and parents will tire of. Instead, use plain painted walls as a canvas that will endure fads and fancies. Walls may be painted in a bold shade or simply in white. It's more fun (and easier to make changes) using patterned bed linen, floor cushions, curtains, or an upholstered chair.**

Clockwise, from above: **These days, there's a huge choice of bed style. Don't just look at what is available in the mall: consider reconditioned or antique thrift-store buys, or commission a carpenter to custom-make a design. For a contemporary look, opt for built-in styles with under-bed storage in painted board, plywood, or tongue-and-groove paneling. Older boys will be happier with a classic design in wood, or composite that can be repainted in different colors over the years. The beauty of providing plain walls is that jolly items, from a punchbag to a football table, space hopper to a giant flag, become decorative, colorful accessories in their own right.**

clothing items such as sweaters and shoes. If there is no space for cabinets, look at shallow toy crates on castors that can hide underneath the bed.

Don't be swayed into decorating a boy's room in the latest cartoon craze; he'll grow out of Batman very fast. Help your son choose appropriate paint colors, and indulge the cartoon phase with a framed poster instead. A generic theme can endure for several years and will please younger boys—perhaps porthole-painted circles and ship's decking for would-be sailors. Don't spend much money, and you won't mind decorative changes when the time comes.

CHILDREN'S ROOMS **125**

Left, top to bottom:
When very young or same-sex children share, the easiest decorative choice is to pick identical bedsteads, lamps, chests of drawers, and shelves, which stops arguments and makes life simpler all around. Subtle ways to personalize special things include an embroidered initial on a cushion or laundry bag, color-coding for comforters and towels, or wooden letters spelling the child's name above each bed.

Above: If two or more kids share, it can be fun to pick a dormitory or summer-camp theme. Choose reconditioned metal-framed beds, old school lockers, utility-style chairs, and a trunk for each child's toys, emblazoned with their initials. Allow individuality, too. Their own choice of cartoon quilt cover, a set of framed sports certificates, or a car collection displayed on a shelf near the bed gives each sleeping area a real sense of personality.

Above right and right:
Avoid arguments when a boy and a girl share by picking identical contemporary-style furniture and allowing each to dress his or her space with personal colors, bedding, and picture displays. For girls, the ideal color combinations are bright, pretty shades, from pink to orange, and, for boys, strong neutrals from khaki to dark gray. Such tones combine well together, so everyone is happy.

Shared rooms

Most children enjoy sharing a bedroom, but parents need to employ rigorous space-planning and a modicum of tact to create successful shared spaces. Demarcation of territory is crucially important. Even a young child needs to know he has his or her own space. Whether you divide a room down the middle or employ other criteria—one child gets the door, the other the window—make the division fun but fair. Little ones will enjoy color-coding to delineate each side (red for one, pink for another) or a painted, dotted line on the floor; older children may prefer a physical division between beds. A plasterboard wall with cutout portholes, sliding panels, or mobile screens on castors are possibilities.

Arrange the beds to suit the personalities and ages of the children. Younger ones might prefer identical bedsteads sharing a bedside table, or cozily placed at a right angle. Bunk beds or a shared, raised platform bed—with a mattress at each end—are amusing options. Older children might prefer a single bed on either side of the room.

Aim to pick decoration that pleases everyone. Provided colors harmonize, each child might pick their own paint shade for one wall. Choice of pattern may be a thorny issue if boys and girls are sharing, and the safest bets are checks, dots, or abstracts. If tastes differ, concentrate pattern on the bed linen, in coordinated colors if possible. For younger children, a fantasy mural is an excellent compromise. Devoting a wall to a woodland grotto or cityscape with cars and stores will entertain everyone and arguments will cease.

Left and right: **The ideal storage combination combines closets for clothes and bulkier toys; open shelves for books; and a low chest of drawers. Furnishing a bedroom is much more fun if you look beyond the chain stores. Retro pieces often come in primary shades, and may already be a little worn. Distressed painted furniture, likewise, will take plenty of hard wear without showing its age!**

halls & awkward
spaces

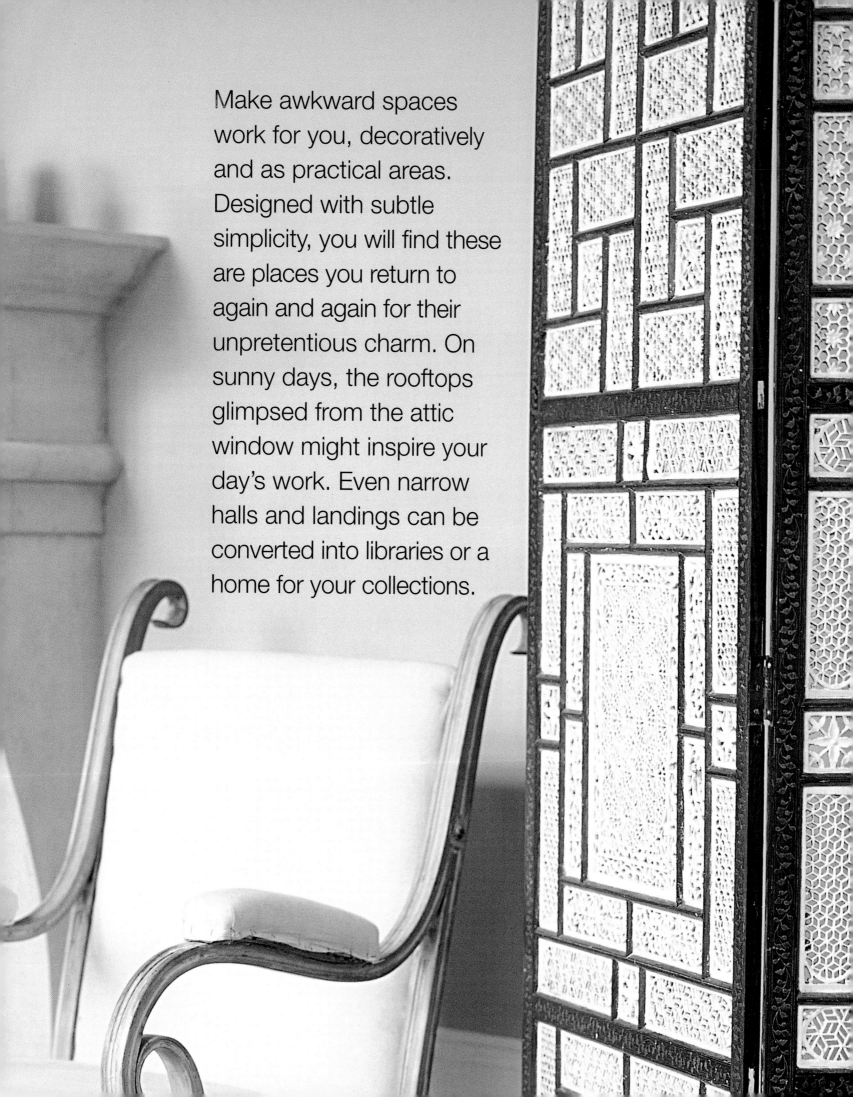

Make awkward spaces work for you, decoratively and as practical areas. Designed with subtle simplicity, you will find these are places you return to again and again for their unpretentious charm. On sunny days, the rooftops glimpsed from the attic window might inspire your day's work. Even narrow halls and landings can be converted into libraries or a home for your collections.

It is the entrances, halls, and landings of a house that create its atmosphere, not the set-piece living rooms or kitchens on which so much care is lavished. The instant you arrive in a house, through the front door into the staircase hall, you can spot what the whole place will be like and you can find out quite a lot about the owner, too.

Therefore, these difficult spaces—often narrow, full of odd corners or vistas, and sparsely lit—are very important. Not only that, but they have to be practical enough to take the constant pounding of feet, the arrival of boxes, bags, and paraphernalia—anything from groceries to mountain bikes— and also to give a great welcome.

The answer is to make these areas an extract of your overall style—minimalist, authentically period, shabby chic, or whatever you fancy—while keeping clutter to a minimum. Stairways can also be used to adapt the feeling of the rooms as you go up—paintings on the walls changing gradually from black-and-white eighteenth-century prints, say, to very twenty-first-century modern abstracts.

It's also worth remembering that entrances are also exits and have to look inviting whether you are arriving or leaving. So make sure that areas above doors that lead outside are taken into account, too.

Entrances, halls, & landings

Above: **Leaving your home should be as interesting as arriving. Seen from the stairs, this elegant hall combines soft neutral colors with a practical floor mat and basket for canes. The urns on the hall table make a classical statement, while leaving enough room for the mail.**

Above right: **Plants, strictly symmetrical, are echoed in the mirror, increasing the feeling of space.**

Below right: **Even a tiny space can be cheered with pale walls and furniture— plus welcoming plants.**

Far right: **This hall reveals its owner's interests, from old doors to exotic lanterns. Hydrangeas add a touch of color.**

Above: **Halls and landings needn't be wasted spaces: shelves are a stylish way to add interest. Cleverly lit, they are ideal for pictures and other collections.**

Above right: **This exotic hall is an extension of the library beyond—not only housing extra books, but encouraging you on. The hall shelves are painted a dark shade, in contrast to the inviting white ones beyond.**

Left: **Mirrors, carefully positioned, always create a feeling of space.**

Right: **An upstairs landing becomes a hideaway with old furniture, a crammed bookshelf, and a daybed —a perfect place to relax.**

Those awkward spaces that seem to need such ingenuity to get right are very rewarding. These are the places where you show your bravura, color sense, and style. What's more, they offer small havens, unexpected views, and privacy, plus the sense that you have created something from nothing.

For years, people have thought garrets are romantic, artists' eyries. The top of the house offers the best light, the best views, and complete privacy. Add to that the sloping ceilings, the unfussy detailing in what architects have often seen as merely utilitarian spaces, and the crisscross of open

Attics, under stairs, & awkward spaces

beams, and you can easily recognize the charm of an attic, whatever the period of the building.

Like under the stairs and small storage rooms, attics are best kept simple. Materials should also be kept natural—sanded, waxed wooden floors, or boards painted pale gray or stone, brushed steel for joists, or stairs left bare, and fabrics as neutral and uncluttered as you can make them. Let the complex spaces speak for themselves.

Attics, in particular, lend themselves to modern treatment. Even if the main house is full of eighteenth-century furniture, up at the top you can burst into Bauhaus or Sixties Italian—both styles where shape is crucial—and abstract expressionism. Or you can suddenly turn rustic after all the elegance of the floors below. Alternatively, use these rooms to house prized but bulky collections, from fossil dinosaur parts to train sets.

Below left: **Someone has had fun creating a garret with cane chairs, carefully arranged treasures, and colorful old books. Note the neutral background.**

Below: **Louver blinds create patterns, and control the light from the many windows in this narrow corridor. The room beyond is much brighter —this and the carefully placed rocking chair make the whole scheme inviting.**

Bottom: **Pure white paint and fabrics exaggerate the angles and textures of this attic room and add light.**

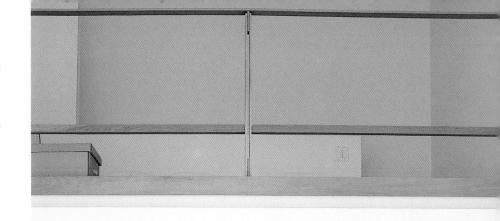

Under stairs and other awkward spaces need a bit more control—they must conform to the rooms around them—but they can be both useful and inviting. Small spaces benefit from generous treatment—building in shelves or including large bits of furniture can actually make them seem bigger. Finally, you can turn a forgotten space into a practical one: a home office, ironing or sewing area, plunge sink for flowers.

Practical areas really don't need to look scruffy. Modern tools and equipment mean that you can buy color-coordinated computers, paint a cheap desk to match and team with desk accessories; flower-arranging equipment always looks charming; while sewing kept in pretty baskets around a comfortable Victorian chair is both cozily domestic and a reminder of diligence. And, yes, even ironing has its own charm as the picture below demonstrates. Think of the bliss of never having to fold up that ironing board again...

Above left: **A large, squashy sofa is swathed in a quilt that matches the banisters above.**

Above right: **Wood and metal are the only colors in this cool kitchen-dining space with its plain ladder leading to a gallery above. Kitchen equipment and tableware should be kept metallic or white, too.**

Left: **Ironing as an art. The pretty yellow cupboard and wood board tone with the stairs. Hide violently colored laundry here.**

Right: **The simplicity of white and wood is cozy and cool in this attic eyrie.**

essential elements

color

Choosing the right color is at once the most exciting and the most daunting of decisions. It is also one of the least expensive ways to achieve a near-instant effect. Paint a room spotless white and you have light and space. Paint the same room plum red and its walls will wrap around you. The difference is dramatic, and all you need is a pot of paint.

Above: The colors here might appear to break the rules, mixing dark red with deep pink and purple. But rather than clashing, these warm, rosy hues work in harmony because they are similar in tone. No single shade dominates.

Left: A quiet combination of white walls, bleached floorboards, and the cool, soft green of paintwork in this timeless kitchen is clean, fresh, and calm.

Right: The bright, strong forget-me-not blue walls of this period living room make a perfect foil for the marble and gilt of picture frames and fireplace.

Color principles

Color is light, as discovered by Newton and revealed in the rainbow. The human eye is astonishingly sensitive to light, able to detect the presence of light equivalent to one candle ten miles away, and capable of discerning between several million colors of varying hue. Some colors make you smile, others make you cringe; but they might have a completely different effect on someone else. Little wonder that poring over color charts can be a fraught business.

If we arrange colors in a color wheel (left), putting the three primaries—red, blue, and yellow—at equal distances and filling the gaps between them with secondary colors mixed from them, and the gaps between these by mixing secondary to make tertiary colors and so on, some general principles are easy to see. Colors on the blue and green side, for example, are thought of as "cool" and "receding," while colors on the red and orange side are "warm" and "advancing." Greens and blues are calm and contemplative, hence the "green rooms" of theaters and television studios. At the other end of the spectrum, bright red is the color of danger, of traffic and brake lights, of warning, and of passion.

The color wheel can be enlarged almost ad infinitum but, even so, it shows only one dimension of color, known as the hue. Color has two further areas of differentiation: saturation, which refers to the vividness of a hue, and lightness, which refers to the amount of white or black mixed in with it. This is one of the reasons that some of the basic "rules" about color have so many exceptions. While a pure yellow hue is generally thought of as warm and welcoming, there are just as many shades of yellow that are sharp, acidic, and decidedly cool. Likewise, there are icy blues and sunny blues, harsh whites and gentle whites. And, just to complicate matters even more, the same color can look quite different at different times of day, on different walls of the same room, placed against another color, matt or shiny, in daylight or under electric light.

Color charts offer a great choice, but they only give an indication of what a paint will look like on a wall or door. This is why sample pots are so invaluable. Paint as large a patch as possible of any color you are considering, ideally on more than one wall, and live with it for several days. Look at it in bright sunlight and by the light of a table lamp; and if you still like it, it is probably a good choice. Remember, mistakes can usually be rectified. Get it right, and your colorful room will be a source of intense visual pleasure.

Above: **The color wheel puts the primary colors—red, blue, and yellow—at equal distances and fills the gaps with secondary colors mixed from the primaries on either side of them. More colors can be introduced by filling the gaps between secondary colors with tertiary colors mixed from the secondaries, and so on, until the gradations of color are very small. The color wheel is useful to decorators because it can be divided into the warm colors, here on the right, and the cool colors on the left. "Complementary" colors are found opposite one another on the wheel.**

Left: **This period dining room owes its theatrical effect to the use of complementary colors, here red and green.**

Paint finishes

By the end of the last century, paint finishes had got a bad name for themselves. Thanks partly to the Eighties vogue for authentic period interiors, and encouraged by do-it-yourself paint finish books, it seemed that no kitchen was complete without a coating of dragged yellow paintwork, no bedroom finished until it had a stenciled border or two, no fireplace grand enough until it had been marbled. Suddenly everyone was experimenting with rag-rolling, stippling, and sponging. Paint finishes became victims of their own success, used indiscriminately, executed badly, and just too commonplace to be interesting.

Twenty years on, there is still a place for paint finishes in fashionable interiors. Used with restraint and applied with appropriate skill, paint finishes offer ways of manipulating and playing with color, treating a wall like an artist's canvas, achieving illusions of depth and texture on a flat surface with thin layers of paint or glaze.

Not all paint finishes require professional skills; sponging, stippling, dragging, and rag-rolling are self-explanatory paint effects that demand practice but, happily, not a particularly high level of skill. You will get best results if you make sure the background color and applied broken color are a close match. Too much contrast between the two tends to look clumsy unless it is applied by a professional. You can also have fun with different textures in paint: try blackboard paint, metallics, or whitewashes.

The decorative effect of all these techniques should not be to call attention to the effect itself, but to achieve a softer, "distressed" color that looks gently aged. For this reason, these paint effects are particularly appropriate for traditional and period interiors, where the uniformity of modern paint can look too flat and unforgiving.

More testing types of paint finish include those designed to imitate another material such as stone, wood, marble, or even tortoiseshell. These are not effects to attempt yourself. However, done well, they are a relatively inexpensive way to achieve a rich and exotic interior finish. *Trompe l'oeil* can also be used to emphasize and highlight existing paneling, for example, by using a lighter shade for the raised border of a fielded panel and a slightly darker one for the panel itself. Or, more ambitiously, you can add instant period glamour to plain walls by painting your own paneling using lines of diluted latex to imitate moldings. And don't forget floors. Even the most dreary blockboard can be transformed by a simple painted design.

Above left: **A mottled paint finish using three shades of antique yellow makes a continuum of walls and door. The effect is like parchment, adding depth and textural interest to a featureless surface.**

Below left: **The fielded paneling of these doors is accentuated by the use of three different colors and paint effects. The central panel has been painted pink and combed to imitate watered silk.**

Left: A detail of the silver and gold leaf on the paneling, far left. Laid directly onto the dark blue paint, the metal leaf has been gently buffed with steel wool for a softer, distressed look. The same technique can be applied to any paint finish for an appearance of instant aging.

Above: This eighteenth-century interior with original paneling has been given a glitzy facelift with a bold combination of dark blue paint and reflective silver leaf. Gold leaf is used for luxurious highlights.

Right: Paint effects can add atmosphere and warmth to spaces that might otherwise feel too hard-edged and industrial. The concrete pillars of this old factory have been painted to look like heavily textured stone.

Neutrals

Some of the most stylish and sophisticated contemporary interiors are those that confine themselves to a palette of the gentle, natural colors we term neutral. In between the extremes of black and white, these are the tones of stone, sand, wood, fur, and earth; browns, grays, and creams and all their subtle variations.

Accepting the discipline of a palette that excludes the bright and the primary has many aesthetic advantages. Like the woman who only wears black, thereby sidestepping the problems of matching shoes and handbags, a room decorated in neutral colors will never look vulgar.

Neutrals, unlike stronger colors, don't clash or fight each other for the eye's attention. This is why neutral color schemes are so often described as harmonious. Traditional Japanese interiors, with their reliance on the soft tones of self-colored materials such as rush, wood, and unbleached paper, have a quiet beauty that has long inspired many Western designers.

Since the Eighties, when decorative interiors —with patterned fabrics and rugs, busy wallpapers, and fussy paint finishes—were the height of fashion, the trend in interior design has been a steady move away from pattern and clutter

Right: **Neutrals can create interiors of surprising warmth, as well as sophistication. In this sleek living room, the walls are a mid-gray. Far from being cold, this is a gentle, welcoming shade. Contrasts of texture are provided by the ribbed rug and pale tan upholstery, while the shiny, reflective whites of the coffee table and the satin pillows also provide color contrasts.**

Left: **Deep chocolate brown and white is a classic combination of colors, as chic as black and white but not quite so hard-edged. In a living room dominated by the pale gold of wood, there are browns from honey to nearly black, while white walls maximize the light flooding in through the huge window. Tactile fabrics including luxurious heavy velvet curtains and thick-ribbed corduroy upholstery make the room cozy and homey.**

Left and top right:
Two views of an ultra-smart New York living room in a disciplined palette of black, brown, and white. The hard and soft, and the shiny and matt, contrast and complement one another, while the bold, bright scarlet of the ranunculus stands out as if under a spotlight.

Right center and above: **Pale, creamy browns, grays, and ivories are cool and classy, but high maintenance—not for dogs or toddlers.**

toward a look that is much more simple, empty, and plain. Natural materials have come into their own; wooden floors are stained or polished, left bare of rugs; pale limestone has ousted tiles or linoleum as the kitchen flooring of choice; cream muslin or taupe linen has replaced chintz, and seagrass and sisal the room carpet. Instead of painted bookshelves and dragged kitchen cabinets, wood is being left bare, oiled, or lightly

waxed, celebrated for its own color and grain. Basing a neutral color scheme around the warm shades of these natural materials is one way to make sure they are shown off to best advantage.

This might imply that creating a neutral color scheme is easy. In fact—even though matching the different colors in a room may be less of a juggling act—neutrals are demanding in other ways. Choosing the right shades of paint, carpet, and upholstery can be just as taxing as if you are using a cocktail of blues, reds, and greens. White, the basis of so many neutral color schemes, sounds straightforward enough until you start to explore its myriad possibilities.

There are dozens of shades of white available to bewildered householders, including "historical" whites that aren't white at all: do you want bright white or old white, gray-white or brown-white, white with a hint of peach or white with a hint of periwinkle? John Fowler, the great twentieth-century interior decorator, softened white by adding a touch of raw umber (very dark brown). A less artistic solution is to choose a cheap brand of brilliant white and wait for it to fade. Taupe is another difficult color to find in a perfect shade—some are too pink, some are too blue, some are too yellow. As with any other color, a neutral should be tried out and tested, however tiny the variations between shades of beige appear to be.

While the eye may find a neutral color scheme pleasantly restful, there is conversely a danger

that lack of color and contrast will result in a boring blandness. To avoid this you need to take extra care with form and texture. Just as bone structure and skin quality show up more in a black-and-white photograph than in color, the eye will concentrate more on shape, arrangement, and the effects of light and shade in a space where color is not a distraction. For this reason, neutral color schemes are particularly effective in rooms of real architectural merit, allowing you to concentrate on the beauties of proportion and focus on features such as windows and fireplaces.

Your eye enjoys contrast and, when this is not provided by color, differences in texture between the smooth and the rough, the soft and the hard, the hairy and the silky, can be just as satisfying. A room with a shiny wood floor, glossy leather

upholstery, and smooth plastered walls offers no variety for the sense of touch. Add some big gray velvet cushions, a thick creamy sheepskin rug, and a lamp with a parchment shade, and it is transformed from clinically sleek to welcoming and tactile. Textiles play a very important role in these pared-down interiors; thick corduroys with slippery satins, coarse linens with supple suede, rough tweed with flat, matt felt—the opportunities for mixing and matching fabrics by feel as opposed to color are endless.

A successful scheme of neutrals looks chic, timeless, and expensive. And, if you tire of the perfect good taste of your sepia-toned interior landscape, you can make a dramatic statement with a mere splash of color, be it a vase of poppies or a pair of beaded slippers.

Left: **In this open-plan space, the kitchen area is loosely defined by chunky natural oak shelving. Its warm honey color and strong, straight grain unify the whole room, as it is also used for the kitchen cabinets and the floor. Touches of fresh green enhance the organic, natural feel, while the pale walls and rug and cream dishes reflect an abundance of light.**

Below: **The discipline of a limited palette is key to the perfect elegance of this room. Black, deep blue, and two browns make a stark contrast with white paintwork and the pale putty of the bedspread. In between these extremes of light and dark are balancing mid tones of the wood floor and gray walls.**

Opposite left: **The glow of auburn cherrywood dominates in a room without strong colors. Cream upholstery looks cool and contemporary, but is practical only as washable slipcovers.**

Above: **A poised, modern living room. Natural materials are a strong element, in color and texture—the wood of the staircase, antique ladder, and the modular coffee table—and in the pale sand of the limestone floor. Other gentle colors of similar tone include soft green and the smoky blue of the striped upholstery.**

Cool colors

Cool colors are whites, grays, and those pale, watery blues and greens that remind us of glassy pools and icy streams and the bleached dawn of winter mornings. Their effect in an interior can be cold or even bleak, but used with care, these pretty, pure shades have a delicate beauty.

Bright white, the color of snow, frost, and cloud, must be the most enduringly popular of all interior paint colors, whether it is the whitewash of a simple country cottage or the flat white latex used to accentuate the soaring classical architecture of a Federal entrance hall. White is almost as effective a reflector of light as mirrors are, and it not only reflects light, but also expands space. White walls seem to recede and white ceilings lift, which is why we almost always choose it for a ceiling, whatever other colors we have used in a room. Small dark spaces, low-ceilinged basements, cramped attics, internal bathrooms—all can be transformed to give an illusion of light and increased volume by the simple application of white paint.

Even in homes that are otherwise a riot of color, white is often first choice for the bathroom. Plain white sanitaryware has long been classic bathroom style, but when it was first introduced at the beginning of the twentieth century, it was the relatively recent importance of hygiene that made white the fashionable choice. A white bathroom feels clean; indeed, it demands to be cleaned. Just as crisp white linen sheets, laundered white shirts, and fluffy white towels are ruined by the smallest stain, a white interior is high maintenance. However, looked after and kept free of grubby fingermarks and smears, the all-white room is reassuringly fresh.

Some of the most successful interiors that use white harmoniously, together with other cool colors, are the Swedish interiors of the late eighteenth century (the style known as Gustavian). Enlivened by touches of gilt and the milky gleam of white-tiled stoves, the appeal of these homes relies on the brightness of a pale palette combined with the inherent warmth of scrubbed wooden

floors, flat-weave rugs, and the faded patina of old painted furniture. Complemented by fabrics in simple stripes and checks, this is a look that combines the restrained simplicity of modernism with a homey, traditional feel.

A more contemporary effect can be achieved by using the same range of cool colors with modern furnishings in pale wood, graceful metal, or even plexiglass. Black-and-white photographs, pencil and pen-and-ink sketches, or engravings will all fit well into this type of scheme.

Top left: **Soft fondant blue woodwork and faintly yellow walls maximize light and space in this airy hall. Even the floorboards reflect light, stained white with a thin coat of latex.**

Above left: **Old blue and white china looks good in a sunny kitchen that is largely white. A paler blue links the hutch with the tables.**

Opposite: **The greens, blues, and whites of this room are refreshing and light, rather than cold.**

Above: **Different blues, from the dark navy of the striped bed canopy to the smoky blue of the runner, are contrasted in this pristinely pretty bedroom with the dazzling white paint of the furniture and other woodwork.**

Left: **White, the color of purity and cleanliness, always seems very appropriate in the bathroom. White towels, like white shirts, have an air of luxury—largely because they demand regular laundering.**

Hot colors

Opposite above left: **This living room glows. While the walls are a relatively subdued primrose yellow, the sofas buzz with fruity oranges and pinks.**

Opposite above right: **A saturated imperial yellow is a bold color for a kitchen. Framed by white tiles and the warm toffee of the wooden floor, cabinets and walls strike the eye like slices of bright sunshine.**

Opposite below: **Red is good for nighttime rooms because it is warm and enclosing. Here, raspberry-red makes a womblike library and sitting area.**

Right: **Orange and black is a classic combination. Here the effect is lightened by pale wood cupboards and furnishings.**

Below: **Bright colors with this much punch are only for the brave.**

At the red, yellow, and orange end of the spectrum are the bold, vibrant hot colors. These are colors to make you smile; cheerful, extrovert colors, impossible to ignore. Because they are so strong, they are not to everyone's taste, but given enough confidence and panache they can create the illusion of sunshine on the grayest day and make the most unprepossessing space cozy.

Of all the hot colors, yellow is probably the most approachable. However, it is also one of those colors that can go horribly wrong; a warm buttercup or imperial yellow is uplifting, but there are other shades of bright yellow that are so acidic as to be nauseating. Yellows containing even the tiniest hint of blue or green are generally to be avoided, but as with all elusive shades, the only way to be certain you have found the right one is to paint some on your wall.

Yellow's nearest color cousin is orange, a particular shade of which, combined with dark brown, was a favorite kitchen color of the Seventies. Subsequently outcast as irredeemably naff, orange has recently seen a revival, thanks to the resurgence of interest in Seventies style. In fact, orange is an easier color to use than yellow. While its yellower, neon varieties might be a bit too dazzling, there are dozens of more subtle shades of orange, ranging from the safely traditional terracotta to clear mid-oranges that work well with wood and stone.

Which brings us to red, the most versatile of all the hot colors and one that can soothe or excite in equal measure, depending on its hue, saturation, or lightness. Bright fire-engine red is such a forceful color it is rarely used in interior decoration; add white and yellow, however, and you have pink, which is always popular, whether for sophisticated drawing rooms or little girls' bedrooms. Pink may be pretty, but in its darker hues red seems to glow with a warmth that can seem as comforting as a crackling log fire.

Contrasts of color, texture, and even styles of furnishing make for interiors that are lively and visually engrossing. It can seem much simpler to give yourself rules: only cutting-edge modern furniture; only authentic Federal antiques; only shades of white or only shades of blue. While even the strictest rules don't make decorating easy, you can at least achieve a certain coherence. Going for a mix is always more of a challenge, and combining colors is a challenge many don't feel equal to.

However, there are some tried and trusted color combinations that never seem to go out of fashion. Yellow, blue, and white, as used by Monet in his house at Giverny, or green and red, as used by the architect Sir John Soane in his London dining room (and by all of us at holiday time), are two examples. But it would help if there were some guidelines to apply to combining colors. "Blue and green should never be seen," "pink and orange always clash," or "never use primary colors and pastels in the same room," perhaps. But we can all think of glorious exceptions that prove these rules meaningless. As with any aspect of interior design, the key is balance. This is something you can learn through experience, by looking at rooms you admire, and by living with schemes of your own devising, by experimenting and tweaking and being prepared to start again.

Mixing gentle, faded colors in one room is more straightforward than mixing more vibrant shades. Bleached or tea-stained shades of almost any

Combining colors

Above: **Mixing subdued colors in similar tones is easier than combining vibrant shades, and can look charming. Areas of broken color, such as stripes and checks, incorporate some of the more dominant hues and cohere the scheme.**

Left: **Primary colors make a surprisingly sophisticated Shaker-style dining room.**

color will blend with one another without fighting for attention. This is the effect achieved in the crowded drawing rooms of well-worn English stately homes. There is no obvious color scheme, just a motley collection of sun-washed damasks and tapestries, subdued chintzes, and sober rugs. A modern version to try yourself might be to use a selection of pastel shades. To avoid a sugary, baby-sweet effect, choose stronger, purer versions of these pale colors—forget-me-not blue rather than duck's-egg, pale yellow with a hint of ocher rather than primrose, for example—and introduce small amounts of deeper color, perhaps in soft furnishings, to add depth.

Above: **Powerful, jewel-bright colors from the hottest section of the color wheel contrast with the cool, reflective aquamarine of glass screens and wall panels. In a converted home with a sharp industrial edge, the warmth of red, orange, and yellow is very welcome.**

Left: **Subdued checks on this sofa are echoed in panels of brighter color on the wall behind, for an effect that is as subtle as it is arresting.**

Faded colors work well together because they tend to share the same tonal values; if you half-close your eyes to look at them, they all appear to have a similar level of brightness. This balance can also be achieved with stronger colors by deliberately paying attention to tone, thereby making sure no single color will grab all the attention to the detriment of the rest.

When combining forceful colors, you might find it useful to return to the color wheel to consider the effect of complementary colors, found opposite one another on the wheel. They are often used by decorators to provide maximum contrast and definition. (A good way to darken a shade is to add a little of its darker

Above: **Mixing hues that are close on the color wheel looks harmonious. In this appealing period dining room, everything seems to have a patina of age. Bright peacock blue is complemented by the softer blue-gray of the woodwork, painted chairs, and the large fruitbowl.**

Right: **A dining room in rich shades of purple and blue, its regal feel enhanced by a crownlike chandelier.**

Above right: **This funky kitchen-diner seems to mix color with abandon— clover pink, orange, royal blue, turquoise, and powder blue. Handled with less skill, the effect could be messy. Instead, strong shapes and a careful balance of areas of dark and light color give the room the poise of an abstract painting.**

complementary color. This gives a softer result than adding black.) Purple and yellow, red and green, and blue and orange are all pairs of complementary colors. Placed together, they intensify each other, so if the effect you seek is drama, you might choose to scatter your navy sofa with orange cushions or to lay your table with yellow china on a purple tablecloth. Used together over large areas, these are not color combinations for the fainthearted. However, they can be deployed more subtly, for piping on upholstery or as a statement vase of flowers.

Such pointed contrasts may not be to your taste, but you can be sure that complementary colors will not detract from the vividness of each other. This is not true for other color combinations—something to bear in mind when putting colors together. Light shades next to very dark ones have the effect of deepening the darker shade. Shell-pink pillows on a deep-red sofa will enrich the red and make it appear to recede from the eye. Replace the shell pink with black velvet, however, and the red of the sofa will seem lighter. To make matters more difficult, reds tend to look as if they are closer than they really are, while blues tend to seem farther away.

Giving equal weight to more than two or three colors in an interior is always a difficult decorating trick to pull off. However, as these illustrations show, the reward can be a room full of life and unexpected harmonies.

Opposite below:
Complementary colors—red and green—used to dramatic effect.

Below left:
Colors combine between rooms, too. Looking into this bathroom, with its vibrant red walls and dark marble floor, you also see a blue door and outside wall.

Below: **The dominant color in this daring scheme is a deep, bright, saturated cobalt blue, to which stripes and slices of even stronger color have been added.**

Light adds shape and form to our world. It defines color and texture, and has a powerful influence over our moods. Electricity has given us the opportunity to design with artificial light. In addition to providing practical illumination so we can navigate spaces, artificial light can enhance interiors, highlighting beautiful objects and details, opening up or closing off spaces, sculpting rooms, and providing ways of enjoying our homes to the full.

lighting

Lighting principles

Lighting is a powerful interior design tool. Well-planned lighting can add enormously to the quality of a space: poorly planned, it can spoil a room, so it's worth careful thought.

When planning lighting, take into account the size, shape, and decoration of the room, how it is to be used, what effects you'd like to achieve, and the size of your budget. As a general rule, the larger the room, the more light sources you'll need. Many older homes have a central ceiling light. This is useful, but should be supported by a range of other fixtures and lights at different levels. Remember that darker decorative schemes require more light sources than pale ones, because dark walls and fabrics absorb light.

Having a clear idea of a room's use is vital to planning a good scheme—a family kitchen, for example, is used from

Opposite: **This is clearly a carefully considered scheme, with its trio of hanging lamps over the dining table, good task lighting in the kitchen, recessed fixtures up the lower stairs, soft reading light by the upstairs sofa, and natural light cascading downstairs and through the skylight.**

Above right: **This scheme makes the most of decorative lighting. To complement the modern interior, there are intriguing Seventies-style table and hanging lamps with multicolored glass shades. Here lighting is one of the room's main features.**

Center right: **Dimmer switches give you maximum control. In this hall, lights are turned up full to spotlight details such as the beautiful bunch of flowers sitting in its alcove.**

Below right: **This flight of stairs is given extra visual interest, and is safer to climb, with the addition of recessed fixtures at the base of the wall. Light washes across the stairs, making it easy to see the outline of the steps, and also makes the staircase a sculptural feature.**

morning to night and may include lights for the dining area, the work surfaces, and inside the cabinets. The scheme will be quite different for a guest bedroom where you may need just a central light or wall lights and a reading lamp. With the use in mind, you can also start to build in subtleties such as different moods. For example, in the family kitchen you'll probably want plenty of bright light to get people up and going in the morning, but you may also want to tone down the atmosphere for grown-up suppers. Dimmer controls are a good idea here: there is only one thing more disturbing than too little light, and that is too much.

And then there is your budget. Essentially, the sky is the limit for any lighting scheme. The most lavish might include recessed light fixtures, expensive classic designer lamps, and a computer-controlled system board. However, you can still achieve great results with a modest array of stylish freestanding floor and table lamps, found in chain stores, mixed with some built-in wall and hanging fixtures.

To create a basic lighting scheme, consider starting with a central fixture for a general wash of light, and adding interest to the room with wall lights, table lamps, and tall floor lamps. Remember that the quality, intensity, and spread of this illumination will react with your room's color scheme. Once the space is filled with a fairly even spread of light, add in points of interest. For real drama, spotlight architectural details or focus on paintings. While beams of light are at their most intense on a subject, at their edges are the dense shadows that give form to objects and underline a scheme's dramatic tension.

Far left: A white decorative scheme is given a crisp edge with sparkling halogen lighting. Tungsten bulbs would give a softer, yellower light.

Left: Tranquil, period-style lighting to enhance a room's traditional style of furnishings and colors. The glass lantern hanging over the table produces a soft wash of ambient light. Below it, the splendid candlesticks bear altar candles for some gentle tabletop illumination.

Below left: A lighting plan that turns the beautiful cantilevered stair into a stunning sculptural element. The simple table lamp creates a sunburst of light under the stair that falls on the tabletop below and reaches across the objects on display. To balance this table lamp, there is a softer wall light casting its beam of light from top right.

Armed with the basics of how to plan your scheme, you can then use light to create different moods. Because our ancestors relied heavily on the natural rhythms of sunlight and moonlight, we respond well to bright sunlight or electric light when we need to get up in the morning and, as darkness draws in, our bodies begin to slow down for sleep. Of course, electric light has artificially extended our days, but we remain sensitive to light levels. We know instinctively that bright light means action and soft light is restful.

A knowledge of the types of light available is useful for creating moods. There are three main sources—tungsten, halogen, and fluorescent.

The familiar household lightbulb is tungsten. It is the world's most ubiquitous electric light source. The inexpensive tungsten bulb has a filament housed in a glass dome that glows when

Creating moods with lighting

charged with electricity, producing the soft, creamy light found in most homes. This type of bulb is now made in a variety of shapes and sizes, including slim tubes. In recent years, the most significant competitor to arrive on the scene is the halogen bulb, available in low-voltage and main-voltage varieties. This light source was first used to add sparkle to retail displays. It gives a hard, crisp, white light. Halogen fixtures are small, but provide a powerful beam of crystalline light. However, they are difficult to fit into the ceilings of older properties, the low-voltage variety requires the use of hefty transformers, and they are still relatively expensive. Completing the trio is fluorescent lighting, now much kinder on the eye than the flickering bleak light most people have experienced in kitchens or garages.

When you create moods with lighting, remember that the calmer and more laidback the scheme, the lower you should set the light levels; for a lively, upbeat atmosphere, turn up the brightness. This versatility is best achieved by having a series of lights on different circuits—for example, ceiling lights on one, wall lights on another, and plug-in floor and table lamps on a third. And make full use of dimmer switches.

Main picture:
This room has many light sources, with a mixture of tungsten and halogen bulbs. Each lamp is turned to a low setting, to create a restful, laidback feeling in the space.

Above: **A quiet corner is created with a soft sofa, a fake-fur throw, plenty of pillows, and a low table lamp with an ordinary tungsten bulb and cream shade —the ideal place to curl up and read.**

Top: **Simple drama. A single spotlight just above and left of this intriguingly shaped vase draws attention to it and enhances its shape. The vase and shelf shadows create a dramatic effect.**

Above: **Lighting is key in making small room settings. Here three sources make a cozy corner: a small picture light, glowing table lamp, and a floor lamp with a movable arm, ideal for reading.**

Task lighting

As its name suggests, task lighting is the type of illumination we need for carrying out everyday tasks. As a general rule, task lighting needs to be brighter than the surrounding room lighting; tungsten or halogen bulbs are both suitable sources. We need greater levels of illumination to work efficiently and safely, and to be able to see important details. Brighter light also keeps us sharper and more alert; it is stimulating, and it helps prevent eye strain and headaches when doing close work like writing, sewing, or using a computer. And as we grow older, our eyesight becomes weaker, and we need more light for any close activity—including reading the newspaper.

In a well-lit home, there is task lighting in every room. In the kitchen it is needed primarily for the work surfaces, but also for any other work area, including the sink and stove. The very best sort of task lighting here is a series of good strong lights, tungsten or halogen, suspended over the work area just above and in front of you. It is important that the light is cast directly downward without any interruptions that may cause shadows.

In the bedroom and bathroom, task lighting for dressing and make-up is usually put around mirrors—the best light is that cast from both sides of a mirror, giving even illumination across your face. Lights positioned above or below can produce unflattering shadows. In the bedroom, task lighting also includes reading lights. Table lamps provide just enough light for reading, but lamps with jointed arms that let you manipulate the beam of light to the page are far better. Among the best types of reading light for double beds are those installed on the wall between the sleepers—this way, you can angle the light away from a partner who may want to sleep without being disturbed by bright light.

The last main category of task light is for the home office or workroom. The best solution for these areas is to buy one or two desk lamps that can be focused on the work surface. For those using a computer, the light should be placed at an angle to the screen to minimize glare.

Above: **This simple, beautiful, and practical scheme incorporates a pair of large hanging lamps with industrial-style aluminum shades for the dining area, plus a track of smaller task lamps, also given aluminum shades, over the work surface. The track system is based on sturdy metal tubing suspended from the very high ceiling.**

Right: **Concealed and recessed task lamps are wired here into the extractor hood above the stove; a very useful type of task light. Most modern extractor hoods have integral lighting, but it is worth checking before you buy.**

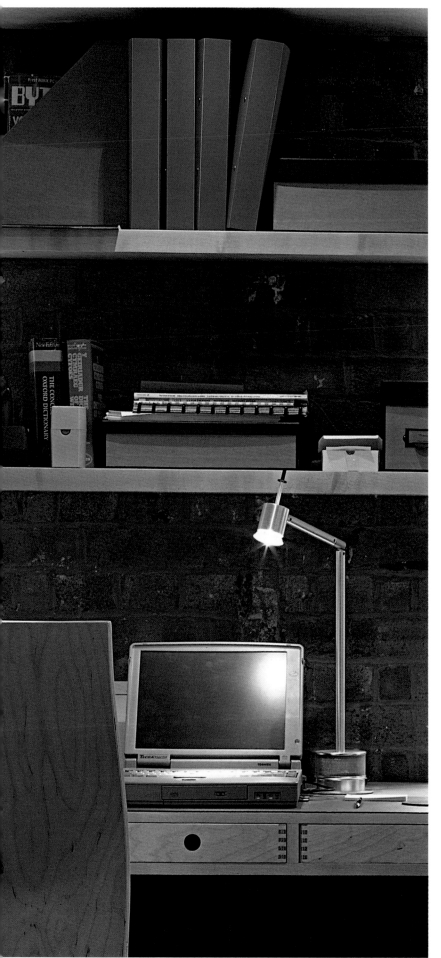

Above: **Wall-mounted reading lamps are a good idea for bedrooms because they are space-efficient and can't be knocked over in the dark. This design has a useful movable arm.**

Left: **This home office area in a converted industrial building has large windows on each side, so it benefits from plenty of natural light. However, it is always a good idea to have an adjustable lamp actually on the desk. This will provide high levels of targeted illumination for your work area.**

Right: **Bathroom lighting needs to be kind— this is where you see yourself first and last thing. For lighting around mirrors, two side lights are always better than one, because they cast an even light across the face without creating shadows.**

Right: **This small area of tabletop is made into an interesting tableau with two stylish lamps.**

Center right: **The clever positioning of this sequence of fish pictures—following the arc of a fishing line—is given extra emphasis by the lighting, which highlights the lowest-level picture. Positioning an uplighter on the floor at the start of the sequence helps the eye read the pictures correctly, from the bottom up.**

Below: **Light fixtures set into shelving units provide really exciting illumination. Borrowing from the techniques of retail lighting designers, these tiny recessed lamps cast a sparkling light downward onto the items displayed beneath them.**

Above: **Ceiling-recessed lights come in several varieties, including ones with an "eyeball" at their center, seen here. The lights wash down the walls across these exquisite screens.**

Right: **This disk of light shows off the textures and details of the surrounding objects.**

Opposite above: **Unusual illumination for a large picture. Rather than providing an even wash of light, different areas of the canvas have been highlighted.**

Opposite below: **In large, open-plan homes, accent lights (like this clip-on design) create little moments of intimacy.**

Accent lighting

When you are designing a basic lighting scheme for any room, try to think like a painter. Be aware of adding washes or layers of light—then finishing with highlights. Accent lighting has a crucially important role to play in bringing out the best of your carefully planned, decorated, and furnished home. You can add interest, drama, and the highlights to complete the overall picture. Finally, shadows and low lights will modulate the scheme.

Accent lighting is a hard-working element that needs to be added to your plan. With your ambient lighting in place and the task lighting set up, accents work to draw the eye through a space. This lighting category is very broad and includes table lamps, uplighters, downlighters, and spotlights. A useful definition of an accent light is that it should draw attention to the object or area to be lit, rather than the light fixture itself.

Table lamps are the odd man out of accent lighting. They are not directional, but they cast a fairly contained pool of light that can be deployed to add drama to the corner of a room, a table, or a chest of drawers. They have the ability to add life to a whole area of room that may be out of reach of the rest of the lighting scheme. Table lamps also cross over into decorative lighting (see page 170 for more).

Other accent lights are all directed to illuminate their subject. Uplighters and downlighters are fairly self-explanatory. Probably the most common type of uplighter is the wall-mounted light with a solid shade, which prevents light flooding out below and instead concentrates the lightfall upward, perhaps to illuminate a pretty decorative molding. Another type of uplighter is a fixture set into the floor, or a floor-standing lamp, both of which have the job of sending light up. A final design to mention here is the big, industrial-style flood lamp, often seen in loft apartments, placed on beams and blasting light upward to show off the rafters, or, in a conversion, old factory pipe- and ductwork.

As you might expect, the reverse is true of downlighters. These include ceiling-recessed fixtures with "eyeball" centers that enable the light beam to be used as a spotlight and can therefore be focused on objects around the room. They can be directed at paintings or architectural features. Contemporary floor lamps can also be used as downlighters, since their main purpose is to focus a beam of light downward. Accent downlighters include those small light fixtures, many of which often started life destined for use in retail displays, which are built into cupboards and shelf units to add an extra glow or sparkle to the objects on show.

Spotlights are also true accent lights. They can be deployed anywhere in the home to add some extra interest or definition and liven up any space. They are also extremely versatile, available in various widths of beam.

Finally, don't forget your visitors. When you are looking at a building from outside, accent lights by windows or lining the path to the front door will make your home look warm and inviting.

Ceiling lighting

The ceiling-mounted light is essentially a substitute for the sun inside the home. It is a poor imitation of the real thing, but most interiors do benefit from light cascading from above.

When electric lighting was first introduced, the standard lighting scheme was based around a central light hanging from the ceiling. These tend to cast a rather gloomy light, with a pool of illumination in the middle, leaving the corners in shadow. Today's schemes are a great deal more sophisticated and pleasing to the eye, although the main type of ceiling lighting is still the traditional one—a light suspended from the ceiling (usually its center) from a cable. There are also fixtures that are recessed into the ceiling, and tracks that are mounted on its surface.

The hanging lamp has a long and glamorous history: in its heyday, chandeliers adorned the world's most prestigious buildings, all illuminated with candles. Now it is electric light that makes the crystals twinkle. Since these days of glory, the hanging lamp has become a rather prosaic lighting element and has spent decades in the doldrums of dreary design. The Sixties and Seventies saw the invention of the hanging light on a spring or cable mechanism, which allowed it to be raised or lowered over the dining table, and there are signs that the hanging lamp could once again be reborn as a thing of beauty. Lighting designers are now bringing plenty of new hanging lights, which successfully lift the spirits, to the market.

Meanwhile, the recessed ceiling fixture has become extremely popular. This type of light, whether it features a tungsten bulb (usually a fairly large fixture) or a halogen bulb (much neater fixtures), has been used in just about every setting. It is extremely useful in bathrooms, where sealed units can be set flush with the ceiling and remain protected from damp or accidental bumps. They are much used in kitchens and living rooms, where the wide-beam versions provide good ambient light, dispensing with the need for hanging lights. And they are particularly

Left: **In circulation areas such as corridors and passageways, a ceiling studded with recessed lamps marks out the route. In this very modern apartment, the use of so many lights is not just practical, but also decorative.**

Above right: **The traditional-style chandelier still has strong appeal. While only purists would insist on using real candles, most of us are happy to install a design suitable for electric light.**

Center right: **This ceiling uplighter is one way of using a traditional light source, the central ceiling fixture.**

Right: **The elegance of this cream hall, with its paneled doors and polished dark wood floor, is enhanced by the large metal-framed glass feature lamps. The glass lamp covers diffuse the light, which fills the entire space with a soft, inviting glow.**

Above left: **In this kitchen-dining room, an elegant track system features small, low-voltage halogen lamps at ceiling level, as well as a lamp on a longer cord, which is suspended over the dining table.**

Above: **Here a track system becomes a decorative feature. This snaking track features a scattering of low-voltage halogen lamps on jointed stems, so light beams can be angled to any area of the room.**

Left: **A Scandinavian-style ceiling lamp is the perfect complement to the style of this crisp modern interior.**

useful in rooms with low ceilings. Recessed fixtures are most often associated with contemporary-style interior design schemes, largely because they can be set quickly and easily into modern wallboard ceilings. It is difficult and messy, and sometimes impossible, to put recessed fixtures into old ceilings.

And, finally, the track. There was a time when track systems were rather ugly, large rafters mounted on or hanging from the ceiling. They enjoyed a fashionable flourish in the Seventies, when substantial tracks were suspended across ceilings with bulky spotlights set into them. Nowadays, the choice of designs on offer is refined and elegant. Track systems usually consist of pairs of fine wires that can be mounted in straight or curved lines, and the lamps themselves are often neat and compact in design. The most popular form of track system is the low-voltage or main-voltage halogen variety, where any number of bulbs in their reflective holders can be suspended from the track. Where the system features low-voltage halogen lamps, you will also have to accommodate the big, usually black, transformer box that this type of system requires.

Lighting mounted on the walls of a room usually provides a very sympathetic quality of light. For those evenings when a restful atmosphere is desired, turn off the main central light and keep wall lights on for a soft, laidback glow.

Most wall lights are a permanent part of the lighting design scheme, so it is important to make sure they are in the right position, at the right height on the wall, and in an appropriate style for the room. It is also common sense to make sure they are in place before you redecorate.

In most rooms, wall lights look best when seen in pairs; for example, either side of a fireplace or window. If you are using them to flank a picture, make sure you are happy to live with it in the same place for a long time. The electrical cable will be set into the wall and then plastered over so that no trace of it remains. Note where these cables run, so there are no accidents later when you are driving in nails to hang pictures.

Stores are now bursting with stunning designs for wall lights—anything from the most traditional designs to truly modern, abstract shapes. Plenty of contemporary designs make use of recesses dug into the wall where the back of the light is let into the wall and then the front panel sits flush with the wall surface.

Wall lighting

Opposite top row: **Decorative sconces, left, and unusual wall lamps.**

Opposite center right: **Low-level recessed wall lamps act as guide lights along a corridor.**

Opposite below left: **A wall light with a bendable arm can be swung over a sofa for reading, or moved back against the wall to provide general light.**

Opposite below right: **A soft, warm glow is provided by a wall light, left; a neat, modern low-voltage halogen lamp that can be angled to cast light where it is required, right.**

Left: **An unusual wall light that climbs, plantlike, up the wall between these two large windows. The yellow shade produces a warm, light tone.**

Right: **Providing extra light in a stairway, this wall-recessed lamp is a welcome departure from the usual ceiling-hung fixtures.**

Wall lighting is particularly well suited to living rooms, but it is also increasingly found in other areas of the home. It looks very effective used to line and illuminate corridors and stairs—also making it a useful safety feature—and is a handsome addition close to the dining table or even in the bedroom. It is worth carefully considering at what height to mount wall lights in dining rooms and bedrooms. Think about setting them at a lower level on the wall than you might in other rooms because, in the dining room, people spend most of their time sitting down and, in the bedroom, lying down. Lights set at a lower level here will provide more useful illumination.

Floor lamps

There was a time when the traditional standing lamp was virtually the only type of floor-based lighting in common use. However, in recent years there has been an explosion of interesting new designs and innovative ways of using these highly versatile lights.

Floor lighting can incorporate a vast spectrum of design ideas and functions. There are tall designs based on the traditional floor lamp, intended to provide a three-quarter-height downward light in the corner of a room or close to a seat for reading. Floor lamps are a handsome addition to many lighting schemes. Another version is the freestanding uplighter—a light that casts its beam to wash upward across a wall or ceiling, reflecting soft, diffused light back into the room. There are also floor lights that provide light halfway up a room and which are intended mainly for reading. All these types of lamp look great when they are used in pairs. They look especially grand at each end of a large sofa or standing sentry on each side of a doorway, window, or fireplace.

The other main category of floor lights are those that are intended to cast their illumination around the lower part of the room. These fixtures are often highly sculptural, with a lovely brooding presence. In addition to providing an interesting

Far left: **Lighting as sculpture: a floor-standing column of light, in a corrugated paper design.**

Left: **Reading lights are always welcome by chairs and sofas— here, a classic floor lamp can be angled to where light is required.**

Below far left: **Providing a warm glow in the lower level of the room is this fabulous Glo-ball lamp by Jasper Morrison, also made as a table lamp.**

Below left: **Floor lamps are a handsome addition to the lighting of any room, and are particularly attractive used in pairs.**

Above right: **Arco, a design classic by the Castiglioni brothers. This great arched floor lamp is a sculptural feature.**

Right: **This egg-shaped lamp looks stunning in a contemporary setting.**

Right: **This wild-looking, treelike floor lamp has three light sources, which can be angled where needed. The conical lampshades give this design the look of a large plant.**

Below right: **Standing guard by this distinctive metal bookshelf is a floor-standing uplighter that casts its illumination up to wash the walls.**

Below far right: **Glowing light globes make a stunning addition to any room and look particularly striking in simple modern settings.**

Below: **This tripod lamp features an unusual loose-fitting cloth shade.**

glow at the base of the room, they can also be positioned behind furniture such as sofas, from where they will cast light up across the lower part of the wall. Used at floor level, they add a welcome wash of light up the wall, but are not a glaring intrusion into the room.

Floor-standing lights are incredibly versatile. They don't need to be set permanently in one position, so they can be moved around the room or indeed the house. And of course you can take them with you when you move.

Like wall lights, floor lights are most often associated with use in the living room, but they also make useful additions to lighting schemes elsewhere in the home. Both the high- and low-level versions can look extremely good in a bedroom or a dining room. You might also consider powerful, freestanding lamps, originally intended

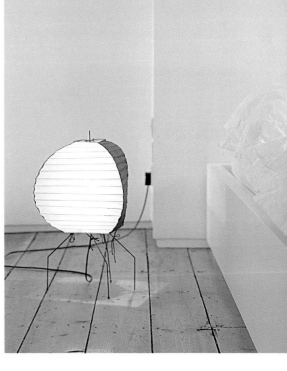

for use in commercial offices, as part of the artificial lighting of a home office.

Lighting can help mold our perception of space, and floor-standing lamps are helpful for manipulating large areas. For example, if a room is very tall and you want to accentuate its height, build in floor-standing uplighters to wash the ceilings. To achieve the opposite effect of lowering

a high ceiling, use floor-standing lamps at a lower level in the room, add hanging lamps that cast a downward light, and perhaps also paint the ceiling a darker shade. To make a low ceiling appear higher than it is, remove hanging lamps, install ceiling-recessed light fixtures, and keep floor lamps at a low level (at or below half the wall height) in the room.

Above far left: **This utterly charming lamp—Lucellino, by Ingo Maurer—features a standard tungsten lightbulb flanked by a pair of wings made of real goose feathers. The name is a play on words, from the Italian *luce* for "light" and *uccellino* for "little bird."**

Above left: **This multi-faceted metal and glass lamp sits on the polished tabletop like a glowing crystal or starburst.**

Center left: **A distinctive tower of light has been created with this stack of cubes that climbs up the wall. Some of the cubes glow more brightly than others.**

Left: **Frank Lloyd Wright's sculptural Taliesin lamp resembles an architectural model.**

Far left: **Vertical strings of light can be incredibly beautiful and highly decorative. Here the tall space features two very different designs, one string with round shades and another with dozens of tiny illuminated cubes.**

Above: **Tom Dixon's polyethylene Jack light looks great on the floor or on a large tabletop. It comes in different colors, doubles as a seat, and can be stacked into tall towers.**

Above center: **A classic of the Seventies, the lava lamp contains colored liquids that move slowly when the light is switched on.**

Above right: **A dome-shaped fiber-optic lamp, also dating from the Seventies. A sheaf of fiber-optic threads is held vertically at the center of the lamp, and splays out to make this perfect dome of tiny points of light.**

Below left: **An Art Nouveau-inspired double lamp with flower-head glass shades.**

Below center left: **A table lamp to complement the ethnic style of this room, with a dark-wood base and a two-tiered, neutral circular shade.**

Below center right: **This boulder-shaped, molded all-in-one lamp glows subtly to illuminate a corner.**

Below right: **Rows of small colored pointed lightbulbs make an unusual "picture" of light.**

Decorative lights

The world of decorative lighting embraces all lamp designs and fixtures that you choose for the sheer joy of their presence. Decorative lighting is not compelled to perform any particular practical function; it is there by the merit of its design (although many examples are invaluable light sources, too). It demonstrates that artificial lighting can add poetry to a space.

It is not surprising, then, that decorative lighting can encompass a huge variety of lamps and light fixtures. Pretty table lamps can be chosen to enhance and complement the overall design and decor of a room. Others, like the classic retro lava lamp or the fiber-optic lamp, can be included for their novelty value. Floor lamps, such as Tom Dixon's Jack light, and even table lamps such as Ingo Maurer's Lucellino (both featured here), can be intriguing sculptural presences in a room—just as beautiful switched off as they are when they're switched on. Even in the simplest of spaces, one glorious light fixture can add real magic. In recent years many independent design studios have started to provide the market with stunning, sometimes highly idiosyncratic, lamps.

When you set out to buy decorative lighting, always make sure you see what each light looks like when it is switched on. And instead of opting for the safer, more staid designs, consider lamps or fixtures with real presence. A single room can't withstand too much eccentricity, unless it is in tune with the room's theme, but one or two unusual pieces of lighting design can have the impact of an artwork. And consider lights featuring colored bulbs. They can add points of interest even in the most neglected corners.

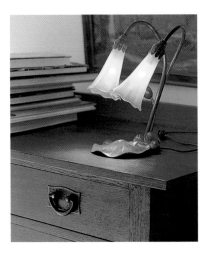

flooring

Flooring is a prominent element in any home. As the foundation of a decorative scheme, it helps to set the tone of the entire room. It must be attractive and practical, so your choice should balance looks with function. Flooring can easily devour a large portion of your decorating budget, so take care to research well and choose wisely.

Above: **Rugs can help to define spaces. Here a pair of pebble-colored rugs is used as the base for the dining table and also for the sitting area. Dark-stained wooden flooring underneath provides a color and texture contrast.**

Above left: **Ceramic tiles have long been used in high-traffic areas like halls because they can withstand heavy wear and tear. The threshold marks the divide between the hall, finished in black and white ceramic tiles, and a rich wood floor.**

Left: **A terrazzo hall. This durable stone composite is made of small stone, marble, or colored glass chips set in concrete and then cut and polished to produce a shiny, smooth surface.**

Main picture: **The simple modern furniture in this room is echoed in the**

plain, short-pile, stone-colored rug. The color theme of stone and dark brown, seen in the furniture, is repeated on the floor in the large rug placed over a dark parquet flooring.

Right: **This open-plan space is clearly split into the circulation area and dining area. The gleaming polished wood boards are solid oak, giving a warm honey-colored glow. This hard wood makes a very durable surface for a key circulation area.**

Above right: **A satisfying pairing of materials where neat, narrow-plank flooring meets a sisal rug. The tones of the stained wood work beautifully with the woven sisal.**

Center right: **This floor demonstrates how you can give a classic design a fresh new edge. Here, instead of the more usual square tiles, rectangular white floor tiles are laid in a pattern with contrasting tiny square black tiles.**

Below right: **To delineate areas in this compact apartment, wood is used for the main circulation routes and soft carpet is inset for other areas.**

Below: **The luxurious and supple quality of leather, seen to good effect in the safari chairs, is echoed in the unusual leather floor rug composed of neat squares. Leather, although expensive, is a particularly hard-wearing and beautiful flooring material.**

Flooring principles

Flooring finishes and materials range from the plain and understated, such as sleek polished wood, to the most flamboyant mosaics or wild-patterned rugs. Today's choice is very extensive.

The main considerations when planning new flooring are what sort of finish is in place already, how the room or area is to be used in future, how it is to be decorated, and the size of your budget. Think, too, about your room's dimensions. It is possible for a flooring material to alter the way a room is perceived—for example, long rectangular stone tiles will have the optical effect of lengthening a space.

Essential to the success of any flooring is what lies underneath, an ideal base being level and sound. For best results, you need to know how that base has been constructed. A solid concrete floor gives the greatest scope, as just about any flooring can be laid on top. Even if the floor is in an upper part of a building in an apartment or converted loft building, reinforced concrete should have the structural strength to carry the additional weight of heavy materials such as ceramic or stone tiles.

However, in most homes, particularly those that have been built traditionally, the floor substructure is made of long wooden joists finished with softwood (usually pine) floorboards. This type of construction is not usually strong enough to bear the weight of stone slabs or tiles. One option here is to salvage and clean up the existing boards if they are not too badly damaged by wear and tear and the disturbance caused by plumbers and electricians installing wires and pipes underneath. Alternatively, remove the old boards and replace them with new wood, or consider any of the lighter flooring options such as cork, vinyl, or linoleum, wall-to-wall carpet, or natural grass coverings such as sisal. On the ground level of a traditionally built house, the old wood floor can usually be replaced with concrete, which then provides a base for stone or ceramic tiles. If you are in any doubt, ask the advice of an architect or structural engineer.

Hard floors

Hard floors—made of stone, ceramic, or brick—provide a glorious palette of texture and color and look equally good in period or contemporary settings (first check that your subfloor can carry the additional weight of a hard floor).

Hard flooring is traditionally used in areas with high traffic, such as halls and corridors, or in wet areas such as kitchens and bathrooms. Flagstones and terracotta quarry tiles are kitchen classics; stone flagstones or encaustic and black-and-white ceramic tiles are often found in halls; and marble always adds a splash of luxury to the bathroom. Recently stone, particularly creamy-colored limestone, has been very popular for dining areas, living rooms, and even bedrooms.

The secret of a long-lasting, good-looking hard floor is to start with a solid base and then make sure the material is laid correctly. A stone floor is expensive, so budget for a professional to lay it. This is not a job for the inexperienced, especially where floors need to be leveled and stones or tiles cut to fit a room's shape.

When choosing a material, think about your room's decorative scheme. You can buy stone, marble, or slate in just about any color, so choose with your general color scheme in mind. Do you want a (dark or pale) neutral base, a floor with a subtle pattern, or a heavily veined marble? Perhaps a composite material will answer your needs. Composites include terrazzo, made of large or small stone chips suspended in cement; poured concrete, which can be mixed with an aggregate to produce a flecked but smooth finish; and marble chips suspended in resin, for a textured finish. The last type of flooring (used in car showrooms) is unusual and less expensive than other solid stone floors.

All stone is porous to some extent. During your research, it's useful to ask how the floor can be sealed so it can repel stains and spills.

Similar advice also applies to ceramic tiles and bricks. These are available in a huge choice of colors, textures, shapes, and sizes. Ceramic can be as tough and long lasting as stone, and where

Above: **Square white tiles make a neat grid on this professional-style kitchen floor. Glazed ceramic tiles are easy to clean, hard-wearing, and can withstand kitchen spills.**

Details, clockwise from top left: **Large white stone tiles with a diamond-shaped black slate inset; handmade Spanish terracotta tiles; a gray, yellow, and white floor of tile fragments; outdoor courtyard tiles sporting a star design; nonslip tiles for a shower floor, featuring a fish design; a subtle bathroom floor in small dark and light blue tiles.**

Opposite above left: **A combination of cream and brick-red tiles is unusual, but looks stunning in this kitchen.**

Opposite above right: **This modern island unit divides a kitchen and dining area. Its white marble continues on the floor and in the steps down to the table. Either side is a wide ribbon of long, red-brick pavers.**

Opposite below left: **A wild-looking crazy paving effect created by combining a spectrum of different-colored marble to make an abstract pattern.**

Opposite below right: **Huge creamy limestone tiles have been laid in this bathroom. As the tiles are so large, they look considerably more exciting than their regular-sized cousins. The limestone complements the marble used on the wall and bathtub side.**

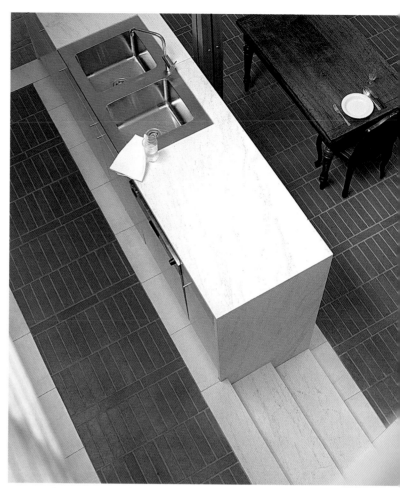

it is glazed, the surface is impervious to stains. Terracotta tiles are made from a variety of clays and have a glazed or unglazed finish. Very hard-baked quarry tiles have a densely textured, matt surface that repels most stains. Glazed terracotta will act in the same way. Unglazed terracotta is softer and can be finished with brushed-on linseed oil or floor wax for a flat finish. Gloss floor varnish will give a shine. With tiled flooring, especially in the kitchen and bathroom, always pay special attention to grouting. While the tiles may be glazed, grouting is often porous and will absorb spills; waterproof varieties are available. It's also a good idea to choose a color that won't show every mark.

Flooring bricks usually require some sort of finishing because they are porous and produce lots of dust for months after being laid. Again, linseed oil or wax can be used as a gentle sealant that maintains a natural look. More drastic treatments include polyurethane-based varnish and sealant, but they can look artificial. Suppliers should offer advice on finishes and maintenance.

Finally, stone, ceramic, and brick flooring is expensive. Even finding what you want in a salvage yard is no guarantee of a bargain. However, investment in a beautiful floor, expertly laid, will give years of pleasure, withstand plenty of wear and tear, and should improve with age.

Opposite above left: **This unusual but extremely elegant floor is made of poured concrete colored with yellow pigment and then inset with lines of tiny pebbles to make a simple diamond pattern.**

Opposite above right: **The same floor shown in context. The pebble pattern stops short of the edges of the room, making a "rug" for the center of the floor.**

Opposite below: **In warm climates, a stone or ceramic floor is a cooler option than carpet. In this period house the scheme is classically simple with pale whitewashed walls, well-worn terracotta-tiled floor, and comfortable furniture upholstered in white linen—just the place to escape the sun.**

Details, clockwise from top left: **The smooth, shiny surface of well-worn rectangular flagstones; a minimal interior set off by extra large, pale honey-colored stone pavers; black-and-white speckled terrazzo tiles; a stunning tile floor using small pieces of colored stone set in a cement base.**

Right: **A dark-tiled floor gives a solid base to a design scheme. The rich color "anchors" the white walls hung with abstract pictures and the modern furniture.**

Left: **Small terrazzo tiles are laid with contrasting dark border strips. The two-tone colors of the speckled tiles are found again in the woven stool seats.**

Above right: **An unusual form of parquet flooring, using recycled hardwood to make a large herringbone pattern. It captures the feeling of American Colonial buildings.**

Center right: **Bleached teak gives this unusual silvery finish, complemented by silvery upholstery fabric and Venetian blinds made of cedar.**

Below right: **Flooring as beautiful as the best cabinetwork. Here the handsome solid oak parquet is finished with a stunning border featuring fine lines of dark hardwood inlay.**

Above far right: **This subtle finish is achieved with small, square wood tiles laid in a diamond pattern. The slight variations in the wood color create a lovely dappled effect in a floor that extends throughout this home.**

Below far right: **Where the original boards are good enough quality, as in this period building, they can be sanded, finished, and simply left bare.**

Opposite: **An all-white modern interior is complemented by pale wooden floorboards. You can achieve this light finish in several ways, including painting with diluted pastel-pale or white paint before varnishing, or rubbing pickling paste into the wood grain with a cloth.**

Wood floors

Wood is perhaps the most versatile of all flooring materials and can be used in just about any setting. It is warm and welcoming, hard-wearing, and almost always stunning to look at.

In its most elemental form, wood is used as simple planking or boarding. During the twentieth century, decorative wood flooring achieved mass popularity laid in block or parquet form. Hardwood blocks or "tiles" were laid in tight geometric designs, often in a herringbone pattern, to make a decorative and hard-wearing floor covering. Among the most recent innovations in the use of wood for flooring has been laminate, where slim wood veneers are stuck to a backing board and given a protective coating, usually clear vinyl. These are then formed into panels or tongue-and-groove boards.

Because it is so versatile, wood flooring can be used just about anywhere in the home, with the possible exception of areas where exposure to water may produce stains, warping, and rot. Wood is not always the best choice in a family kitchen or bathroom, where spills are inevitable.

If you are considering wood flooring, think about your decorative scheme—old pine floorboards that have been sanded and stained will probably not suit an interior that is highly finished, sophisticated, and furnished with state-of-the-art contemporary furniture. In this case, a thoroughly planed new hardwood floor with a sheer, flawless finish might be a better option.

Also take into account the existing floor. A solid, stable concrete slab is the perfect base for wood flooring. The usual process is to lay strips of wood and then anchor boards across them. This allows air to circulate between the concrete and the wood, preventing rot. Another option for a concrete base is to use wood blocks that can be set in place with adhesive.

Where there is an existing boarded floor, first decide whether it is in good enough condition to be saved and revived. Consider whether any damaged boards can be repaired (and try to imagine whether the final result will be what you had in mind). Be aware that plenty of old pine boards, when sanded, reveal themselves to be an unattractive orange color—this can be obscured with dark stainer, or painted over, but is unlikely to improve with just a coat of varnish. Laminated flooring can be laid directly onto a base, whether it is concrete or old floorboards, as long as the base is stable.

Laying wood floors takes time, patience, and skill, but the surface finishing is often key to making sure the floor looks its best. Most laminate flooring comes prefinished, saving the extra work of staining or varnishing. However, with solid blocks and boards, the finish is usually added after laying. Remember to try out your stains, paints, and varnishes on spare pieces of the lumber, especially if you are new to the techniques. While a particular stain might look quite wonderful on pale oak, it can produce an altogether different result when applied to pine or ash. Varnish is a good all-round finish—it is tough, hard-wearing, and easy to clean—but it is unlikely to improve with age. Wax-polished wood does improve with age, but requires regular, time-consuming maintenance.

Like all flooring materials, wood is expensive, but prices vary enormously between different materials. Prices also vary between suppliers, so it is always worth shopping around. You may even

Above: **In this converted warehouse the wooden boards have been restored—sanded, stained, and varnished. They bear the knocks and scrapes of use, retaining something of an industrial quality.**

Right: **Neat, slim boards, stained and glossily varnished, make this room gleam beautifully.**

Left: **Perfectly smooth, finely finished boards— the hallmark of a brand-new floor. The high-quality finish makes a wonderful dark base for white-painted rooms.**

be lucky and find just what you want in an architectural salvage yard, but don't expect rock-bottom prices even there. When calculating the cost of the whole floor, take account of how time-consuming and tricky the wood will be to lay and to finish, since it may add considerably to the overall price. For example, some architectural salvage yards sell block flooring in its freshly reclaimed state still coated with sticky, black, tarlike adhesive. The prices may seem a bargain, but it can take days to chip off the glue and clean up these blocks before they are usable. They will also need to be fully sanded and finished once laid, so that, too, adds to the bill.

Finally, when buying wood for flooring, check its provenance. Make sure your wood comes only from sustainable and managed sources.

Above: **Original broad floorboards, sanded and finished but retaining a worn look to contrast with elegant furniture.**

Above right: **This highly unusual floor is just one of many factory-made wood finishes available.**

Below right: **A marquetry border. Colored woods —here, cherry—are inlaid into contrasting wood to make complex geometrical patterns.**

Far right: **Narrow strip flooring, sophisticated and markedly different from wide floorboards.**

Left above and below: **New pale floorboards make a simple, crisp base in this contemporary home. Nonslip textured vinyl in deep cherry red covers the stairs.**

Opposite above: **In this comfortable, old-style kitchen, the floor has been covered in a checkerboard of blue and white linoleum tiles. Linoleum is popular because it is extremely hard-wearing and composed largely of non-irritant ingredients.**

Soft sheet & tiled floors

Opposite below left and right: **Soft tiles are incredibly versatile and are easy to cut to fit. Vinyl and linoleum (shown here) were once used only in bathrooms and kitchens, but they are now found in all corners of the home— even in home offices. These patterns have been made using the latest linoleum-cutting technology, which makes it possible to produce quite finely detailed designs.**

The recent fashion for wood and stone floors has left soft sheet and tile finishes rather in the shade. However, manufacturers of soft flooring are fighting back with new products in great colors and interesting, subtle patterns.

This category of flooring includes four main groups—linoleum, vinyl, cork, and rubber. After a couple of decades as an unfashionable outcast, linoleum is now recognized as a warm, tough, attractive material that has found favor with many, including those who suffer from asthma or allergies. Linoleum is a composite material made with natural ingredients including linseed oil, chalk, cork, and wood powder. Many asthma and allergy sufferers find it one of the few flooring materials they can tolerate. It is also fairly easy to lay, and very easy to keep clean. As demand has increased, so has the choice of colors and patterns, and hi-tech cutting equipment makes complex floor patterns possible.

Like linoleum, vinyl can be cut to form patterns, and is sold in sheets and tiles. Vinyl can also be solid or cushioned. It is a plastic-based material that is warm to the touch, strong, and stain resistant. Vinyl is sold in many different grades, from very thin and easy-to-manipulate cheap sheeting to an incredibly tough, high-grade material that commands substantial prices.

Cork enjoyed huge popularity in the Sixties and Seventies. It is sold mainly as tiles— prefinished with a tough transparent vinyl coating, or left in its natural state for finishing once it is laid. It can be stained and varnished to make a resilient surface. The appeal of cork is that it is warm, natural, characterful, acts as a fairly efficient soundproofing material, and is inexpensive, easy to cut, and very hard-wearing.

Finally, there is rubber. Sold in sheet and tile form, this material enjoyed huge popularity in the Eighties, when it made the transition from commercial use in hospitals, warehouses, and factories to the home. Rubber is a very tough material, also warm to the touch, fairly pliable, easy to lay, and available in a great selection of colors and textured finishes.

The very good news about these materials is that they are virtually maintenance free and can be forgiving of slightly uneven floors. Before you

lay the tiles or sheet, prepare the area by putting down a base layer of plywood or masonite. The soft flooring can then be stuck to this surface; always use the adhesive recommended by the manufacturer.

Laying sheeting (once you have maneuvered the material into the space) is usually straightforward, although the thicker the material, the more difficult it is to manipulate. If the floor to be covered is an unusual shape or involves cutting around doors or cabinets, make a full-size cardboard or thick paper pattern. Cut the sheet material outside the room, then bring it back in when you are ready to lay it.

Left and far left:
Textured sheet and tile materials like these rubber sheets were developed for high-traffic areas in commercial buildings such as hospitals and warehouses. Their excellent track record for withstanding heavy wear and tear can be transferred usefully to the average kitchen. Now they have entered the home market, they are available in extensive choices of interesting textures and colors.

The secret of success in laying soft tiles is to measure the room and mark a cross at the exact center of the floor, place four tiles in a square with its center at this cross, and continue laying tiles outward. The logic behind working this way is that the lines of seams run absolutely straight and parallel to each other across the center of the room. The eye reads these straight lines and doesn't notice that the walls may be out of kilter.

Leather floor tiles are luxury items in this category. They are obviously expensive, but leather is warm and hard-wearing, and like wood, it tends to improve with age. Leather tiles are available naturally colored or dyed in a variety of dark shades.

The latest type of sheet flooring to enter the home is metal. This is a fairly recent innovation and has found favor in contemporary-style interiors. The success of the finish is dependent, as ever, on careful installation. Metal flooring is sold in large sheets or tiles. Like all flooring, it requires a solid, level base. Metal flooring can be stuck directly onto a concrete base. If the subfloor is wood, it is advisable to create a masonite base; then the tiles can be stuck or screwed to this. Always make sure metal flooring is isolated from any electrical source.

Sheet and soft tile products are good news for anyone on a tight budget, as they tend to be considerably cheaper than stone or wood floors.

Below: **In this refurbished Sixties apartment, a thoroughly modern style has been adopted. The industrial look of the pale wood and stainless-steel dining table and shaped plywood chairs is echoed in the smooth rubber tiling used on the floor.**

Sitting under the expanse of glass, the bright yellow is a sunny addition.

Above right:
Leather flooring might seem impractical, but it has a long life and can improve with age. It should be treated like a wooden floor, cleaned regularly, and waxed and polished about every three to six months.

Below right:
Luxurious leather in the bedroom. Its soft, flat-finish surface feels great under bare feet.

Left: In this landing and corridor, perfectly plain walls and a generous amount of wood sit on a neutral carpet base. The plain carpet means that attention is focused on the fine detailing of the space, the lighting, and objects on display.

Below: Pale wooden flooring as the backdrop to an abstract-patterned rug. In carefully controlled interiors featuring pale colors and plain upholstery, rugs and carpets in dynamic patterns can add drama.

Right: The all-white theme of this contemporary home is broken only by the check throw and collection of pottery. The backdrop is entirely white—including the wall-to-wall carpet. A plain backdrop gives objects on display increased prominence.

Below right: Recreating period interiors includes finding suitable furnishings. Here an understated cream rug adds a perfectly authentic note to this Sixties-style living room.

Above left and right: **Pattern in carpet can be purely decorative, as in the rug (left), with its neat graphic design in black. Pattern can also be used to emphasize architecture and define a route (right).**

Left: **Real presence: the ponyskin rug takes pride of place in a white room.**

Far left: **The geometric pattern in this tufted wool rug complements the modern sofas.**

Carpets & rugs

There is something undeniably warm and cozy about soft flooring. The choice is awesome, from the finest close-weave wool carpets, to jewel-bright stitched rugs, inexpensive cotton runners, and humble rag rugs.

The perennially popular wall-to-wall carpet dipped out of view when stripped wood floors and stone came to dominate fashion underfoot. However, it is now back in favor. And rugs have never diminished in their popularity, because they are available in such a vast choice of colors, shapes, sizes, and patterns—and portable from home to home.

Recent decades have also seen the rise in popularity of natural, woven-fiber flooring such as seagrass, sisal, coir, jute, and even paper. These tough, neutral-colored materials are stuck in place. Among the toughest wearing is sisal, sold either as a wall-to-wall finish or in the form of rugs.

Top row, left to right:
A gray-and-cream-striped woven cotton rug looks good with pale natural wood.

In a room with plain furnishings, pattern is added in the rug.

Sisal floor covering is tough and hard-wearing.

The pattern of the striped red wool stair carpet is complemented by the Venetian flat-weave wool runner on the hall floor.

Left: **In this light, sunny room furnished with natural wood and pale, plain upholstery, the seating area is defined by the addition of a neutral flat-weave rug over the plain, neutral carpet. The restrained color palette means this slight variation of texture is enough to delineate an area.**

Above right: **Real drama is added here with these bold stripes in red, black, and cream. The rug is a heavy flat-weave material, and its red stripe is picked up in the throw over the sofa and the pictures on the wall. In contrast, the rest of the room is simply furnished.**

Right: **Here the emphasis is on layers, with piles of books and cushions. On the wooden floor is a creamy stone-colored rug. On top is a pale gray-green rug, made of squares of heavy felted wool.**

Consider a room's decoration and use when selecting carpet. Wall-to-wall carpet is suitable for most areas except kitchens and perhaps bathrooms—excessive water spills will cause rot. Pale carpet is best reserved for child-free rooms to avoid the inevitable sticky fingermarks. Natural-fiber carpets, except sisal, are slightly slippery, not recommended for use on stairs, and will not withstand damp conditions. Meanwhile, rugs look great just about anywhere in the home—they can add softness to a wooden floor, and look chic laid over wool or natural-fiber carpets.

When it comes to budgeting for soft flooring, the sky is the limit. The best rugs and wool carpets can cost as much as a family car, but it is possible to pick up flat-weave cotton rugs for a very modest outlay.

storage & display

Well-considered storage solutions can change your life. Imagine—no more frantic searching for a belt, a book, or a bag of flour, and closets that look as good inside as out. Indeed, there's only a fine line between storage and display—bags of flour can look as good as books on open shelves. Stylish solutions come with patience and practice and a willingness to work out what you want in advance. Careful storage planning can make all the difference between a home that works and one that doesn't.

The theory behind successful storage and display is that ugly or pedestrian objects should be hidden and beautiful ones shown to their best advantage. It's not easy to get it right—and storage is generally harder than display.

The point about good storage is that it not only conceals things, but also makes best use of available space and keeps anything from hoisin sauce to hundred-dollar hats in the best possible condition and, of course, easy to find. Apart from the disciplined control freaks among us, very few people can honestly say that they have solved their storage problems.

The principles behind successful storage are to keep like with like (all keys together, all cookie jars, all sneakers) and to have special places to which objects are always returned after use. Thus, a pantry can be both attractive and useful if all Italian foods are kept separate from Chinese ones and jellies kept apart from relishes. Clothes look better in closets and on shelves if organized by color, ranging from, say, black to white via deep blue, pink, and cream. Shoes should be arranged by height of heel and use, preferably with their own trees and on special racks. It may involve fuss and expense, but knowing that—behind closed doors—order reigns is very satisfying. It also saves time—imagine waking up knowing just where your black jacket is, or calmly cooking with ingredients immediately at hand.

While storage is complex, display is simpler. You are trying to improve the look of a room by showing off the objects you love, whether beautiful, curious, funny, or valuable. People who are really skilled at display tend to work instinctively. Too much thought creates contrivance. But do not despair; instinct is honed by practice and lots of observation. Look at displays around

Storage & display principles

you, consider what you like, and try to analyze why. Analyze, too, what you want to display. Don't be conventional—a pyramid of Heinz baked bean cans looks terrific, and so do piles of old boxes and exercise books. Both are cheap and are useful, too. You can also display your storage,

Above far left: **Storage can also be display. These old cases are good homes for unwieldy belts or bags.**

Center far left: **There is plenty of good-looking storage—even for tricky items. It pays for itself in saved time and temper.**

Below far left: **One way to display is to theme objects. Lighthouse, bottle boat, and lantern recall maritime vacations.**

Left: **The best storage, like these open shelves, is custom-made.**

Right: **Much clever display is instinctive. Uniting factors here are blue (pictures and walls) and gold colors.**

Below right: **This library combines working books, set at eye level and lower, with elegant bindings, set above. The higher books are for display, the lower in use.**

from huge black and gilded Chinese chests stuffed with ugly work files to rows of identical rosewater bottles with old-fashioned labels. Foods stored in identical glass jars are always interesting and colorful.

Objects can be grouped by common colors: a brilliant red stamp in a painting can be echoed in a red lacquer box below; blue-and-white china can be matched with indigo hangings and a glass vase of hydrangeas; ebony and silver have an affinity. Other groups may have a theme: Cape May souvenir lighthouses beside marine pictures; lots of animals in prints, fabrics, and carvings; books about mushrooms along with botanical illustrations of fungi; sepia family photographs hung in huge groups.

Make jokes. Play around with scale: set a large pigeon next to a small elephant, have pottery dogs beadily eyeing painted foxes, or hang a delicate kimono by a rack of galoshes.

We're talking about adorning walls here. Though pictures can be propped on shelves and textiles spread on beds and chairs, the best way both to see a picture or an embroidery and to conserve it from damage and wear is to hang it up.

Before you get into the enjoyable part of making patterns on the walls, make sure each item is kept in the best possible conditions you can give it: no direct sun on fragile pastels, watercolors, or tapestries; no damp seeping into oil paintings around fireplaces or causing rot

Left: **If you have a really special picture—not necessarily valuable—display it simply. Here a plain, dark wall allows a picture full impact.**

Right: **This group above a retro cabinet works because each item harks back to the Sixties.**

Far right: **An old console table holds Chinese porcelain, in mixed shapes and sizes, but all deep cobalt blue. Behind stands a linen and mother-of-pearl artwork.**

Displaying pictures & textiles

behind impermeable plastics; no old string or wonky nails to break and let pictures fall.

Then you need to decide what to put together, how good a light you want on any object (bad pictures can look good in a gloomy corner), and whether to hang in large or small groups or singly. Pictures can be teamed with textiles—a fine old damask behind an old master (or a reproduction of one)—but, generally, they are best separated.

When grouping pictures that are all of a set—same size, similar subject—the best solution is to give them matching frames and hang them an inch or so apart. Each picture has a pattern, and the group makes a second pattern. Diverse shapes and sizes need different frames, but they should have something in common. It's no good putting flat aluminum frames beside ornate gilded versions. Pictures don't need to conform to a period or style, but do need a point of contact: any black-and-white etchings may well suit, as will dashed-off charcoal sketches—eighteenth century or twenty-first.

Before you hang them, experiment by laying out the intended group on the floor. Here you will spot obvious mistakes—wrong colors, wrong subjects, the fact that you'll run out of wall. You can also adjust the space designated for each and spot whether the best picture in the group has enough prominence. For instance, you may have one genuine Piranesi and eight cheap copies—make sure the real thing is center stage.

Hanging is best done by eye, not carpenter's level. Walls are not perfect rectangles, and old

Above: **Floral fabrics include a beautiful tapestry and rose-strewn shoes, set off by a bright pink chair.**

Above left: **Black-and-white photos, identically framed, are close hung above a heavily carved Eastern cabinet. The simplicity of the pictures points up the complexity of the chest.**

Main picture: **This decor is deliberately simple—white walls, sisal floor—to show off the shapes of the objects and metal sculpture (which follows the black abstract).**

ones may defy the sturdiest drill, which means that the level-and-ruler approach will never work. The look of the whole is more important.

Textiles, being generally bigger, lighter, and floppier, need fewer load-bearing nails, but will often require loops sewn on at the top and threaded through a rod (bamboo from garden centers is good) to hold them flat. Never put nails through the fabric itself—they may rust and damage the cloth permanently.

Finally, work out the lighting: a table lamp for soft focus, concealed ceiling lights angled down on the display, or spots mounted on walls and ceilings are all good. But, unless your pieces are museum standard, don't bother with picture strip lights or those cunning devices that illumine only the area of the picture. It's too elaborate.

Far left: **A collection of beautiful vintage shoes, carefully racked and color themed.**

Left: **The forms of these wood skittles recall natural seaweeds and underwater growth. They are grouped on a display cabinet of similar tone.**

Center left: **This collector has made a virtue of security by giving each valuable fossil a stand in its own plexiglass cubicle. The whole display becomes a wall of objects.**

Right: **Holes have been made in the wall to display specific objects; do this only if you are confident in your choice.**

Below left: **Throw away convention and put your old knives and forks in matching black frames. In this instance, the frames probably cost more than the flatware.**

Below: **A low Indian table is the perfect foil for a group of dark, interesting shapes. The whole is echoed by the pots in the background on chunky cupboards.**

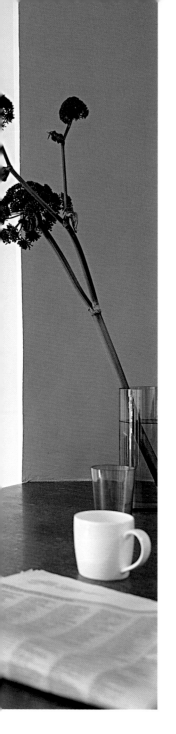

The first rule in displaying objects is never to think of them as ornaments. Ornaments are tiddly little things you've been given by various relations and would really like to consign to the wastebasket. Objects, on the other hand, are pieces you love and cherish, maybe collect in all their forms, and which have at least one thing in common: your own taste. Be true to yourself and toss out auntie's Copenhagen blue bird (or put it in a drawer until next time she visits) and make the most of your favorite things.

In deciding how far to go with the display, remember that you'll probably buy new things and discard old ones, so any really expensive shelving, lighting, and stands should be adaptable. By leaving plenty of space around each piece, you are also showing it to best advantage, in that every beautiful pot, sculpture, or shell will have an interesting silhouette. You can decide whether this shape should be emphasized by back lighting or its patterns and textures made focal by side lights or raking light. You can also decide whether the object looks at its best standing alone or whether it is enhanced by being part of a group of similar pieces.

Another consideration is the fragility and value of each piece. You will never enjoy your Tang horse if, every time your eye rests on it, you worry about it falling off the mantelpiece. Instead, construct secure cabinets with glass doors or deep shelves, which protect the piece from accidents. If you have children, even visiting ones, you may need locked doors for security.

Displaying objects

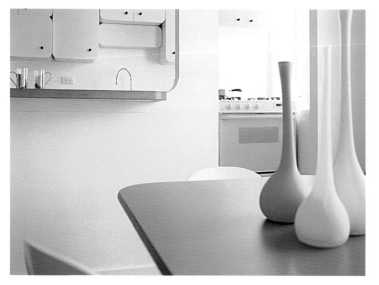

Above and left:
It takes skill to arrange these colorful twentieth-century glass vases, and discipline to allow their tones to be the main color in the room. Those in the picture above all have lips and similar shapes and autumnal colors. They are divided from the flat bowls below. The three (left) recall the shape of onions and are in citrus colors.

The best displays, however, are not necessarily the most valuable ones. A bowl full of mah-jong counters, a line of jars filled with dried chiles, a pile of sea-washed glass—all are beautiful, as are seedheads arrayed in tiny boxes or old buttons still sewn onto their cards.

The skill is to spot the varieties of shape, form, texture, rarity, and age in what you collect and then team them together. Fossils and modern stoneware pottery have much in common, as do modern sculpture and Tang figures. Have confidence in your own eye, see beauty in the unexpected—and your displays will be full of vigor and charm.

Displaying books

Above left: **If your shelves are too generous to fill, hide the empty space with a carefully sited picture. But never hang a picture over shelves that are in full use.**

Above: **Books of many different colors are given cohesion by a few similarly colored box files, chosen to match the office chairs.**

Left: **A working library may need closed shelves for filing cuttings, thin paperbacks, and ugly magazines, and an adjustable ladder to reach higher shelves.**

Main picture: **These cube shelves impose control by preventing books from flopping to one side. Yellow on the shelves is picked up in cushions.**

Opposite right: **This all-white room makes bright books a focal point. Tan archive boxes and art emphasize their colors.**

The purpose of books is to be read, and the purpose of a book collection, if you're lucky enough to have room for a library, is to have all your books about you, each in its proper place. In a display of books, therefore, content is more important than appearance.

That being said—and there's nothing more obvious and sterile than a library collected for its looks alone—there are a number of things you can do to display books to best advantage. One is to go to a good bookbinder and have all your books bound in a similar color buckram with gold lettering on their spines. Wildly expensive, of course. Next, you can repair only those that are falling apart, again in matching bindings. Third, you can give your books new dust jackets in heavy paper of your choice (there's a good deep turquoise that builders use with insulation) and, fourth, you can buy books of similar bindings and put them together. Old Bantams, book club choices, and collections of reprints are all valid, as are runs of the *World Book Encyclopaedia* (well worth reading), auction catalogs, or magazines. It is these groups that will provide the backbone for the shelves. Your books are not—should not be—all identical, but a few feet here and there look good and solid.

When you have an idea of what will be on your shelves—small paperbacks, large illustrated books, hefty reference works—design their height and depth accordingly, since books look best if they fit neatly. Allow a good inch above the book height to fit your questing finger. If you have lots of tall, floppy books, make the shelf length shorter, though this will reduce the number you can fit in. Then graduate the shelf height so the largest books are at the bottom and the shortest at the top—making sure the top shelf is tall enough for paperbacks. If you have some extra-deep books, you may need a breakfront section.

While most books look good on open shelves, you may have some that are very thin, floppy, or dog-eared. These can be hidden behind doors or even slung in files. Elsewhere, if you have the space, books can be interspersed with propped pictures and photographs, sculptures, or heavy objects like fossils, stones, or old brass weights.

It is important to be able to find the reference book of the moment. You may want to arrange books together for their looks—runs of similar bindings are obvious—but keep an eye out for theme as well. It's as easy to search through books arranged by subject as through those that are classified alphabetically.

But the best thing of all about libraries and serious bookshelves is that they should never be too neat. Use your books well and let it show.

Above: **Despite apparent disorder, the shelves of this kitchen hold objects in only a few neutral colors—white, ocher, tan, blue, and silver—which calms the whole.**

Left: **Curvy cubes stack up to display modern glass (note how the doors echo their colors). Books and records live in the rest.**

Right: **This shelving unit uses black for coherence: black book spines, drawer knobs, and a dark focal vase.**

Opposite: **Children's toys, especially well-loved and worn ones, have a charm of their own. Here they are well spaced on plain white shelves.**

Shelves

Shelves are for both display and storage, and the way to get the best out of them is to unite the two purposes. But the objects, rather than the shelves themselves, should be the attraction.

Shelves, therefore, should be seen but not scream. They should be neat, workmanlike, carefully designed to do their job, but not obtrusive or so over-designed that they become more important than what they hold. The more shelves are used for display — especially of collections — the more they should be custom-designed. Equally, the more their purpose is to house kitchen equipment, box files, piles of sweaters, or garden tools, the simpler they should be.

Ideally, shelves should be wide enough to hold only one layer of objects. This almost never happens, but in a perfect world we'd have all our canned tomatoes lined up on one-can-deep shelves and never have to rummage in the depths of a dark pantry again. At the same time, a row of canned tomatoes would look extravagantly Andy Warhol and thus a display in its own right.

The most mundane objects take on attraction when well grouped. Huge aluminum pots and pans, set on a white shelf, have interesting silhouettes, as do children's toys; piles of matching cheap archive boxes are as good as a sculpture, and collections of modern blue-and-white plates, used every day, will give a hutch as much presence as pieces of old Staffordshire.

The shelves should complement the collection. Thus, if you are going for eighteenth-century pottery, design a built-in hutch to suit the period; if you want a modernist kitchen, hide all but a few shelves of stainless-steel equipment. A rustic kitchen lets it all hang out with lots of woven willow baskets, bread bins, and bowls of fruit on the shelves. Children's toys need deep, deep chests to keep the primary-colored plastics at bay, with just a few matching pieces on open shelves, while old toys from your own childhood deserve a good show.

Keep looking at your shelf life carefully, edit, and rearrange. Otherwise, it will get out of hand.

Left: **Stores of cans, boxes, and bags of food should ideally be visible from all sides. This clever system of metal racks within sliding doors is a perfect answer.**

Main picture: **The perfect closet for a well-organized man has areas for hanging ties and suits and open shelves for shirts. There are deep drawers and a mirror, too.**

Below far left: **Mundane objects such as older hi-fi equipment can still be housed in interesting cupboards.**

Below left: **Hi-fi systems are more attractively designed today. This one is on shelves behind sliding doors so you can conceal—or admire—it.**

Below right: **Even large, chunky armoires can be made to vanish—or nearly—by painting them like the room walls and reducing their handles to a minimum.**

Opposite below left: **Ranks of useful drawers are given small but obtrusive knobs in a Shaker-inspired scheme. They are painted the same color as the door and hanging rack.**

Opposite right: **The whole wall of this bedroom is a closet, made to blend with the wall. The upper ones are for rarely used luggage, hats, and so on.**

Opposite far right: **A series of cupboards with internal shelves stands above drawers of all shapes and sizes made for specific items.**

Closets & drawers

If most of us were asked unexpectedly to open up our closets, there would be a small avalanche as objects stuffed away to create the illusion of neatness cascaded around us. Ideally, of course, the proud owner would open the doors to a fanfare of applause for meticulousness.

Yes, neatness is achievable and desirable, even if we all slip back on bad days. The secret is to use all the devices that clever designers are inventing to hold such disparate shapes as shoes, hats, kitchen utensils, and Pokémon cards. Look at catalogs and spend money buying sock separators and pan-hanging racks, because it will save time and stress in the end.

Closets and drawers are designed not just to hide the unwieldy, the bad, and the ugly; they are intended to reduce dirt and dust, to keep moths and cooking grease at bay, and to allow easy access to books, disks, files, and soy sauce. An important byproduct (because no one puts up cabinets for their looks alone) is that they give interest and variety to a plain wall with their panels, handles, and planking. They also provide insulation against

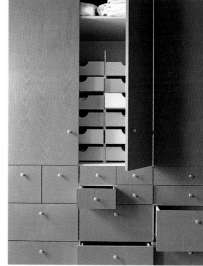

cold and noise. It's true that closets may reduce the size of a room, but the reduction in clutter will make the lack of space less evident.

Closets should be designed to suit the style of a room. Minimalists may want the doors to match the walls and have no handles (hidden magnets hold the doors shut), while classical rooms often look good with a giant freestanding mahogany armoire complete with camphor-lined drawers. Rural rooms can go the Shaker route or use built-in closets constructed from old paneled doors, while hard-working areas, like work spaces, bathrooms, and kitchens, can benefit from neat metal cabinets with sliding pull-out shelves.

Once you get the design right and figure out how to use the hidden space—remembering that even an antique cupboard can benefit from up-to-date wheezes for socks and CDs—your life will be transformed. Honest.

Freeform storage

Storage needn't cost a mint. Of course, it's nice to have spacious walk-in closets and pantries with cool slate shelves, but there's satisfaction, too, in using your ingenuity and a sure eye to achieve the same effects.

The catalogs of office equipment firms have some surprisingly good-value unstructured storage solutions. Flat-pack archive boxes made of strong cardboard are cheap and make excellent storage for shirts and sweaters, children's toys, and newspaper clippings, as well as for real archives and files. Pick solid, handsome ones, make sure they are all identical, and pile them high. Antique black tin boxes look even better, and are also inexpensive.

Real baskets are another excellent source, and there are craftsman basketmakers around who will weave to your exact measurements. Cheaper, however, are ready-made baskets—especially Eastern ones—which can be found to fit onto your shelves (unless you make the shelves to fit the baskets). Baskets also have an advantage over drawers—you can pull them right out to see what lurks at the back.

If you are neat by nature, you can find trolleys to wheel under counters—from the archetypal Twenties trolley of fumed oak to modern versions of steel and aluminum, and office designs with lots of pockets and shelves. Trolleys are excellent in the office. Pile them with your current work, then wheel them under a shelf at the end of the day.

Shallower mobile boxes and baskets are ideal when space is tight: shove them under the bed—often a forgotten area—or pile them up in cupboards under the stairs, carefully marked with attractive labels. Pack them with completed projects—again well labeled—and put them in the attic or garage in neat towers. If you throw important papers away, you are bound to regret it.

In these days of cramped houses, space is valuable. Do you have objects to store, and furniture that is empty? Not just drawers and cabinets, but decorative chests and elegant boxes. They can be filled with flea-market finds

such as old quilts and bits of antique fabric, and photographs and negatives, carefully sorted.

Luggage also tends to lie empty after a vacation. Why not use it all year round? Modern suitcases are an excellent place for clothes, toiletries bags, or shoes that are only ever used on vacation. Pile them in the bottom of closets, out of sight. But old-fashioned luggage—the sort with brass locks and handles that needs a redcap's trolley to move—is now put on display.

It's still possible to find nice pieces in secondhand stores or flea markets, especially if you don't mind that the locks have burst and the handle has snapped. Buy them when you see them and pile them in graduated heaps—perhaps with old labels describing what they hold.

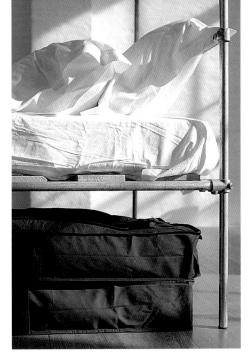

Above right: **The space under a bed may be wasted. There are modern boxes and good-looking bags designed specifically to take advantage of this area.**

Below right: **Heavy-duty cardboard, or light laminated wood as here, makes attractively neutral and surprisingly strong drawers and boxes. They are very cheap, and stackable.**

Main picture:
Old suitcases in piles are a fashionable way to store anything from photos to sweaters. Look for those with funny old labels and don't worry if they are battered.

Opposite above:
Baskets are an attractive alternative to drawers. They can be made to measure, as can the shelves. Freestanding baskets are more adaptable than conventional drawers.

Opposite below left:
Attractive piles of matching dishes, spices, and kitchen equipment look good on open steel shelves—making your everyday equipment act as a display while it is neatly in storage.

Opposite below right:
Baskets are very adaptable. They can fit under a bed as easily as in the kitchen and are also attractive piled on the floor. Use them for office work as well as vegetables and towels.

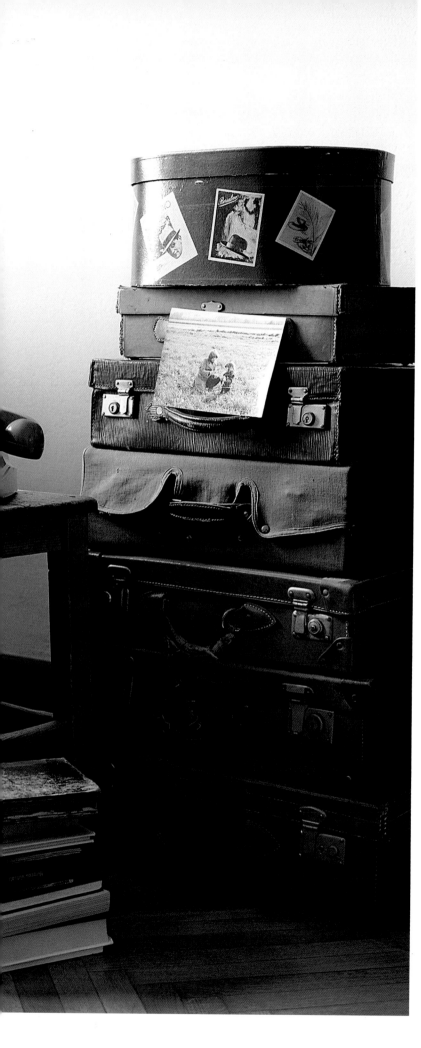

window treatments

Windows are one of the most important architectural features, whether you look at a house from outside or in. Thus it is important to treat them right. There's a huge choice of styles, from authentic eighteenth-century curtains with all the trimmings to minimalist translucent blinds. With attention to detail and a clear idea of the style you want to achieve, dressing up your windows can be great fun.

Window treatment principles

Windows are the most visible parts of a room. Because they are the main light source during the day, it is to them that the eye first travels. Get the look of your windows right and you are well on the way to getting the rest of the room right, too.

The first thing to consider when you are deciding how to dress your windows is whether you want to go along with the immutable style of the window itself, whether you are somehow going to obscure its shape, frame, and glazing bars, or whether you will impose a foreign style upon it. If, for instance, you have a large and beautiful Colonial window that looks out on an unfortunate view, will you let it be itself or, in trying to hide the view, impose a casbah-type fret or Louisiana louvers over its surface?

It is, of course, always best to let the window be itself. This way, you will make few period or design errors. But if this is impossible, try to impose as sympathetic a solution as you can. The Louisiana louvers are a much better answer than the casbah fret because real Louisiana windows approximate to Colonial ones, while Moroccan ones do not.

A second principle in window dressing is to decide how to change the window space by night. The beautiful daytime light source becomes a cold black space after dark. What's more, uncovered, who knows who's watching you.

If you are lucky enough to have shutters, curtains may not be necessary and will, anyway, detract from the architectural features. If there are none, but the window is beautiful, try the plainest shades possible. They will disappear by day and simply block the window glass by night. Another minimal solution, good for any style of house (as are shades), is to have the plainest available white cotton or linen curtains. No valance, no fancy hangings, but a sheer sheet of fabric to pull across by night.

If, however, the windows are ugly or you want a cozier approach, then curtains are the better option. The shape of the opening can easily be hidden by voluminous curtains that disguise the window area, and other ugly features minimized by making the curtain more important than the window. An equally good solution is to have a dramatic fake curtain covering the window frame with, behind it, another, simpler curtain or shade to close at night.

When you take the trouble to think hard about windows, solutions come easily. Consider the pros and cons in your home, decide what would be ideal, copy other people's ideas—then add your own style to the mix.

Clockwise from right:
Sheer voile curtains, toned with walls and floor, will hide an ugly view or difficult window shape, yet allow in muted light.

Detailed heavy curtains in a strong color distract the eye from a dull view.

Deep windows are made important by three treatments: shutters and louvers minimize the light and outside noise, while a single dramatic curtain is swept to one side. The mirror between adds light and space.

Only a glimpse of the window and a garden outside is allowed through a white Venetian blind. A perfect solution on a hot day.

A half-drawn shade controls both the light in the room and the shape of the window behind it. The dark frame adds a modern, geometric touch.

Shades can be as sheer or thick as you need. Here a pleated shade minimizes outside noise. A pink curtain softens the scheme.

Three beautiful floor-to-ceiling windows have been given extra prominence by the white furniture and surrounds. The shades, pulled to different levels, emphasize their shape, as do the bookshelves between.

Window styles

The shapes and materials used for windows are one of the most important aspects of house design—whether they are seen from inside or out. In the past, window styles were dictated by the cost of glass, its technology (large areas of glass became possible when the Victorians invented rolled plate glass), the need for warmth or cool, and the available materials for the frames.

Curiously, countries with extremely high or low temperatures opted for very small windows. In the tropics windows were pierced and shaded to keep heat out but allow breezes in, while in the far north they were shuttered both inside and out to conserve what warmth there was.

Today, with the increasing use of central heating and air conditioning, it's possible to have huge areas of glass where the view is exciting. But we still need the solace of heavy curtains and shutters in winter, or louvers and voiles to keep blinding sun out in summer. If you do have huge areas of plate glass in your house, remember that they can be unpleasant in climatic extremes.

Small windows, by contrast, need to be opened out. If you can, make a vista to stretch beyond the glass so the small area seems to widen into a view. Make sure maximum light penetrates by keeping curtains, blinds, and ornaments from encroaching into the glass area. Paint sills, frames, and reveals as light a shade as you can to enhance the incoming light. In Mediterranean climates, consider different curtains for summer and winter: hot summers need light voiles, but it may get cold enough in winter to warrant fabrics heavy enough to be unmoved by drafts.

If your windows' shapes are interesting or elegant, don't disguise them with fussy curtains or fabrics. Most of us have rather dull, rectangular windows or, worse still, positively ugly ones. If you are lucky enough to have round arches or Gothic points, Corbusier-type wraparounds with metal frames (increasingly fashionable), stone mullions, or Shaker panes, celebrate your luck. This means subordinating the window treatment to the window. If need be, do without curtains and rely on interior or exterior shutters. Paint the window a strong color to contrast with pale or neutral walls, or draw attention to the window by placing the furniture around it.

Curtains

There was a time—and the fabric manufacturers must have thrown their hats in the air with glee—when curtains seemed about to take over the world. No designer could look at a window without seeing gilded dolphins disporting over curtain poles and tassels big enough for a state visit. Everybody got the bug in the way that, at one time, every woman had shoulder pads big enough for a linebacker. Today, we're in reaction against these excesses, and generally curtains are as slimmed down as our jacket shoulders. Indeed, many people now live without any curtains at all, relying on built-in shutters or blinds so neutral as to be practically invisible. It has done wonders for our bank balances.

So, window treatments are as much the creatures of fashion as hemlines and hats—the only difference being that they change more slowly. It is possible to ignore the trends, but this requires the willingness to stick with what you have until it becomes fashionably retro.

Curtains today are very understated. You will see that many of those illustrated here are

unpatterned, and many have no strong color. Most are translucent enough to let light through and fine enough to blow in the wind. The inspiration for this trend came from Sweden, where light is precious. As can be seen in the nineteenth-century paintings of Swedish interiors, curtains were even then intended to let in any light available, while closed shutters provided insulation at night.

Of course, translucent curtains are not a good choice in bedrooms, where darkness is essential, but curtains can be backed with shades and still retain their fragility. An alternative is to have two sets of curtains—the inner ones light and airy and the outer ones heavy and shady (or vice versa). Other areas of the house are less complex. These gauzy styles can be left closed all day where the view is poor and tranquility important, or partly drawn to admit as much of a view as you want.

Far left: **A Swedish-inspired curtain—soft, billowing, pale, and translucent. Ideal for lightness and privacy.**

Left: **These curtains, made of contrasting sheer fabrics sewn in wide vertical stripes,** are a dramatic feature. The lightness of the fabric encourages them to billow in the breeze.

Above: **More translucent curtains serve to screen the bathroom without loss of light. Everything else is in pale shades.**

Above: **Curtains don't have to cover all the glass. This neat scheme leaves the top of the windows free, giving the impression that only a small part of the glazed wall is actually window. Pure white, slightly** scrimped curtains cover two smaller side windows. Only enough of the third, larger window is revealed to show an interesting garden view.

Above right: **Very plain, preferably washable,** curtains suit kitchens, which will inevitably become messy at times. These semi-translucent curtains are an unassuming backdrop, and screen the room from passersby. They run smoothly on a concealed track.

Right: **French-style windows can open fully to reveal balconies and gardens beyond, so curtains have to be able to hang inside the window frame as well as out. They can push right back before the windows are opened.**

Opposite above left:
The light streaming in from this generous window gives definition to an exotic antique lantern by showing off its colors and lines. Its ornate shape cleverly echoes that of the balcony outside.

Opposite right: **If this were the Eighties, these complex curtains would be shiny, trimmed, and multicolored. Today's treatment of swags and folds is just as romantic, but the use of a plain off-white fabric adds a touch of poverty chic.**

Top: **Strong and overscaled scallops in dark fabric edge these pale neutral curtains to give them shape and form. They also serve to draw attention to the window's shape and the view beyond.**

Above: **This Thirties-style living room high in the city is composed of blond woods, leathers, fabrics, and wall. The curtains, just a shade lighter, are hung from an integral valance for maximum translucency.**

Top right: **Eighteenth-century windows adapt beautifully to modern living. These have been treated with the utmost simplicity, yet the room's restraint means that they and the view beyond become the focal point.**

Opposite below left:
The designer of these subtle lime-green curtains has allowed a hint of floor creep, but allied it with very narrow, simple hangings. Plain shades, knotted at the base for weight, diffuse the light.

While the current trend is for plain and pale, it's still possible to admit a little color in your curtains. Pure white is lovely, especially in an all-white room or one painted a slightly darker pale gray. It contrasts well, too, with primary colors and touches of black. Otherwise, neutrals can veer to cream for a warmer effect, or to pretty lime greens and old rose pinks, once again teamed with whites and grays. Because simplicity is important in this style, keep valances and curtain poles to a minimum. Black iron, brushed steel, and painted metal rods are good, as are built-in valances that disguise the hooks and other workings while being painted in with the room.

If you love patterns, don't despair. Patterns haven't vanished entirely, but are more restrained. Stripes, checks, tickings, and self-colored patterns are perfectly in keeping with twenty-first-century simplicity, but all used with a tweak of difference. Gingham need not be confined to the country—imagine it with full-length nineteenth-century townhouse windows backed by a matching plain lining. Urban damasks turn up in country farmhouses, and toiles have been revived in overscaled form, every detail of the print enlarged.

The traditional country look lives on, with modern chintz bleached to look worn or its background tea-stained to seem aged. And authentic window treatments are always acceptable, so these chintzes can be lined with pretty cottons patterned with tiny all-over floral designs as were used in the eighteenth century.

Authenticity has, however, less power than before. Once, purists would suck in their cheeks if you dared to deck your period window with something incongruous, but that's now a valid choice. As a result, all sorts of unconventional fabrics are being used, helped by the fact that, when the treatment of the material is simple, the fabric itself can be unconventional. Don't do both

—fake leopardskin is lovely, but not when ruched. Designers are now looking at crossovers between fashion fabrics and soft furnishings. Yards of men's suiting—gray flannel, chalk and pinstriped worsted, even cavalry twill—make fine curtains because the cloth is simple, strong, and fluid when hung in long lengths (don't try it for cottage windows, though). Designers also love checked tattersalls, Viyella shirtings, and denim. Cashmeres and silks can be very expensive, but sari silks, beautifully embroidered, can sometimes be picked up cheaply on trips or in ethnic neighborhoods. Likewise, beautiful batik cottons can be bought cheaply by the bolt. Many flea markets, at home or abroad, have exciting and cheap fabrics on offer.

The best way to spot them is simply to look at other people's windows, clothes, and curtains when you are on vacation. In India it will be fine and fiery silks, in Sweden stripes and checks in subtle shades, while Italy has narrow white appliquéd strips intended for glazed cupboard doors. West Africa offers stylized portraits of important politicians and the British love chintz. What you see around the place can usually be found in the markets and local stores.

Then, of course, you can put your nous and your needle to the job. Plain fabrics can be cut into overscaled checks and stripes, quilted, or blanket-stitched around the edges with contrasting thread. Pedestrian materials such as dishcloths, linen dishtowels, sailcloth, or terrycloth can be stitched together and mixed and matched. Borders can be added, top or bottom, around the edges or even in the center, the fabric fringed by removing the warp or weft, or appliquéd with matching or contrasting motifs. Fine cloth can be pleated or tucked, horizontally or vertically, to make darker bands against the light, or it can be hung halfway down the window or folded at the top to create a self-valance.

Once you start to assess the possibilities— helped, perhaps, by pictures in magazines to start the imagination flowing—you can come up with window treatments that are not just elegant, subtle, and clever, but ones that are entirely your own invention.

Use your ingenuity. You'll find it's fun.

Above: **A mix of patterns adds weight and grandeur. The curtain fabric here complements the two French chairs.**

Left: **In this pleasant, French-inspired living room, the wallpaper pattern is repeated as a curtain border. But the curtains themselves are quite plain.**

Opposite below left: **Checks are really only doubled stripes. In this bedroom, a striped wall dilutes the impact of heavy checks. A ruffled valance adds form.**

Left: Though this room contains busy patterns, control is exerted by the use of few colors. The curtains are a strong element—the stripes are more assertive than the other patterns.

Above right: If you find antique hangings or needlework to fit a window or door, snap them up. Deficencies in the width can always be made up with secondary curtains or shades.

Right: A window of maximum theatricality. The translucent dark curtains against a somber wall pull back to reveal the glass framed by bright contrast lining.

Below center: Here's a clever mix of scarlet geraniums and checked red gingham.

Below right: Note how even the curtain pole matches this neat soft pink treatment.

Huge expanses of windows can be tamed by plain shades. Some of these are pulled down, allowing only a few panels of glass to remain visible.

Far left:
Roman shades are sympathetic to many fabrics. Here a busy paisley is let down at varying levels. The colors are echoed in the furnishings.

Shades & blinds

Don't even consider ruched shades. They should have been consigned to the pages of history long ago. Into the same black hole throw any shade with frilly ruffles around the edge, shades made of glass-curtain material, and unless you insist on retro kitsch, all-plastic Venetian blinds. Despite this wholesale slaughter, there are plenty more that are not only useful and good-looking, but also stylish. The tendency here is towards simplicity—minimalism has finally been adopted and adapted by the mainstream—camouflage, and lack of pattern.

Virtually all shades are better professionally made. Don't think about making your own sprung shades, for you will spend your life winding them back and forth by hand or leaving them hanging at half-mast or wherever they decide to stop. Properly made, however, shades are unobtrusive when rolled up, can be mounted on the window frame, and do not deprive the room of light. Thus, they are excellent for dark rooms where every ray of light is needed. Roll-ups are good, too, when you want a neutral shade. A roll-up in a plain white or off-white fabric, teamed with the color of the room or in a dull dark material, is the most recessive shade possible. No strings, pleats, loops, or hangings. Just a stretch of material. Some years ago, there was a fashion for making shades into rectangles of jolly scenery or faux stained-glass windows. Drop these into history's trash can, too.

Roman shades are a mite easier to make and easier, too, to rescue when things go wrong. But all those strings that make the shades ascend and descend in their required pleats need something of a mathematical genius to make, so a professional job is a good idea here, too.

Romans are one step away from plainness. If the fabric is translucent, the pleats will double the color intensity; if opaque, the lines of the pleats are pleasingly visible. They look more like blinds than the roll-ups do and they shut out a bit more light by hanging over the top of the window. They do, however, allow for a pattern (overscaled ones

Above: **Most shades are calming. These Roman shades are made of a neutral fabric, but are given form by red borders. The wider shade has a border a few inches in from the edge, making the three widths appear less varied.**

Left: **Floppy fabric works well in Roman shades, allowing a casual note in a formal dining room.**

Above: **Roman shades are excellent for noisy rooms—the fabric can be heavily padded to keep out both drafts and the roar of traffic. This all-white scheme emphasizes the comfort of the shade and pillows.**

Left: **These shades have doubled fabric to make borders around their edges. Their plainness sets off the artwork below.**

look startling) and a contrasting fabric as a lining. And, unlike roll-ups, they can be made in virtually any fabric.

Roman shades are also good for reducing noise levels since they can be lined and interlined, padded, or even quilted. These shades can also be given extra touches by adding contrasting borders, sewn lines of contrasting fabric at the point of the pleat, and irregular bamboo poles at the back to give interesting silhouettes.

While plastic Venetian blinds are definitely Fifties (except in pure white, when they are acceptable), slatted blinds in various natural fabrics are very much of today. They include wooden louvered blinds, which are sometimes used on cabinet doors, and exotic slatted versions made from oriental grasses, split bamboo, and rattans. These work very well if carefully sited, because they have all the subtle variations of natural stems. They may be uneven, blotched, or veined in subtle browns and beiges.

The caveat is that such blinds are quite definitely oriental. They work well in a scheme that has oriental qualities, be it a Manhattan loft sparsely decorated with Chinese furniture or a garden room filled with exotic orchids. You may even get away with them in a French farmhouse if the fabrics are Provençal (these were originally imported from India) or a stark modern home dedicated to the grains of wood and sheen of metal, but they are not suitable in every room.

Wooden louvers are an easier choice because they have been used extensively all over the South and the Caribbean. Thus they work in period buildings in warm climates. They even add to old farmhouses and townhouses, especially if the idea is to keep them shut and allow the light to make patterns on corridor walls.

All such blinds can happily be teamed with curtains. The blind does the work of keeping the light at an acceptable level while the curtains add color, texture, and a certain coziness. This is also a good solution to using incredibly expensive curtain fabric—cut the amount to a minimum and never close the curtain. However, in all cases, the blind and curtain should have something in common—color, pattern, trimming, texture—or a good strong contrast.

Opposite below left: **Very thin strips of bamboo (as used in cheap beach mats) make delightfully cool, textured blinds, fragile enough to blow in the wind.**

Opposite below right: **Strips of a rough form of hemp make these unusual shades. They let the light through, but are strong enough to withstand constant rolling. The edges** are bound in white and the whole is raised from a single central cord and pulley. It is an ideal complement to the wooden walls.

Opposite above: **Roll-up shades, in a fabric just a tad darker than the walls and table, are hung at half mast to give low light levels and, just maybe, hide something nasty higher up.**

Top left: **An all-white scheme with a deep window has plastic shutters that mimic the lines of wooden ones. They are translucent enough to glow in the sun.**

Above left: **Plain white Venetian blinds make a virtue of narrow windows in a calm living area. Dark spaces between slats emphasize the black patterns of the pillows and lamp.**

Above: **The virtue of louvered blinds is that they keep out the heat of strong sunlight, but even when closed, tiny slivers of light creep in to create shadows on the walls.**

Right: **White Venetian blinds create rays and patterns both on the walls and on their own slats. The shade they offer is far less than the louvers, above.**

Trimmings

One of life's pleasures is to find old trimmings and impedimenta for curtains in flea markets, French *brocantes*, and antique stores. French ones are rich sources because the French have made an art of dressing up curtains, shades, and other fabrics.

Tiebacks of gilded tin, brass, or iron are common sights and are an excellent way of controlling heavy curtains with style; punched lines of brass can be discovered to tack together into valances, while the range and exuberance of passementerie is immense. Keen trufflers will also find ancient, curvy valances of quilted *toile de Jouy*, once intended for four-poster beds, but just as good for windows.

French manufacturers still make both passementerie and metalwork curtain trimmings, and they are sold worldwide, with other producers following suit. It's now possible to find whole lines of colorful bobbles, tassels, bullion fringes, and embroidered borders to complement your curtains, along with little brass clips, Victorian-style wood and metal rings on curtain poles, and curly iron tiebacks and poles.

All these are intended to disguise the boring fact that curtains and shades have to hang above the window and behave themselves as they drop to the floor. The ruches and hooks at the top of the curtain, all those white tapes and strings, need to be hidden, and frankly, the old pleated valance in a matching fabric is pretty old hat.

This page: **A complex window treatment with dramatic detailing. Contrasted with the brilliant white molding, which is a focal point, the curtains and shades make a border for each window, then divide it. The curtain fabric hides the space between the windows, and the hangings of the shades imitate the geometrics of the window frame (echoed in the striped mat on the table). The curtains are lush and very full, encroaching on the floor, which softens the stark effect of the window treatment itself.**

Opposite main picture: **This very feminine window combines soft colors, translucency, and a swagged, trimmed valance. It is saved from over-sweetness by the window's formality and the view of the yard.**

Details, clockwise from top left: **From a distance, this chic curtain looks like voile, but it is in fact a dimpled plastic fabric. Decorative dark ties keep the carefully formed pleats neat.**

This curtain is a fringed throw whose tassels have been tied over the curtain pole—a trick that works as long as the curtains are not pulled too often. The back lighting exposes the throw's texture.

This rich ornamental scheme combines a painted ceiling detail above the molding

with heavy satin curtains, hung with gilded wooden rings on a gilded curtain pole.

A heavy red pattern and matching tassels make a dramatic valance.

Roman shades are, at once, formal and casual in their folds. This one tends to formality with its rich silky gray fabric and contrast backing.

Fragile-looking net material forms a striped shade. A deep but insubstantial fringe belongs to curtains of the same material that hang in front of it.

Top: **Curly iron tiebacks work best with simple fabrics, either as a contrast or harmonizing.**

Above: **The ruched valance made of the same fabric as the curtain is now obsolete. A much neater version is to use the curtain fabric attached to a stiff backing, with not a pleat in sight. You could also trim the edges to define the border.**

Trimmings should be chosen to suit the decorative scheme. Thus iron poles and tiebacks work both in ancient houses with small windows and in modern schemes where ornament is reduced to a minimum. Gilded valances and tiebacks are for grandeur—though they can be modern as well as classical—while fabric trimmings can be found to suit virtually everything but a cottage. Silk tassels and bobbles are best suited to classical rooms filled with antiques, while burlap and velvet versions are excellent in more contemporary settings. That's not to say you can't have fun going against convention— imagine brilliantly mixed primary-color bobbles *à la* Damien Hirst on a modern shade, for instance, or brushed-steel poles in a modern log cabin. Both, with care, will work well.

With a few basic rules, trimming curtains and shades isn't difficult. The first rule is to determine your style and stick to it—don't be seduced by the charm of the passementerie. Second is to be disciplined and keep trimmings under control (the price will help you to do this). Third is to consider the options for some days before you take the plunge. There's lots of choice out there, and you need time to make wise decisions.

Genius is in the detail. It is just as important to put a final effort into the last tweak of a curtain or shade as it is to pick the fabric in the first place.

Working with fabrics is like dressing up. It's the fun part of creating a room, where you can allow your fantasies full rein. Rooms can be completely altered by different fabric furnishings—and changed for summer and winter—while clever use of color and contrast will highlight good points and disguise bad. If furniture is the underpinning of a design scheme, then fabric furnishings provide the fashionable touches.

fabric furnishings

Fabric furnishing principles

It is a rare house or apartment that completely ignores fabric furnishings. And it will be one that is poorer for doing so. We've all been in those minimalist restaurants where the walls and floors are concrete and the tables metal. What is the result? It is brutal cacophony as sound waves caused by noisy conversation meet hard surfaces to bounce and echo back. As the ornate interiors of the Vienna Opera House prove, large areas of matt fabric make a great acoustic.

Fabric furnishings are also the most adaptable, the most frequently altered, and the most variable element of any decorative scheme. If you take a plain white cube, with the simple use of fabrics—gingham, French toile, cut-velvet brocade, or hazy voile—you could change its style to anything from country to Provençal, from palazzo to Gustavian Swedish. Equally, with the misuse of clashing colors, overactive or inappropriate patterns, and a wild assortment of textures, even the most perfectly proportioned room and the best furniture are overwhelmed.

It's important not to try so hard that your cleverness is more apparent than the room itself. The flouncing Eighties are a dire example of what can happen when too much money meets too much design. Yards of ornate fabrics writhed and twisted around curtain poles and oozed, lavalike, across floors. Edges were bobbled, trimmed, and ruffled—a truly overplayed style.

Below: **Remnant boxes or obsolete swatch books are good places for fabric finds. This generous throw of squares of soft tweed in browns, beiges, and grays has been sewn together with a luxurious velvet border. The pillows—not an economy suggestion— are covered in cashmere. Their neutral tones perfectly complement the natural dyes of the tweed and the stone fireplace.**

Above: **Clever ideas often spring from necessary economy. Designers search for scraps of expensive fabric and eke them out with appliqué work. This cushion is covered with glowing silk sari fabric embroidered and bordered in gold, the whole contrasted with a wide central band of black. It is cunningly teamed with a neutral silk pillow as backing.**

Fashion, even in interior design, is a fickle beast, and it's pretty certain that, after today's spare and neutral themes, we will return again to something a bit fussier. Thus, if you still love your Eighties curtains and can keep your nerve, you may well find you have a delightfully authentic interior forty years on. But expect lots of sniggers before that.

Just like designer clothes, well-thought-out interiors, however neutral, need touches of color, texture, and even eccentricity to be enjoyable. The new trimmed-down curtain, so much cheaper than before, can be changed for winter or summer, entirely altering a room according to season. Winter demands wool, tweed, or velvet; summer, light linen, silk, or cotton. If you decide to have a seasonal look, the two fabrics can obviously be more extreme both in weight and color.

Similarly, covers, throws, and scatter cushions are infinitely variable. Suppose your winter curtains are gray flannel and summer ones French cream linen. In winter, chunky tweed pillows with gray among the colorful threads

Above: **The pillows are the only spot of color in a neutral living room where every other shade is monochrome, from black and dark brown to stone, string, and bone. Their effect is startling.**

Above right: **This living room is colored in exotic shades of red and gold. Yet the only element of pattern is in the pillows and curtains. Their colors pull together the room's various shades.**

Right: **Eastern patterns and rough silks are very chic, and their subtle shades rewarding.**

can be tossed over gray cashmere throws, while as the days lengthen, the linen drapes can be complemented with bright green-and-white gingham slipcovers arrayed with leafy-patterned cotton cushions. And, if that finally bores you, add shocking-pink velvet to your gray flannel scheme and gilded Indian silks for the summer.

Fabrics are equally adept at creating a mood. Bedrooms should be the most heavily clothed areas, and kitchens, where smells and grease are attracted to fabrics, the least. Bedrooms need to be comfort zones, and the colder the climate, the more you need fabrics. In the north, cashmere, silk, muslin, and chintz are all contenders—even a man's bedroom looks fine with dark-brown silks and tobacco-dyed toiles. Warmer climates encourage bedrooms with floating curtains, plain blinds, and pale-covered chairs—all creating a sense of breezy cool. It's always a good idea to take colors from the landscape: brilliant blue by the Pacific coast, terracotta in the Arizona hills, ice and pine in the frozen north, and brilliant primaries along the streets of New York.

Above and below left:
Using fabrics in a room isn't necessarily all about color and cloth; it's about texture and surface, too. These details show how neutral shades can contrast with each other by taking advantage of the variations of surface and how the light reacts to them. Suede and leather are perfect examples of the use of light: suede, with its brushed flat appearance, tends to recede and add comfort, while leather is shiny, glamorous, and assertively hard-edged. Neutrals such as slubbed silk, sheeny satin, and matt velvet can also be combined with the skins.

Patterns often conjure up visions of chintz. But they can be exotic and abstract, too. The cotton fabric *(above left)* is printed in modern blocks of neutrals, while a brilliant painted wall *(above right)* makes a dramatic foil for the purple and pink easy chair and pillows. The leopard-print stool *(left)* would be quite happy in a traditional setting.

Left: **What is it that makes this room so effective? The idea of teaming a sofa covered in a soft, flowery chintz with another in a strong mix of leather and velvet would seem wrong. Yet here it works. The first reason must be the way white has been used for walls, floor, rails, and furniture. The next is that the dark sofa's presence is picked up by the black-and-white pictures. Finally, the pillows on the dark sofa refer back to the pretty chintz. This room has been created by a great eye.**

Below: **If working with fabrics in a room is like dressing up, then someone has had a great deal of fun here with the costume box. Note first that the whole scheme is in variations of a single color and the fun is in the textures. The geometric lines of floorboards and tabletop lead the eye to the wildly appliquéd oatmeal and cream throw, tossed over a plain cover on the sofa and emphasized with pretty cushions. Even the position of the crystal globes is intended to reflect the whole.**

Choosing fabrics

Never let anyone tell you that choosing fabrics for a room is easy. You simply need to look at the photographs of posh houses for sale in upscale magazines to see the many pitfalls. Living rooms are abuzz with chintz, oriental carpets, and fancy cushions; dining-room chairs are dressed up like milkmaids, and everywhere curtains are too short, too grotesque, or look ready for a garden party.

In deciding which fabrics to pick, it's a good idea to approach the whole as you would an outfit. Would you wear matching hat, bag, and gloves? No, you wouldn't—so don't team your curtains with the wallpaper *and* the cushions. Would you add a cotton printed with roses to a touch of chinoiserie with gingham? Not unless you were very experienced at mix and match.

Thus, when you approach the soft fabrics in a room—and you can do this first or last, before or after picking the furniture—the secret is simplicity and relaxation. Decide on the kind of room you want, whether it has to work all year round, morning and night, or whether it can focus on a particular season or lighting pattern. Simplicity means keeping patterns under control—no more than two for the fabrics unless you're an expert, and nothing too dramatic. If you do want to mix patterns, keep them to a theme. This can be the type of fabric—gingham, say, or toile—or it can be the color. Indigo batik fabrics from Africa may team happily with denim or Swedish navy stripes. If in doubt, watch what experienced decorators do and adapt their ideas to suit your home.

Relaxation in picking fabrics means not over-straining. Should you decide on a chintz with a white background covered in purple fuchsias with green leaves, steer clear of designing the rest of the room with matching plain white, purple, and green touches. It's just too contrived. You could, however, pick just the fuchsia shade and play games with it in different tones and textures.

If caution is good in choosing fabrics, so, too, is the unconventional. Fabric furnishings need not be made only from upholstery fabrics. Curiously, it's often cheaper, as well as more

Top: **The secret here is simplicity. When using fabrics, stick to a very limited color palette and be disciplined about pattern. Here, the charming patterned chair cushions are given center stage against the restrained background.**

Above: **A single color choice allows you to mix the patterns on fabrics. A variety of checks, stripes, and plain rose-and-white fabrics has been joined by a single floral, while the rest of the room—even the chair and books—is simply a soft white.**

Top: **Mixing textures —here a leather sofa, velvet cushions, and a mohair and satin throw—is simple if you keep to a color scheme. All are in tones of brown and cream, but vary from shiny to matt.**

Above left: **Plain wool blankets often have a shiny satin edge; an idea to copy for handsewn throws and pillows.**

Above right: **If you cover pillows in shiny silk, cover the furniture in wool. The contrast helps both—and pillows won't slip around.**

Top right: **A very feminine scheme that relies on one color. The femininity comes in textures: a gold-trimmed sari is draped over the gilded sofa, while the pillows are velvet.**

effective, to buy tailoring or dressmaking fabrics. Gray flannel, for instance, looks stunning as long curtains in period windows because it hangs so fluidly; it also works for cushions and chair covers. Tweed is another men's fabric to watch out for. It may be expensive, but it wears well and is full of subtle color variations that will pick out objects in a room. African fabrics are often in restrained, if colorful, combinations, and some will make you laugh for joy—you can't say that for many cushions. Antique cloths are another good source, from characterful old linen sheets, often with cross-stitched monograms, to scraps of tapestry or embroidery to use as collage.

It's important when you are choosing fabrics that you do not see each room in isolation. People will walk from one to another, so there should be a sense of continuity. This doesn't mean you can't switch from sixteenth-century Florentine damask to Nineties plastic sheeting in a single house—but you need to give visual warning of what is about to happen. Once again, complementary colors will do the trick, as will a consistent theme—roses through the centuries, say, or checks and plaids.

Most professional decorators work with a color board, and it makes good sense. Not only

Above: **In a restrained room, the single pattern on the fake fur draws the eye.**

Left: **Real ingenuity has gone into these textured cushions, made from woven elastic bands. The upholstery is bland honey-brown felt.**

Right: **This disciplined bedroom is utterly plain to show off the handblocked throw.**

does a color board look swanky, it actually works. Paint or cover the board with what's going on the walls, then attach to it swatches of the fabrics for curtains, covers, and cushions. If the scale of a fabric's pattern is enormous, try to get a color photocopy of it reduced in scale to give an idea of its entire pattern. Move all the bits around, pin them by your breakfast table, and keep considering whether they work and why. If you are doubtful, make a change or two. If you are still doubtful, scrap the whole thing and think again. The effort will give enormous satisfaction—and a much better result at a tenth of the cost.

Top right: **Lots of antique finds cover this bed, from lace-edged linen to the embroidered and bemirrored spread, but they are all kept in one color palette.**

Center right: **Indigo and white always works, even with complex patterns. Order is kept by the pure white headboard and soft blue walls.**

Above: **Slipcovers are very useful in changing a room's emphasis. Here an old chair has a plain, light slipcover, over which is a neat woolen throw, a shade darker. Darker yet are the cushions on the windowseat. This is a summer scheme that could change utterly for colder weather.**

Above right: **Plain off-white slipcovers reduce the bulk of this large sofa—but keep a spare set to make laundering easier. The pale fabric also increases the light levels in the room.**

Right: **Ugly brown wooden furniture can become beautiful when painted white, revealing its lines. This small table and large seat have been given a Swedish feel by adding cushions in gingham of Gustavian green shadowed with tan.**

Slipcovers

A slipcover is meant to be practical, but it can still look good. The secret is to pick a fabric that can cope with the curves and angles that make up a chair or sofa. Solids are obviously excellent, as are all-over florals of a restrained nature. Geometrics can cause problems—though stripes and checks are generally easy. Another good choice is a faded, tea-stained chintz that looks as though it's had a thousand washes. The secret is to avoid anything too new-looking or over-powering—most armchairs and sofas are not beautiful in themselves and are best dressed discreetly rather than in garish florals.

Once the fabric has been chosen (not all chairs in a room need to match—better if they don't, in fact), decide the style of cover. Ruched petticoats are unfashionable (and ugly) so go for a plain skirt and the minimum of fuss. Edges can be piped to give shape and emphasis, and this works well with chintzes and many geometrics. Solid fabrics rarely look good with contrasting piping.

Cushion covers are a form of slipcover and are extremely adaptable. They are also very easy and cheap to make. In certain rooms—kitchens, dining rooms, and studies—where there are fewer fabric furnishings, a variation in the cushion covers can alter the entire decor. The obvious time to change is between winter and summer. Winter cushions need an element of snuggle and come in heavy fabrics such as tweed, corduroy, velvet, and, if you are very lucky, cashmere, the coziest of all. Colors should suit the season: warm autumnal browns and rusts, scarlets and crimsons. Summer brings silky fabrics, ginghams, tickings, and lightweight linens. Florals come into their own, as do checks, tickings, and maritime colors.

When you've got it all planned, it's tempting to buy two of everything just to provide longer wear, easier washing, and no more hassle for a decade. It depends on how fickle your tastes are and how often you are likely to change whole schemes—but for some, there's nothing more comforting in a room than a squashy old sofa dressed in a floppy cover that welcomes muddy fingers and paws.

Top left: **The complex patterns of ticking make fine cushions and curtains. Back cushions are tied onto casual seats in front of a table in a different version.**

Center left: **When you buy furniture, go for line rather than upholstery. If pieces are good, ugly covers can be disguised by wrapping the backs and seats in soft linen. But keep the fabric simple.**

Above: **Details—how curtains are hung or cushions anchored to chairs—are key. Here, plain dining chairs have cushions with long ties which are cross-gartered down the legs.**

Left: **Big, squashy chairs or sofas seem even more inviting covered in traditional —but worn—chintz. "Faded" or tea-stained floral cottons can now be bought new—and strong.**

Cushions, pillows, & accessories

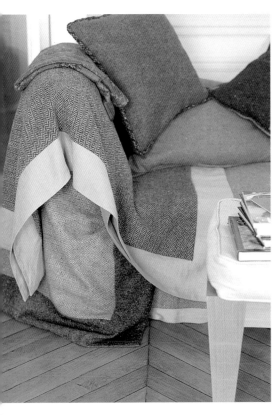

The most changeable parts of any room scheme are the accessories you add at the end. Today's styles mean that lots of these will be made of fabric, as well as plants, flowers, paintings, and tablescapes. Indeed, you can use fabric for realistic silk plants such as orchids or bowls of flowers such as deep magenta lilies, while modern tapestries in bright abstracts are much in vogue, as is the idea of hanging a special antique dress or Chinese costume on the wall. If you have large and important areas of wall, look out for these finely embroidered robes—they are beautifully sewn in brilliant colors, exotic, and what's more, really good value.

More prosaically, modern living has gone overboard on the throw. From cashmere to synthetic fleece, knitted Aran to silk plaid, no fabric designer has ignored the possibilities. They have come up with deeply luxurious alpacas to snuggle up to in winter, glossily handsome fake furs, brilliantly colored Welsh blankets with contrasting stitching, and bright plaids that are as good around your shoulders as on the sofa.

But don't feel the need to buy designer chic if the cost is high; flea-market finds such as old blankets, plaids, and travel rugs can be improved with the addition of a wide, complementary, or contrasting border, with contrast stitching, or by adding appliqué patterns cut from other vintage fabrics. Find faded old curtains and sew them onto plain matching backgrounds for added strength. Buy fake furs from fabric merchants and back them with matching felt.

These throws fulfil multiple purposes: they change the feeling of a room in an instant; they disguise ugly furniture or unfortunate upholstery; they soften the harsh lines of beds and sofas; and they give a casual feeling to a formal room. Use them over sofas and easy chairs, drop them on side tables and dining tables. Layer them over each other as you would shirts and sweaters, or fold them neatly and drape them over chair arms.

Then you can add pillows on top. They must be filled with down or feathers—slightly under-

Above left: **Tweed is the most helpful fabric for furniture because so many patterns, textures, and colors match each other. Here throws have been given presence and formality by heavy contrasting borders.**

Below left: **Don't overlook texture—see how this cube covered in bobbly ostrich skin immediately takes center stage in an all-neutral living room. Place it so it catches the light for full effect.**

Above and center right: **The pretty greens of a fragile sari fabric— with a thin strip of pink—contrast with soft leathers, velvet, and cotton. Notice how the vibrant green plant emphasizes the color in the room.**

Below: **When choosing fabrics for accessories, think what the room already offers. Here it is a thin stripe of blue in the window. Avoiding the obvious (quantities of gingham or blue ticking), a single piped pillow is a bright note.**

Above left: **Dust covers protect stored furniture. But why not dress your chairs in transparent slips, to show their lines —but not their ages?**

Above right: **Texture is key in an off-white living room containing two suede cubes. The chair and sofa are in a slightly sharper cotton.**

Left: **Many materials can make accessories. This tablecloth is made of heavily textured artist's canvas, appliquéd with perky petals and border.**

stuffed if you want the current floppy look—but can be in any size from bolster to handkerchief as long as they are round, square, or rectangular. No triangles, hexagons, or stars, please. The choice of fabrics for scatter cushions should be as carefully chosen as the rest of the scheme, but keeping up the fashion analogy, cushions are like ties in a man's outfit—a chance to show a sense of color and humor, to break away from the formality of the rest. When you have your scheme, pile them high.

Like large sofas, beds benefit from pillow power—especially spare beds, which can look awfully sad. Your bed looks good dressed up, too—if you are prepared to dress it as well as yourself every morning and reverse the process every night. If you are, your bedroom will always be a haven during the day, a comfort zone when things go wrong.

Because fabric around the place helps soften the acoustics, use plenty in rooms that are intended to be comforting. As well as bedrooms, these include living rooms, bathrooms, and children's rooms. Bathrooms should be packed with fleecy white towels and such items as cosmetics bags, make-up boxes, and nests of facecloths, preferably in white with soft touches of color. Gray, beige, stone, and dark brown are very soothing.

Children's rooms, by contrast, thrive on bright primary shades, but keep the scheme under control by sticking to one bright colour—scarlet, denim blue, lemon yellow—and contrasting it with black, white, or neutral stone. Try having toys, bags and boxes, chair cushions, and laundry bags in nothing but shades of scarlet combined with

stone. Both adults and children will appreciate the stunning effect.

Living rooms can be accessorized rather more subtly. Again, pick a color and play games with it. Lacquer red, chocolate brown, or leaf green can be mixed in dozens of tones, textures, and fabrics and teamed with real Chinese lacquer, ebony pieces, or leafy plants. Use fabric for lampshades, as mats under houseplants, as backing to wall-hung mirrors, or to cover piles of notebooks.

Left: **There is absolutely no adornment in this pale green tropical-style bedroom but the ceiling fan and the lines of the mosquito net. Both mattress cover and floor match the walls. Throws and a trail of pillows in a variety of pinks provide the only color interest.**

Above right: **Subtle mixes of natural colors—seashell, granite, cream, string, and straw—are highly fashionable in our environmentally conscious age. And they all work together, as they do in nature.**

Below right: **If you are unenthusiastic about paintings, interesting fabrics make good wall hangings and, as in this bedroom, make sense of an overall color scheme. The hanging should have some pretensions to be more than just a fabric strip. Here, it's the ornate edging.**

Far right: **Fabric can be used not only for wall hangings; it can also act as a frame for a painting, print, or photograph. This two-tone cotton hanging with its monochrome center picture matches the satin bedspread, feathers, lampshade, and even the organized files.**

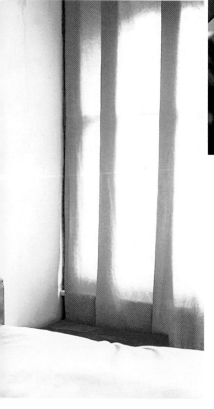

Accessories will pin down the theme of a room. Take plaid: you may want to have a Scottish effect in your dining room without going overboard with plaid curtains and carpets. So use plaid to cover the table and for napkins, emphasized, perhaps, with horn-handled knives and prints of Scottish castles. If you want a seaside effect, the living room can have cushions of bleached, natural canvas and old pennants, ropes, and flags draped over sofas or hung on the wall. Country rooms can take up brilliantly colored horse blankets. Great sources of unusual accessories are specialist outlets such as boating suppliers and riding stores.

Even offices benefit from being cleverly accessorized. Computers come in vibrant colors and their raspberry or aqua shades can be echoed by fabric-covered boxes for papers and files. Ugly reference books can be covered in similar fabrics and marshaled together on a shelf, and even tubs for pencils can be matched in. Don't go over the top, however: aim at a chic, organized office.

RESOURCES

INSPIRATIONAL INTERIORS

Search department stores and home shops for basics. Define your style with finds from boutiques and specialist outlets (see the Living Rooms section for ideas).

ABC Carpet & Home
881–888 Broadway
New York, NY 10003
212 674 1144
For a store near you, call
561 279 7777
www.abchome.com
Exotic collection of home furnishings, fabrics, carpets, and design accessories.

Bloomingdales
1000 Third Avenue
New York, NY 10022
212 705 2000
www.bloomingdales.com
Department store. Twenty-four locations nationwide.

The Conran Shop
407 East 59th Street
New York, NY 10022
212 755 9079
www.conran.com
Cutting-edge design from furniture to forks.

Crate & Barrel
646 N Michigan Avenue
Chicago, IL 60611
800 996 9960
For a retailer near you, call
800 927 9202
www.crateandbarrel.com
A wonderful source of good value furniture and accessories, from simple white china and glass, to chairs and beds.

IKEA
Potomac Mills Mall
2700 Potomac Circle
Suite 888
Woodbridge, VA 22192
For a store near you, call
800 254-IKEA
www.ikea.com
Home basics at great prices, including assembly-kit furniture, and stylish, inexpensive kitchenware.

Kolbe & Kolbe
1323 S 11th Avenue
Wausau, WI 54401
For a retailer near you, call
800 955 8177
Windows and doors.

Macy's
800 BUY-MACY
www.macys.com
Department store. Furniture, bedding, etc. Stores nationwide.

Martha By Mail
P.O. Box 60060
Tampa, FL 33660-0060
800 950 7130
www.marthabymail.com
Tasteful homewares.

Neiman Marcus
For a store near you, call
888 888 4757
For mail order, call
800 825 8000
www.neimanmarcus.com
Department store. Furniture, accessories. Thirty-one stores and catalog.

Pottery Barn
P.O. Box 7044
San Francisco
CA 94120-7044
For a store near you, call
800 922 9934
www.potterybarn.com
Everything from furniture to decoration details, such as muslin curtains, china, pillows, and candlesticks.

Restoration Hardware
935 Broadway
New York, NY 10011
212 260 9479
www.restoration
   hardware.com
Not just hardware, some of the funkiest home furnishings, lighting, and home and garden accessories you'll find.

Target Stores
33 South Sixth Street
Minneapolis, MN 55402
888 304 4000
www.target.com
A chain store with things both funky and functional.

Waverly
Dealer locations:
800 423 5881
www.waverly.com
Complete supply of decorative accessories including fabric, wallpaper, furniture, window treatments, tabletop, paint, and floor coverings.

ROOM BY ROOM

KITCHENS & EATING AREAS

American Woodmark Corp.
Box 1980
Winchester, VA 22604
For a retailer near you, call
800 677 8182
www.american
   woodmark.com
Cabinet and accessory manufacturer.

Becker Zeyko
1030 Marina Village Parkway
Alameda, CA 94501
510 865 1616
www.beckerzeyko.com
This high-end cabinetry is manufactured with the highest environmentally conscious standards using earth-friendly materials and biodegradable products.

DuPont Corian®
Barley Mill Plaza
Price Mill Building
P.O. Box 80012
Wilmington, DE 19880-0012
800 426 7426
www.dupont.com/corian/
This nonporous acrylic surface is used for counters and sinks. Patterns and colors are consistent throughout the piece. Stains or scratches can easily be ground out.

Formica®
10155 Reading Road
Cincinnati, OH 45241
800 367 6422
www.formica.com
This well-known laminate can mimic nearly any matt, shiny, or pattern-textured surface you can think of.

Franke Inc.
3050 Campus Drive,
   Suite 500
Hatfield, PA 19440
For a retailer near you, call
800 626 5771
www.franke.com
Stainless-steel, granite, and titanium sinks and faucets.

Jenn-Air
240 Edwards Street SE
Cleveland, TN 37311
For a retailer near you, call
800 JENN-AIR
www.jennair.com
Stoves and convection ovens.

Just Manufacturing
9233 King Street
Franklin Park, IL 60131
847 678 5150
www.justsinks.com
This company produces over 500 models of stainless-steel sink. All are nonporous and sound deadened.

Kitchen Center
1105 Burke Street
Winston Salem, NC 29101
336 725 2343
www.thekitchencenter.com
Features top-rated products such as Wood-Mode cabinets, DuPont Corian countertops, Hansa faucets, Viking and Thermador ovens and ranges, and Sub-Zero refrigerators.

Modern-Aire Ventilating
7319 Lankershim Boulevard
North Hollywood, CA 91605
818 765 9870
www.modernaire.com
Makers of standard and custom-designed stainless-steel range hoods. Stainless-steel panels can also be designed to fit fronts of other kitchen appliances for a coordinated look.

Salt Marsh Pottery
Dartmouth, MA
800 859 5028
www.saltmarsh.com
Ceramic tile countertops.

Sears, Roebuck and Company
800 MY-SEARS
www.sears.com
Working with local contractors, Sears resurfaces cabinets and drawers to change the look of a kitchen with little fuss and at minimum cost.

Sterling Plumbing
2900 Golf Road
Rolling Meadows, IL 60008
800 783 7546
www.sterlingplumbing.com
Stainless-steel and fiberglass-sheet-molded composite sinks designed to be quiet and kind to china and glass. Matching faucets are part of the line.

Williams-Sonoma
121 East 59th Street
New York, NY 10022
800 541 1262
www.williams-sonoma.com
Cooking utensils, fine linens, and classic china.

LIVING ROOMS

Anthropologie
375 West Broadway
New York, NY
Call 800 309 2500 for your nearest store
www.anthropologie.com
Furniture and home furnishings.

B & B Italia
150 East 58th Street
New York, NY 10155
800 872 1697
www.bebitalia.it
Modern furniture. Specializes in Bellini, Cittero, Pesce, Scarpa, and others.

Barneys
660 Madison Avenue
New York, NY
212 826 8900
www.barneys.com
Home furnishings and accessories.

Classic Leather
P.O. Box 2404
Hickory, NC 28603
828 328 2046
www.classic-leather.com
Manufacturer of leather-upholstered furniture.

Dana Robes
Route 4-A
Lower Shaker Village
Enfield, NH 03748
For a retailer near you,
call 800 722 5036
www.danarobes.com
Shaker-style furniture.

Decorative Crafts
50 Chestnut Street
Greenwich, CT 06830
203 531 1500
www.decorativecrafts.com
Italian furniture.

Design Within Reach
455 Jackson Street
San Francisco, CA 94111
800 944 2233
www.dwr.com
A consumer-friendly shop supplying furniture from over fifty modern designers including Alessi, Gehry, and Knoll.

The Federalist
Greenwich, CT
203 625 4727
Early nineteenth-century Federal-period American furniture.

Ficks Reed
Cincinnati, OH
513 985 0606
www.ficksreed.com
Wicker and rattan furniture.

Full Upright Position
800 431 5134
www.fup.com
Stocks furniture designed by Aalto, Eames, Le Corbusier, van der Rohe and more.

George Smith LA
142 North Robertson
   Boulevard
Los Angeles, CA 90048
310 360 0880
www.georgesmith.com
English sofas and chairs.

Lexington Home Furnishings
P.O. Box 1008
Lexington, N.C. 27293-1008
For a retailer near you, call
800 539 4636
www.lexington.com

Maine Cottage Furniture
P.O. Box 935
Yarmouth, ME 04096
207 846 1430
www.mainecottage.com
Maple, birch, and cherry veneer furniture.

MOMA Design Store
44 West 53rd Street
New York, NY 10022
800 447 6662
www.momastore.org
A finely honed selection of furniture, lighting, kitchen, and tabletop accessories by modern designers including Stark, Wright, and Vasa.

Montis
Hendersonville, NC
919 942 1608
www.montis.nl
Leather and metal furniture.

Pier One Imports
71 Fifth Avenue
New York, NY 10003
212 206 1911
www.pier1.com
Great home accessories, furniture, and outdoor ideas.

Strictly Wood Furniture Co.
301 S. McDowell Street
Suite 811
Charlotte, NC 28204
800 278 2019
www.strictlywood
   furniture.com
Mission-style furniture hand-crafted from solid wood; hardware, lighting, and mirrors.

Thomasville Home Furnishings
15531 South Tamiami Trail
Ft. Myers, FL 33908
941 482 5110
www.thomasville
   furniture.com
Wood and upholstered furniture.

BEDROOMS

Ad Hoc Softwares
136 Wooster Street
New York, NY 10012
212 982 7703
Retailer of imported bed linens in natural fabrics.

Avery Boardman
979 3rd Avenue
New York, NY 10021
212 688 6611
www.averyboardman.com
Headboards, plus sofabeds, daybeds, and trundle beds.

California Closets
1625 York Avenue
New York, NY
212 517 7877
www.calclosets.com
Closet customizations.

Carlyle Custom Convertibles
1375 Third Avenue
New York, NY 10028
212 570 326
Sofabeds.

Charles P. Rogers Brass & Iron Beds
55 West 17th Street
New York, NY
800 272 7726
www.charlesprogers.com
Original and restored brass and iron beds.

Garnet Hill
P.O. Box 262, Main Street
Franconia, NH 03580
www.garnethill.com
Bed linen in natural fibers, wonderful down duvets, and pillows.

Ralph Lauren Home Collection
1185 Avenue of the Americas
New York, NY 10036
For a retailer near you, call
212 642 8700
Bed linen and homewares.

Workbench
470 Park Avenue South
New York, NY 10016
800 380 2370
www.workbench
   furniture.com
Clean and functional imported Danish furniture for bedrooms and dining and living rooms.

BATHROOMS

Acme Brick Co.
P.O. Box 425
Fort Worth, TX 76101
800 932 2263
Glass-block walls.

American Standard
1 Centennial Avenue
Piscataway, NJ 08855
732 980 3000
www.americanstandard.com
Tubs, whirlpools, sinks, and toilets.

Bed, Bath & Beyond
620 6th Avenue
New York, NY 10011
800 GO BEYOND
www.bedbathand
   beyond.com
Modern bathroom accessories.

Burgess International Bathroom Fixtures
6810-B Metroplex
Romulus, MI 48174
800 837 0092
www.burgess
   international.com
Toilets, bidets, vanities, and traditional bathroom furniture.

The Chicago Faucet Co.
2100 S. Clearwater Drive
Des Plaines, IL 60018
847 803 5000
Faucets.

Epanel Inc.
P.O. Box 115
Pennington, NJ 08534
800 537 2635
Electric towel warmers, towel bars, towel rings.

Foremost Industries
906 Murray Road
East Hanover, NJ 07936
973 428 0400
Faucets, vanities, vitreous china.

Kohler Co.
444 Highland Drive
Kohler, WI 53044
800 4-KOHLER
www.kohlerco.com
Bathroom suites in a wide range of styles.

MAAX Inc.
600 Rte Cameron
Ste-Marie-de-Bce
Quebec
Canada G6E 1B2
418 387 4155
Showers, tubs, whirlpools.

Royal Baths Mfg Co.
14635 Chrisman Road
Houston, TX 77039
281 442 3400
www.royalbaths.com
Whirlpools, shower bases, shower seats, toilets.

TFI Corp.
1065 Marauder Street
Chico, CA 95973
530 891 6390
www.tficorp.com
Corian products.

WORK SPACES

The Cabinetmaker
1714 East Owl Hollow Road
Paoli, IN 47454
812 723 3461
www.the-cabinetmaker.com
Reproductions of Greene and Greene furniture and other designs from the American Arts & Crafts movement.

Frederick Cooper Lamps, Inc.
2545 West Diversey
Chicago, IL 60647
773 384 0800
www.frederickcooper.com
Handsomely designed and finished lamps of all types and styles are this American manufacturer's specialty.

Hunter Fan Company
2500 Frisco Avenue
Memphis, TN 38114
800 448 6837
www.hunterfan.com
Silent ceiling fans. Many have built-in lighting and can be installed to replace a standard ceiling light.

CHILDREN'S ROOMS

Babies "R" Us
Call 800 BABY RUS or visit
www.babiesrus.com for a
retailer near you
Complete line of linens for babies.

Crayola Paints
Call 800 344 0400 or visit
www.benjaminmoore.com
for a retailer near you
150 colors of washable latex paint, including glitter, glow in the dark, and chalkboard varieties.

Frick and Frack's Toy Storage
1470 Route 23 North
Wayne, NJ 07470
973 696 6701
www.frickandfrack.com
Toy benches and children's trunks.

Fun Time Designs Inc.
#375–2600 Granville Street
Vancouver, B.C.
Canada V6H 3V3
800 977 3443
Furniture featuring kids' favorite cartoon characters.

Gloria's Kids Beds
180 Post Road East
Westport, CT 06430
888 600 5437
Children's furniture.

Tuffyland
H. Wilson Co.
555 West Taft Drive
South Holland, IL 60473
800 245 7224
www.tuffyland.com
Children's tables and chairs, plus computer workstations.

HALLS & AWKWARD SPACES

The Rug Barn
P.O. Box 1187
Abbeville, SC 29620
864 446 3136
Rugs and runners.

Rug Oasis
115 West Avenue
Kannapolis, NC 28081
800 524 6902
Large selection of Karastan carpets and other brands.

ESSENTIAL ELEMENTS

COLOR

Benjamin Moore & Co.
51 Chestnut Ridge Road
Montvale, NJ 07645
800 826 2623 for
distributors
*Interior and exterior paints,
plus wood stains. Many
palettes, including a wide
selection of whites and over
176 historic paint selections.*

BioShield Paint Co.
1635 Rufina Circle
Santa Fe, NM 87505
800 621 2591 for phone
order or The Natural Choice
Catalog
www.bioshieldpaint.com
www.natchoice.com
*Washes and finishes
packaged in biodegradable
or recyclable containers.
Collection includes stains,
thinners, and waxes, all
made in small batches from
natural materials.*

Cabot Stain
100 Hale Street
Newburyport, MA 01950
800 877 8246 for
distributors
www.cabotstain.com
*Transparent and opaque
wood stains and finishes in
a full spectrum of colors. The
website contains an image
of a house to try color
schemes on.*

Fine Paints of Europe
P.O. Box 419
Route 4 West
Woodstock, VT 05091-0419
For a retailer near you, call
800 332 1556
www.finepaints.com
Dutch oil and acrylic paints.

Finnuren & Haley Inc.
901 Washington Street
Conshohocken, PA 19428
800 843 9800
*Manufacturer of The
American Collection of
historic colors from the
mid-1800s.*

K-Mart
800 635 6278 for your
nearest store
www.kmart.com
*256 everyday latex paint
colors at moderate prices,
coordinated with other
Martha Stewart home
furnishings available at
K-Mart.*

**McCloskey Special Effects
Decorative Finish Center**
6995 Bird Road
Miami, FL 33155
866 666 1935 / 305 666
3300 for distributors or your
nearest store
www.o-geepaint.com/
Faux/McFaux
*The stores carry a huge
range of paints, finishes,
glazes, faux painting
supplies, and paint tools
and brushes. McCloskey's
also manufactures finishes
and supplies for contractors.*

**Old Fashioned Milk
Paint Co.**
P.O. Box 222
Groton, MA 01450
978 448 6336 for
distributors and mail order
www.milkpaint.com
*Manufacturer of authentic
milk-paint powders—add
water and mix. They supply
instructions, lessons, and
photos. They also sell a
milk-paint remover.*

PPG Architectural Finishes
One PPG Plaza
37 West
Pittsburgh, PA 15272
800 441 9695 for
distributors
www.ppgaf.com
www.olympic.com
*Architectural finishes, from
paints to stains and
coatings. Many specialized
color cards. The ppgaf
website has an amazing
color display. Olympic and
Lucite are other brands
manufactured by PPG.*

Shaker Workshops
P.O. Box 8001
Ashburnham
MA 01430-8001
800 840 9121 / 978 827
9000 for mail-order catalog
www.shakerworkshops.com
*Manufacturers of Shaker
furniture. They sell Stulb's
Old Village Paints in colors
to coordinate with Shaker
tradition.*

Sherwin-Williams Co.
101 Prospect Avenue, NW
Cleveland, OH 44115-1075
800 474 3794 for distributors
or your nearest store
www.sherwin-williams.com
*The company also
manufactures Dutch Boy
paints and many special
lines for specific stores, such
as K-Mart. The main website
has useful color wheels.*

LIGHTING

**Baldinger Architectural
Lighting, Inc.**
19–02 Steinway Street
Astoria, NY 11105
718 204 5700
www.baldingerlighting.com
*Some of the world's most
famous architects design
sconces, wall fixtures,
ceiling lights, and
chandeliers in contemporary
vein for this company.*

Baldwin Brass
841 East Wyomissing
   Boulevard
P.O. Box 15048
Reading, PA 19612
800 437 7446
Brass designs.

**Electrics Lighting and
Design**
530 West Francisco, Suite H
San Rafeal, CA 94901
415 258 9996
*This firm distributes over
100 different lighting lines,
most from Italy with
additions from Spain and
America and emphasis on
modern looks.*

Illuminating Experiences
233 Cleveland Avenue
Highland Park, NJ 08904
732 745 5858
*For 26 years this company
has been importing Italian
and Spanish lighting, with
the emphasis on unique
styling. While they are best
known for contemporary
designs, they also feature
classic looks.*

Kichler Lighting Group
7711 East Pleasant
   Valley Road
Cleveland, OH 44131
800 659 9000
216 573 1000
www.kichler.com
*This manufacturer can
provide any type of lighting
in any style, from
chandeliers to under-
counter fluorescents and
everything in between.*

Lava World International
5921 West Dickens Avenue
Chicago, IL 60639
For a retailer near you, call
800 336 5282
www.lavaworld.com
Lava lamps.

The Lighting Center Ltd.
240 East 59th Street
New York, NY 10022
212 888 8388
www.lightingcenter-ny.com
*Representatives of hundreds
of European and American
lines, they provide recessed
and track lighting, plus
chandeliers and
freestanding lamps.*

Lightolier
631 Airport Road
Fall River, MA 02720
800 217 7722
www.lightolier.com
*Whether indoor or out, task
or track, freestanding or
built in, all types of
contemporary lighting are
available from this company.*

Luigi Crystal
7332 Frankford Avenue
Philadelphia, PA 19136
215 338 2978
*Manufacturers of ornate,
hand-cut crystal
chandeliers, candelabras,
hurricane lamps, and aurora
prism lamps. Replacement
parts are also available.*

Lumax Industries Inc.
Chestnut Avenue &
   4th Street
Altona, PA 16603
814 944 2537
*Fluorescent lighting
products.*

Task Lighting Corp.
P.O. Box 1090
Kearney, NE 68848
800 445 6404
*Low-voltage task and
accent lighting.*

Top Brass
3502 Parkdale Avenue
Baltimore, MD 21211
800 359 4135
www.antiquelighting
   fixture.com
*Specializing in fine
craftsmanship, this company
manufactures unique lamps
and lighting, including a
range of interesting sconces,
in styles that range from
antique reproductions to
contemporary.*

W.A.C. Lighting Co.
113–25 14th Avenue
College Point, NY 11356
800 526 2588
www.waclighting.com
*This manufacturer is known
for its discreet and subtle
track and recessed lighting.
Use these products where
you want light but not
obvious fixtures.*

FLOORING

Aged Woods, Inc.
2331 East Market Street
York, PA 17402
800 233 9307
*Antique heart pine, hickory,
ash, and other unusual
domestic flooring. Catalog.*

Amtico
200 Lexington Avenue
Suite 809
New York, NY 10017
800 268 4260
www.amtico.com
*Luxury vinyl tile flooring and
vinyl wall base. Catalog. Call
for nearest retailer.*

**Armstrong World
Industries Inc.**
2500 Columbia Ave
Lancaster, PA 17604
717 569 2259
www.armstrongfloors.com
Vinyl and laminate flooring

Authentic Pine Floors, Inc.
P.O. Box 206
Locust Grove, GA 30248
800 283 6038
*Wide-plank and heart pine
flooring. Catalog.*

The Burruss Company
P.O. Box 6
Brookneal, VA 24528
800 334 2495
*Oak, pine, maple, ash,
walnut, and cherry floors.
Catalog.*

Country Floors
8735 Melrose Avenue
Los Angeles, CA 90069
For a store near you, call
310 657 0510
www.countryfloors.com
*Handcrafted and decorative
floors.*

Dixon Lumber Co.
P.O. Box 907
Galax, VA 24333
540 236 9963
*Refinished, laminated, and
unfinished oak and maple
flooring.*

Endura
P.O. Box 9045
Waltham, MA 02254-9045
800 643 7463
*Rubber flooring and stair
treads, including for the
visually impaired. Catalog.
Call for nearest retailer.*

Granitewerks Inc.
2218 North Elston Ave
Chicago, IL 60614
773 292 1202
Natural stone.

Interceramic USA
2333 S. Jupiter Road
Garland, TX 75041
214 503 5500
Ceramic floor and wall tiles.

Linoleum City
5657 Santa Monica
 Boulevard
Hollywood, CA 90038
213 469 0063
Selection of linoleum styles.

Lonseal
928 East 238th Street,
 Building A
Carson, CA 90745
800 832 7111
Sheet vinyl flooring.

Paris Ceramics
979 Third Avenue
New York, NY 10022
888 845 3487
*Limestone, terracotta,
antique stone, and hand-
painted tiles. Catalog. Call
for nearest retailer.*

Sullivan Floors
506 East 118th Street
New York, NY 10035
212 353 3490
*All types of wood flooring.
Catalogs.*

Walker & Zanger Inc.
31 Warren Place
Mt Vernon, NY 10550
914 667 1600
*Marble, granite, slate,
limestone.*

STORAGE & DISPLAY

Dutch Armoire
P.O. Box 301
Cary, NC 27511
888 636 0660
www.DutchArmoire.com
Armoires.

Hold Everything
P.O. Box 7807
San Francisco, CA 94120
800 840 3596
www.holdeverything.com
*Everything for storage from
baskets to shoe holders.*

IKEA
Call 800 254-IKEA or visit
www.ikea.com for a retailer
near you.
*Storage, furniture, and
accessories.*

Inside Out Productions
10836 Washington
 Boulevard
Culver City, CA 90232
310 838 0255
www.insideout
 productions.com
Children's storage chairs.

WINDOW TREATMENTS

**Blaine Window Hardware
Inc.**
17319 Blaine Drive
Hagerstown, MD 21740
301 797 6500
*Replacements parts for
windows and patio doors.*

Country Curtains
The Red Lion Inn
Stockbridge, MA 01262
413 298 5565
800 876 6123
www.countrycurtains.com
*Extensive assortment of
hardware. There is a wide
selection of fabric and
lace curtains on offer as
well as swags and other
accessories. Mail order.
Catalog.*

Gige Interiors Ltd.
170 South Main Street
Yardley, PA 19067
215 493 8052
*Custom-made window
treatments.*

Hollywood Trims
Prym-Dritz Corporation
P.O. Box 5028
Spartanburg, SC 29304
800 845 4948
www.prymdritz.com
*Rayon, cotton, and metallic
trims, cords, tassels, and
thread. Mail order. Catalog.*

Hunter Douglas
One Duette Way
Broomfield, CO 80020
888 501 8364
www.hunterdouglas.com
*Manufacturer of all kinds
of shades and window
treatments.*

Materials Unlimited
2 West Michigan Avenue
Ypsilanti, MI 48197
800 299 9462
*Antique and reproduction
window hardware.*

**Notions and Trims
Conso Products**
P.O. Box 326
Union, SC 29379
800 845 4948
www.conso.com
*Enormous collection of
decorative trims, tassels,
and fringes of all types.
Call for local distributor.*

Renovator's Supply
P.O. Box 2515
Conway, NH 03818
800 659 0203
Wooden window hardware.

Smith & Noble
P.O. Box 1387
Corona, CA 91718
800 248 8888
www.smithandnoble.com
*Vertical and horizontal
shades and blinds in all
materials, Roman shades,
cornice boxes. Mail order.
Catalog.*

Springs Window Fashions
7549 Graber Road
Middleton, WI 53562
800 521 8071
www.springs.com
*Vinyl, metal, and fabric
vertical and horizontal
blinds and shades. Fashion
and pleated shades are also
available. Mail order.
Catalog.*

Tinsel Trading Co.
47 West 38th Street
New York, NY 10018
212 730 1030
*Vintage to contemporary
trims, tassels, flowers,
fringes, buttons, cords,
metallics, and military trims.
Mail order. Catalog.*

The Warm Co.
954 East Union
Seattle, WA 98122
For a retailer near you, call
800 234 9276
www.warmcompany.com
*Insulated fabric for window
shades.*

FABRIC FURNISHINGS

Anichini
466 North Robertson
 Boulevard
Los Angeles, CA 90048
800 553 5309
www.anichini.com
*Manufacturer of fabrics,
decorative pillows,
and upholstered sofas
and chairs.*

Calico Corners
203 Gale Lane
Kennett Square, PA 19348
800 213 6366
www.calicocorners.com
*Retailer of fabric from
manufacturers such as
Waverly, Ralph Lauren,
plus furniture. Many
stores nationwide. Mail
order. Catalog.*

DJC Design Studio
800 554 7890
www.djcDESIGN.com
*Manufacturer of decorative
pillows and throws.*

The Fabric Center
485 Electric Avenue
Fitchburg, MA 01420
978 343 4402
*A wide variety of decorator
fabrics at discounted prices.
Mail order. Catalog.*

Fabrics To Dye For
Two River Road
Pawcatuck, CT 06379
800 322 1319
www.fabricstodyefor.com
*Hand-painted fabrics, dyes,
and kits, also available at a
variety of retail locations.*

Hancock Fabrics
2605A West Main Street
Tupelo, MS 38801
662 844 7368
www.hancockfabrics.com
*America's largest fabric
store, good for all basic
decoration needs.*

Keepsake Quilting
Route 25B
P.O. Box 1618
Center Harbor
NH 03226-1618
800 865 9458
www.keepsakequilting.com
*Good selection of
lightweight cottons. There is
also a wide range of threads
as well as notions available.
Mail order. Catalog.*

The Lampshade Shop
661 327 2145
www.lampshadeshop.com
*Manufacturer and retailer
of custom shades and
supplies for making all
kinds of shades.*

Laura Ashley
Call 800 367 2000 or visit
www.lauraashley.com for a
retailer near you.
*Floral, striped, checked,
and solid cottons in a
range of colors.*

Michaelian & Kohlberg
225 7th Avenue East
Hendersonville, NC 28792
800 258 3977 x10
www.mkhome.com
*Manufacturer of decorative
pillows.*

On Board Fabrics
Route 27
P.O. Box 14
Edgecomb, ME 04556
207 882 7536
www.onboardfabrics.com
*Everything from Balinese
cottons to Italian tapestry,
botanical prints, and woven
plaids.*

Oppenheim's
P.O. Box 29
120 East Main Street
North Manchester
IN 469-62-0052
800 461 6728
*Fabric retailer. Country
prints, denim, chambray,
flannel fabrics, and mill
remnants.*

Silk Trading Co.
360 South La Brea Avenue
Los Angeles, CA 90036
800 854 0396, or visit
www.silktrading.com
*Retailer and catalog. More
than 2,000 silk fabrics, from
taffeta to classic damask,
readymade curtains,
trimmings, lampshades.
Nine stores nationwide.*

Tinsel Trading Co.
47 West 38th Street
New York, NY 10018
212 730 1030
*Retailer of vintage to
contemporary trims, tassels,
flowers, fringes, buttons,
cords, metallics, and
military trims.*

Thai Silks!
252 State Street
Los Altos, CA 94022
800 722 7455
www.thaisilks.com
*Large selection of silk,
velvet, organza, jacquard,
and taffeta. There are also
imported fabrics, including
batik. Mail order. Catalog.*

PICTURE CREDITS

KEY: **a**=above, **b**=below, **c**=center, **l**=left, **r**=right, *ph*=photographer.

1 *ph* Andrew Wood/the Shell Beach, California home of Chuck & Evelyn Plemons; **2–3** *ph* Chris Everard/an apartment in London designed by Littman Goddard Hoggarth, light courtesy of Skandium; **4** *ph* Polly Wreford/Courtney Brennan's apartment in New York designed by Ken Foreman; **6–7** *ph* Polly Wreford/Mary Foley's house in Connecticut; **8–9** *ph* Chris Everard/Reuben Barrett's apartment in London, light courtesy of Coexistence; **10l** *ph* James Merrell; **10–11** *ph* James Merrell/Gabriele Sanders's apartment in New York; **11a** *ph* Tom Leighton/blanket and candle, Interiors Bis; **11b** *ph* Andrew Wood/a house near Antwerp designed by Claire Bataille & Paul ibens; **12l** *ph* Tom Leighton/Roger & Fay Oates' house in Herefordshire, The Long Barn, Eastnor, Ledbury, Herefordshire HR8 1EL (+44 1531 632718); **12–13** *ph* Andrew Wood/Bernie de Le Cuona's home in Windsor; **13a** *ph* James Merrell/a house in Sydney designed by Larcombe & Soloman; **13b** *ph* Andrew Wood/a house near Antwerp designed by Claire Bataille & Paul ibens; **14al** *ph* Catherine Gratwicke/Kimball Mayer & Meghan Hughes's apartment in New York designed by L. A. Morgan, painting by Erin Parrish; **14ar** *ph* James Merrell; **14b** *ph* David Montgomery/Sheila Scholes's house near Cambridge; **15al** *ph* Chris Everard/the Sugarman–Behun house on Long Island; **15ar** *ph* Andrew Wood/Roger & Suzy Black's apartment in London designed by Johnson Naylor; **15cl & bl** *ph* Andrew Wood/Bernie de Le Cuona's home in Windsor; **15cr** *ph* Chris Everard/a house in Hampstead, London designed by Orefelt Associates; **15br** *ph* Chris Everard/a house in London by Seth Stein; **16al** *ph* Alan Williams/the architect Voon Wong's own apartment in London; **16ar** *ph* Andrew Wood/Alastair Hendy and John Clinch's apartment in London designed by Alastair Hendy; **16bl** *ph* Chris Everard/Jonathan Wilson's apartment in London, light courtesy of SCP; **16br** *ph* Alan Williams/Jennifer & Geoffrey Symonds's apartment in New York designed by Jennifer Post Design; **17** *ph* David Montgomery/Carlton Gardens apartment in London designed by Claire Nelson at Nelson Design; **18al** *ph* James Merrell/Dominique Lubar for IPL Interiors; **18ar** *ph* Alan Williams/private apartment in West London, designed by Hugh Broughton Architects; **18bl** *ph* James Merrell/Rose Gray's flat in London designed by Hester Gray; **19al** *ph* Alan Williams/apartment for Richard Oyarzarbal by Urban Research Laboratory, London; **19ar** *ph* Alan Williams/the architect Voon Wong's own apartment in London; **19bl** *ph* Alan Williams/Alannah Weston's house in London designed by Stickland Coombe Architecture; **19br** *ph* Ray Main/an apartment in London designed by Circus Architects; **20al** *ph* Tom Leighton/a house in London designed by Charles Rutherfoord; **20ac** *ph* Chris Everard/Paul Brazier & Diane Lever's house in London designed by Carden & Cunietti; **20ar** *ph* Chris Everard/Calvin Tsao & Zack McKown's apartment in New York designed by Tsao and McKown; **20b** *ph* Alan Williams/Alannah Weston's house in London designed by Stickland Coombe Architecture; **21al** *ph* Chris Everard/Mark Weinstein's apartment in New York designed by Lloyd Schwan; **21ar** *ph* Alan Williams/Selworthy apartment in London designed by Gordana Mandic and Peter Tyler at Buildburo (www.buildburo.co.uk); **21b** *ph* Andrew Wood/Alastair Hendy and John Clinch's apartment in London designed by Alastair Hendy; **22al** *ph* Christopher Drake/Nelly Guyot's house in Ramatuelle, France, styled by Nelly Guyot; **22ar** *ph* Christopher Drake/designer Barbara Davis's own home in upstate New York; **22cl** *ph* Fritz von der Schulenburg/Robert Kinnaman & Brian Ramaekers' house in Wainscott; **22cr** *ph* Simon Upton; **22bl** *ph* Christopher Drake/Ali Sharland's home in Gloucestershire; **22br** *ph* Tom Leighton; **24a** *ph* Christopher Drake/designer Barbara Davis's own home in upstate New York; **24b** *ph* Alan Williams/the Arbuthnott family's house near Cirencester designed by Nicholas Arbuthnott, fabrics designed by Vanessa Arbuthnott; **25al** *ph* Simon Upton; **25ar** *ph* Tom Leighton; **25bl** *ph* Christopher Drake/Enrica Stabile's house in Brunello; **25br** *ph* Jan Baldwin/Elena Colombo's cottage on the east end side of Long Island; **26a** *ph* Simon Upton; **26c** *ph* David Montgomery/a house in Connecticut designed by Lynn Morgan Design; **26bl** *ph* Christopher Drake/designer Barbara Davis's own home in upstate New York; **26br** *ph* Christopher Drake/refurbishment & interior design by Chicchi Meroni Fassio, Parnassus; **27a** *ph* Simon Upton; **27ar** *ph* Christopher Drake/Enrica Stabile's house in Milan; **27cr** *ph* Christopher Drake/designed by Lorraine Kirke; **27br** *ph* Tom Leighton; **28a** *ph* Chris Everard/Bob & Maureen Macris's apartment on Fifth Avenue in New York designed by Sage Wimer Coombe Architects; **28bl** *ph* Andrew Wood/Norma Holland's house in London; **28br** *ph* Chris Everard/the London apartment of The Sheppard Day Design Partnership; **29al** *ph* Chris Everard/an apartment in Milan designed by Daniela Micol Wajskol, interior decorator, prints from Cristina Ballini Antiquario, Milan; **29ar** *ph* Alan Williams/Stanley and Nancy Grossman's apartment in New York designed by Jennifer Post Design; **29br** *ph* Tom Leighton/Keith Varty & Alan Cleaver's apartment in London designed by Jonathan Reed/Reed Boyd (+44 20 7565 0066); **30al** *ph* Ray Main/an apartment in New York designed by Laura Bohn Design Associates Inc., light from Lightforms; **30ar** *ph* Ray Main/Jonathan Reed's apartment in London, lighting designed by Sally Storey, Design Director of John Cullen Lighting; **30bl** *ph* Andrew Wood/Chelsea loft apartment in New York, designed by The Moderns; **30br** *ph* Andrew Wood/an apartment in London designed by James Gorst; **31al** *ph* Ray Main/a house in Pennsylvania designed by Jeffrey Bilhuber; **31ar** *ph* Ray Main/Gai Harris's apartment in London designed by François Gilles and Dominique Lubar, IPL Interiors; **31cl** *ph* Ray Main; **31cr** *ph* Chris Everard/Florence Buchanan, Steve Harrison & Octavia Spelman's house in Tribeca, New York, designed by Sage Wimer Coombe Architects; **31b** *ph* Andrew Wood/media executive's house in Los Angeles, architect: Stephen Slan, builder: Russell Simpson, original architect: Carl Maston c.1945; **32a** *ph* Polly Wreford/Mary Foley's house in Connecticut; **32c** *ph* Ray Main/Jonathan Reed's apartment in London, lighting designed by Sally Storey, Design Director of John Cullen Lighting; **32b** *ph* Alan Williams/Stanley and Nancy Grossman's apartment in New York designed by Jennifer Post Design; **33al** *ph* Tom Leighton/Keith Varty & Alan Cleaver's apartment in London designed by Jonathan Reed/Reed Boyd (+44 20 7565 0066); **33ac** *ph* David Montgomery/Annabel Astor's house in London is full of furniture and accessories designed exclusively for her OKA Direct Mail Order Catalogue; **33ar** *ph* David Montgomery/house in South London designed by Todhunter Earle Interiors; **33cr** *ph* David Montgomery/Carlton Gardens apartment in London designed by Claire Nelson at Nelson Design; **33b** *ph* Chris Everard/interior designer Ann Boyd's own apartment in London; **34a** *ph* Verity Welstead/Lulu Guinness's house in London; **34b** *ph* Andrew Wood/the apartment of Michel Hurst & Robert Swope, owners of Full House NYC; **35a** *ph* David Montgomery/Sabina Fay Braxton's apartment in Paris; **35b** *ph* Fritz von der Schulenburg/Michael & Ruth Burke's house in Mississippi designed by Vicente Wolf of Vicente Wolf Associates; **36al** *ph* Chris Everard/Gentucca Bini's apartment in Milan; **36ar** *ph* Polly Wreford/Ros Fairman's house in London; **36b** *ph* Ray Main/Jonathan Leitersdorf's apartment in New York designed by Jonathan Leitersdorf/Just Design Ltd; **37a** *ph* Polly Wreford/The Sawmills Studio; **37bl** *ph* Polly Wreford/Ros Fairman's house in London; **37br** *ph* Chris Everard/Gentucca Bini's apartment in Milan; **38–39** *ph* Andrew Wood/John Cheim's apartment in New York; **39al** *ph* Chris Everard/Gentucca Bini's apartment in Milan; **39ar** *ph* Polly Wreford/Ros Fairman's house in London; **39b** *ph* Polly Wreford/Carol Reid's apartment in Paris; **40–41** *ph* Chris Everard/an apartment in London designed by Littman Goddard Hoggarth, light courtesy of Skandium; **42–43** *ph* Andrew Wood; **44al & br** *ph* Andrew Wood/Phillip Low, New York; **44r** *ph* Andrew Wood/Kurt Brendenbeck's apartment at the Barbican, London; **45** *ph* James Merrell/Sophie Sarin's flat in London; **46** *ph* James Merrell; **47al, cl & ar** *ph* James Merrell/Felix Bonnier's apartment in Paris; **47bl & br** *ph* James Merrell/Christine Walsh & Ian Bartlett's house in London designed by Jack Ingham of Bookworks; **48a** *ph* James Merrell/designed by Interni Interior Design Consultancy; **48b** *ph* James Merrell/Douglas & Dorothy Hamilton's apartment in New York; **49al & ar** *ph* Fritz von der Schulenburg/a house in Pennsylvania designed by Laura Bohn Design Associates; **49b** *ph* James Merrell; **50b** *ph* James Merrell/a house in London designed by François Gilles and Dominique Lubar, IPL Interiors; **50al & 50–51** *ph* Andrew Wood/Norma Holland's house in London; **51** *ph* Andrew Wood/Gabriele Sanders's apartment in New York; **52** *ph* James Merrell/Grant Ford & Jane Bailey's house in London/kitchen by Rhode Design; **53l & ar** *ph* James Merrell/Nigel Rowe's house in Middlesex/kitchen by Crabtree Kitchens; **53b** *ph* Henry Bourne/a mews house in London designed by McDowell & Benedetti; **54al & bl** *ph* James Merrell/Charles Morris Mount & Harold Gordon's house on Long Island designed by Charles Morris Mount; **54r** *ph* Andrew Wood/the loft of Peggy & Steven Learner designed by Steven Learner Studio; **54br** *ph* Andrew Wood/a house in London designed by Guy Stansfeld (+44 20 7727 0133); **54–55** *ph* Ray Main/Alastair Gordon & Barbara de Vries' house near Princeton designed by Smith-Miller + Hawkinson Architects; **55bl & br** *ph* James Merrell/John Alexander & Fiona Waterstreet's loft in New York designed by Lorraine Kirke; **56bl & ac** *ph* Christopher Drake/refurbishment & interior design by Chicchi Meroni Fassio, Parnassus; **56bc** *ph* Christopher Drake/Enrica Stabile's house in Milan; **56r** *ph* Henry Bourne; **57al** *ph* Henry Bourne; **57ar** *ph* James Merrell/Mr & Mrs Barrow's house in Surrey designed by architects Marshall Haines + Barrow/kitchen by Chalon; **57bl & br** *ph* James Merrell/Sally Butler's house in London; **58al & ar** *ph* James Merrell/the Ash house in London designed by Ash Sakula Architects; **58bl** *ph* James Merrell/Etienne and Mary Millner's house in London; **58br** *ph* Polly Wreford/Ann Shore's house in London; **59bl** *ph* James Merrell; **59ar** *ph* Christopher Drake/Melanie Thornton's house in Gloucestershire; **59cr** *ph* Fritz von der Schulenburg/Bunny Williams's house in Connecticut; **59br** *ph* James Merrell/a house in London designed by

François Gilles and Dominique Lubar, IPL Interiors; **60–61** *ph* Andrew Wood/ Robert Kimsey's apartment in London designed by Gavin Jackson (+44 7705 0097561); **62** *ph* Andrew Wood/Bernie de Le Cuona's home in Windsor; **63a** *ph* Andrew Wood/Aude Cardinale's house near Paris; **63bl** *ph* Chris Everard/an apartment in New York designed by Gabellini Associates; **63br** *ph* Tom Leighton; **64–65** *ph* Andrew Wood/Rosa Dean & Ed Baden-Powell's apartment in London designed by Urban Salon (+44 20 7357 8800); **66a** *ph* James Merrell; **66b** *ph* Chris Everard/Mark Weinstein's apartment in New York designed by Lloyd Schwan; **67a** *ph* Simon Upton/Barefoot Elegance; **67b** *ph* Andrew Wood/Andrew Noble's apartment in London designed by Nico Rensch Architeam; **68l** *ph* Andrew Wood/ Brian Johnson's apartment in London designed by Johnson Naylor; **68–69** *ph* Andrew Wood/Roger & Suzy Black's apartment in London designed by Johnson Naylor; **69al & r** *ph* Chris Everard/Eric de Queker's apartment in Antwerp; **70a & 70–71** *ph* Andrew Wood/an apartment in Bath designed by Briffa Phillips Architects; **70cl, bl & br** *ph* Andrew Wood/Jamie Falla & Lynn Graham's house in London; **71a & b** *ph* Andrew Wood/Han Feng's apartment in New York designed by Han Feng; **72** *ph* Andrew Wood/Brian Johnson's apartment in London designed by Johnson Naylor; **73a** *ph* Alan Williams/Gail & Barry Stephens's house in London; **73c** *ph* James Merrell; **73b** *ph* Chris Everard/François Muracciole's apartment in Paris; **74a** *ph* Henry Bourne/Frédéric Mérchiche's apartment in Paris; **74b** *ph* Alan Williams/Margot Feldman's house in New York designed by Patricia Seidman of Mullman Seidman Architects; **74–75** *ph* Ray Main/Vicente Wolf's house on Long Island, lights designed by Vicente Wolf; **76bl** *ph* Alan Williams/designer Barbara Davis's own house in upstate New York; **76ar** *ph* Chris Everard/an apartment in New York designed by Steven Learner; **76br** *ph* James Merrell; **76–77** *ph* Ray Main/Julie Prisca's house in Normandy; **77a** *ph* Alan Williams/ Miv Watts's house in Norfolk; **77b** *ph* Chris Everard/an apartment in Milan designed by Nicoletta Marazza; **78–79** *ph* Tom Leighton; **80** *ph* Andrew Wood/ Nicki de Metz's flat in London designed by de Metz Architects; **81a** *ph* Andrew Wood/Michael Benevento–Orange Group; **81b** *ph* Henry Bourne; **82al & bl** *ph* Andrew Wood/an apartment in London designed by Littman Goddard Hogarth Architects; **82ar** *ph* Andrew Wood/Johanne Riss's house in Brussels; **82–83 & 83al** *ph* Andrew Wood/Brian Johnson's apartment in London designed by Johnson Naylor; **83ar** *ph* Alan Williams/the Arbuthnott family's house near Cirencester designed by Nicholas Arbuthnott, fabrics designed by Vanessa Arbuthnott; **83b** *ph* Chris Everard/the London apartment of the Sheppard Day Design Partnership; **84al** *ph* Jan Baldwin/Fern Mallis's house in Southampton, Long Island; **84bl** *ph* Alan Williams/Stanley and Nancy Grossman's apartment in New York designed by Jennifer Post Design; **84ar** *ph* Andrew Wood/Johanne Riss's house in Brussels; **84–85** *ph* Jan Baldwin/Robert & Gabrielle Reeves's house in Clareville designed by Stutchbury & Pape Architecture + Landscape Architecture; **85al & ac** *ph* Catherine Gratwicke/the brownstone in New York of Bonnie Young, director of global sourcing and inspiration at Donna Karan International, styled by Gaby Karan; **85ar** *ph* Henry Bourne; **86** *ph* Catherine Gratwicke/Bryan Purcell, an artist living in New York; **87al** *ph* Chris Everard/an apartment in New York designed by Gabellini Associates; **87ar** *ph* Fritz von der Schulenburg/Irene & Giorgio Silvagni's house in Provence; **87bl** *ph* Fritz von der Schulenburg/Frank Faulkner's loft in New York; **87br** *ph* Chris Everard/an apartment in New York designed by Steven Learner; **88al** *ph* Polly Wreford/Glenn Carwithen & Sue Miller's house in London; **88al** *ph* Jan Baldwin/Camp Kent designed by Alexandra Champalimaud; **88bl** *ph* Chris Everard/Eric de Queker's apartment in Antwerp; **88br** *ph* Andrew Wood/ Century (+44 20 7487 5100); **89al** *ph* Ray Main/Central London apartment designed by Ben Kelly Design; **89bl** *ph* Andrew Wood/Philip & Barbara Silver's house in Idaho designed by Mark Pynn A.I.A. of McMillen Pynn Architecture L.L.P.; **89r** *ph* Andrew Wood/Jo Shane, John Cooper & family apartment, in New York; **90l** *ph* Polly Wreford/Glenn Carwithen & Sue Miller's house in London; **90ac & ar** *ph* Andrew Wood/Andrew Noble's apartment in London designed by Nico Rensch Architeam; **90c** *ph* Polly Wreford/home of 27.12 Design Ltd, Chelsea, NYC; **90b** *ph* Tom Leighton/a loft in London designed by Robert Dye Associates; **91ar** *ph* Christopher Drake/Josephine Ryan's house in London; **91bl & br** *ph* James Merrell; **92–93** *ph* Andrew Wood; **94** *ph* Polly Wreford/Kimberly Watson's house in London; **94–95a** *ph* Chris Everard/the London apartment of the Sheppard Day Design Partnership; **94–95b** *ph* Andrew Wood/'Melwani House' designed by Bedmar & Shi Designers in Singapore; **95** *ph* Chris Everard/Hilton McConnico's house near Paris; **96al** *ph* Christopher Drake/Ali Sharland's home in Gloucestershire; **96c & br** *ph* Chris Everard/a house in Highbury, London designed by Dale Loth Architects; **96–97** *ph* Andrew Wood/a house near Antwerp designed by Bataille & ibens; **97al** *ph* Chris Everard/the Sugarman–Behun house on Long Island; **97ar** *ph* Fritz von der Schulenburg/Frédéric Méchiche's apartment in Paris; **97bl** *ph* Chris Everard/Emma & Neil's house in London, walls painted by Garth Carter;

97br *ph* Andrew Wood/Roger & Fay Oates's house in Herefordshire, The Long Barn, Eastnor, Ledbury, Herefordshire HR8 1EL (+44 1531 632718); **98** *ph* Chris Everard/ Richard Oyarzarbal's apartment in London designed by Jeff Kirby of Urban Research Laboratory; **99al & ar** *ph* Chris Everard/Fred Wadsworth's flat in London designed by Littman Goddard Hogarth; **99c** *ph* Andrew Wood/an apartment in London designed by Littman Goddard Hogarth Architects; **99b** *ph* Chris Everard/ designer Alan Tanksley's own apartment in Manhattan; **100** *ph* James Morris/ a loft apartment in London designed by Simon Conder Associates; **101al** *ph* Chris Everard/One New Inn Square, a private dining room and home of chef David Vanderhook (all enquiries to +44 20 7729 3645); **101ac & al** *ph* Chris Everard/an apartment in Paris designed by Bruno Tanquerel; **101bl** *ph* Simon Upton; **101br** *ph* Chris Everard/Freddie Daniells's apartment in London designed by Brookes Stacey Randall; **102al** *ph* Andrew Wood/a house in London designed by Bowles & Linares; **102ar** *ph* Chris Everard/One New Inn Square, a private dining room and home of chef David Vanderhook (all enquiries to +44 20 7729 3645); **102bl** *ph* Chris Everard/ Richard Hopkin's apartment in London designed by HM2; **102br** *ph* Andrew Wood/ a house near Antwerp designed by Bataille & ibens; **103al** *ph* Chris Everard/ architect Nigel Smith's apartment in London; **103ar & br** *ph* Simon Upton; **103bl** *ph* Chris Everard/Stephen Schulte's loft apartment in London; **104al** *ph* Andrew Wood/Alastair Hendy and John Clinch's apartment in London designed by Alastair Hendy; **104cl** *ph* Chris Everard/a house in Hampstead, London designed by Orefelt Associates; **104bl** *ph* Chris Everard/a house in Highbury, London designed by Dale Loth Architects; **104ar** *ph* Chris Everard/Tiffany Ogden's house in London designed by Andy Martin of Fin Architects & Designers; **104br** *ph* Tom Leighton/a house in London designed by Charles Rutherfoord, 51 The Chase, London SW4 0NP (+44 20 7627 0182); **105al** *ph* Chris Everard/Richard Oyarzarbal's apartment in London designed by Jeff Kirby of Urban Research Laboratory; **105bl** *ph* Chris Everard/Paul Brazier & Diane Lever's house in London designed by Carden & Cunietti; **105ar** *ph* Chris Everard/Gomez/Murphy loft, London designed by Urban Salon Ltd; **105br** *ph* Chris Everard/Suzanne Slesin & Michael Steinberg's apartment in New York designed by Jean-Louis Ménard; **106l** *ph* Alan Williams/ Gail & Barry Stephens's house in London; **106ar** *ph* Andrew Wood/a house near Antwerp designed by Bataille & ibens; **106br & 107cl** *ph* Andrew Wood/a house in London designed by Guy Stansfeld (+44 20 7727 0133); **107al** *ph* Chris Everard/ an apartment in New York designed by Steven Learner; **107bl & c** *ph* Chris Everard/ Calvin Tsao & Zack McKown's apartment in New York designed by Tsao & McKown; **107r** *ph* Andrew Wood/Dawna & Jerry Walter's house in London; **108–109** *ph* Andrew Wood; **110al** *ph* Andrew Wood/Chelsea studio in New York City, designed by Marino + Giolito; **110ar** *ph* Andrew Wood/Heidi Kingstone's apartment in London; **110bl & br** *ph* Andrew Wood/Kurt Bredenbeck's apartment at the Barbican, London; **111al** *ph* Andrew Wood/Gabriele Sanders's apartment in New York; **111ar** *ph* Catherine Gratwicke; **111bl** *ph* Catherine Gratwicke/Frances Robinson & Eamonn McMahon's house in London; **111bc** *ph* Polly Wreford/Clare Nash's house in London; **111br** *ph* Ray Main/Kenneth Hirst's apartment in New York; **112al** *ph* Ray Main/Thierry Watorek's house near Paris; **112ar** *ph* Ray Main/Century (+44 20 7487 5100); **112b** *ph* James Morris/Joan Barnett's house in West Hollywood, designed by William R Hefner A.I.A., interior design by Sandy Davidson Design; **113bl** *ph* Chris Everard/Bob & Maureen Macris's apartment on Fifth Avenue in New York designed by Sage Wimer Coombe Architects; **113ar & br** *ph* Andrew Wood/Jo Shane, John Cooper & family apartment, in New York; **114al & br** *ph* Andrew Wood/Ian Bartlett & Christine Walsh's house in London; **114bl & ar** *ph* Andrew Wood; **115b** *ph* Andrew Wood/Century (+44 20 7487 5100); **115a** *ph* Andrew Wood/Phillip Low, New York; **116–117** *ph* Debi Treloar/Eben & Nica Cooper's bedroom, the Cooper family playroom; **118al & b** *ph* Debi Treloar/Belén Moneo & Jeff Brock's apartment in New York designed by Moneo Brock Studio; **118ar** *ph* Debi Treloar/Vincent & Frieda Plasschaert's house in Brugge, Belgium; **118c** *ph* Debi Treloar/Ab Rogers & Sophie Braimbridge's house, London, designed by Richard Rogers for his mother. Furniture design by KRD – Kitchen Rogers Design; **118–119** *ph* Debi Treloar/Michele Johnson's house in London designed by Nico Rensch Architeam; **120al** *ph* Debi Treloar/Ab Rogers & Sophie Braimbridge's house, London, designed by Richard Rogers for his mother. Furniture design by KRD – Kitchen Rogers Design; **120a** *ph* Debi Treloar/designed by Sage Wimer Coombe Architects New York; **120br** *ph* Debi Treloar/Sophie Eadie's house in London; **121 al** *ph* Debi Treloar/Rudi, Melissa & Archie Thackry's house in London; **121** *ph* Debi Treloar/Vincent & Frieda Plasschaert's house in Brugge, Belgium; **121bl** *ph* Debi Treloar/Victoria Andreae's house in London; **121br** *ph* Debi Treloar/ an apartment in London, by Malin Iovino Design; **122 & 123al** *ph* Debi Treloar/ the Boyes home in London designed by Circus Architects; **123cl & c** *ph* Debi Treloar/the Zwirner's loft in New York; **123cr** *ph* Debi Treloar/Ben Johns & Deb Waterman Johns's house in Georgetown; **123b** *ph* Christopher Drake/Enrica

Stabile's house in Brunello; **124al & bl** ph Debi Treloar/Sudi Pigott's house in London; **124bc** ph Debi Treloar/Julia & David O'Driscoll's house in London; **124ar** ph Debi Treloar/the Zwirner's loft in New York; **124br** ph Debi Treloar/Victoria Andreae's house in London; **125al** ph Debi Treloar/Elizabeth Alford & Michael Young's loft in New York; **125bl** ph Debi Treloar/Suzanne & Christopher Sharp's house in London; **125ar & br** ph Debi Treloar/Sera Hersham-Loftus's house in London; **126al** ph Christopher Drake/Melanie Thornton's house in Gloucestershire; **126cl** ph Debi Treloar/Suzanne & Christopher Sharp's house in London; **126bl** ph Debi Treloar/Sue & Lars-Christian Brask's house in London designed by Susie Atkinson; **126ca & cb** ph Debi Treloar/Ben Johns & Deb Waterman Johns's house in Georgetown; **126br, 126–127 & 127bl** ph Debi Treloar/Eben & Nica Cooper's bedroom, the Cooper family playroom; **127br** ph Debi Treloar/Victoria Andreae's house in London; **128–129** ph Tom Leighton; **130al** ph Christopher Drake/designer Barbara Davis's own home in upstate New York; **130cl** ph Polly Wreford/Sheila Scholes & Gunter Schmidt's house in Cambridgeshire; **130bl** ph Simon Upton; **130br** ph Christopher Drake/designed by Lorraine Kirke; **131al** ph Chris Everard/Bob & Maureen Macris's apartment on Fifth Avenue in New York designed by Sage Wimer Coombe Architects; **131ar** ph Chris Everard/an apartment in Milan designed by Nicoletta Marazza; **131bl** ph Andrew Wood/Heidi Kingstone's apartment in London; **131br** ph Christopher Drake/designer Barbara Davis's own home in upstate New York; **132l** ph James Merrell; **132ar** ph Ray Main/Marina & Peter Hill's barn in West Sussex designed by Marina Hill, Peter James Construction Management, Chichester, The West Sussex Antique Timber Company, Wisborough Green, and Joanna Jefferson Architects; **132br** ph Simon Upton/Barefoot Elegance; **133al** ph Simon Upton; **133bl** ph Andrew Wood/Vanessa & Robert Fairer's studio in London designed by Woolf Architects (+44 20 7428 9500); **133ar & br** ph Andrew Wood/Patricia Ijaz's house in London designed by Jonathan Woolf of Woolf Architects; **134–135** ph Chris Everard/Jonathan Wilson's apartment in London, light courtesy of SCP; **136–137** ph Alan Williams; **138a** ph James Merrell/Milly de Cabrol's apartment in Paris; **138bl** ph Simon Upton; **138br** ph James Merrell; **138–139** ph Alan Williams/Warner Johnson's apartment in New York designed by Edward Cabot of Cabot Design Ltd; **139a** ph Tom Leighton; **140a** ph Alan Williams/Donata Sartorio's apartment in Milan; **140b** ph Alan Williams/Géraldine Prieur's apartment in Paris, an interior designer fascinated with colour; **140–141 & 141a** ph James Merrell; **141b** ph Andrew Wood/Aude Cardinale's house near Paris; **142** ph Polly Wreford/Clare Nash's house in London; **142–143** ph Chris Everard/an apartment in Antwerp designed by Claire Bataille & Paul ibens; **143bl & ar** ph Alan Williams/Stanley and Nancy Grossman's apartment in New York designed by Jennifer Post Design; **143cr & br** ph Tom Leighton; **144l** ph James Merrell; **144r** ph Alan Williams/Gail & Barry Stephens's house in London; **145a** ph Andrew Wood/a house in London designed by Bowles & Linares; **145b** ph Tom Leighton/bed, bed linens & table Interiors Bis; wooden cylinder David Champion; **146** ph Tom Leighton/paint Farrow & Ball: floor Mouse's Back floor paint no.40, cupboards Green Smoke no.47 and interiors Red Fox no. 48, walls and woodwork String no.8, ceiling Off White no.3; **147al** ph Alan Williams/the Arbuthnott family's house near Cirencester designed by Nicholas Arbuthnott, fabrics designed by Vanessa Arbuthnott; **147bl & ar** ph Simon Upton; **147br** ph Alan Williams/Alannah Weston's house in London designed by Stickland Coombe Architecture; **148al** ph Christopher Drake/Marisa Cavalli's home in Milan; **148ar** ph James Merrell/Sally Butler's house in London; **148b** ph Alan Williams/New York apartment designed by Bruce Bierman; **149l** ph Christopher Drake/Juan Corbella's apartment in London designed by HM2, Richard Webb with Andrew Hanson; **149r** ph James Merrell/an apartment in Paris designed by Hervé Vermesch; **150a** ph Alan Williams/the Arbuthnott family's house near Cirencester designed by Nicholas Arbuthnott, fabrics designed by Vanessa Arbuthnott; **150b** ph Simon Upton; **151a** ph Christopher Drake/Juan Corbella's apartment in London designed by HM2, Richard Webb with Andrew Hanson; **151b** ph Alan Williams/Lindsay Taylor's apartment in Glasgow; **152al** ph Simon Upton; **152bl** ph Alan Williams/interior designer and managing director of the Société Yves Halard, Michelle Halard's own apartment in Paris; **152br** ph Andrew Wood/Neil Bingham's house in Blackheath, London; **152–153** ph Alan Williams/apartment for Richard Oyarzarbal by Urban Research Laboratory, London; **153bl** ph Chris Everard/architect's house in London designed by Dale Loth Architects; **153br** ph Alan Williams/Selworthy apartment in London designed by Gordana Mandic and Peter Tyler at Buildburo (www.buildburo.co.uk); **154–155** ph Ray Main; **156** ph Ray Main/Mark Jennings's apartment in New York designed by Asfour Guzy; **157a** ph Andrew Wood/an apartment in The San Remo on the Upper West Side of Manhattan, designed by John L. Stewart and Michael D'Arcy of SIT; **157c** ph Ray Main/Gai Harris's apartment in London designed by François Gilles and Dominique Lubar, IPL Interiors; **157b** ph Ray Main/John Howell's loft in London

designed by Circus Architects; **158b** ph Ray Main/Vicente Wolf's house on Long Island, lights designed by Vicente Wolf; **158cr** ph Ray Main/Greg Yale's house in Southampton, New York; **158br** ph Ray Main/Nello Renault's loft in Paris; **158–159** ph Ray Main/an apartment in New York designed by Laura Bohn Design Associates, Inc.; **159l** ph Andrew Wood/Jane Collins of Sixty 6 in Marylebone High Street, home in central London; **159ar** ph Ray Main/Lee F. Mindel's apartment in New York, lighting designed by Johnson Schwinghammer; **159br** ph Ray Main/Greg Yale's house in Southampton, New York; **160a** ph Chris Everard/Simon Crookall's apartment in London designed by Urban Salon, light courtesy of London Lighting; **160b** ph Andrew Wood/Heidi Kingstone's apartment in London; **161l** ph Ray Main/a loft in London designed by Nico Rensch; **161ar** ph Ray Main/Malin Iovino's apartment in London; **161br** ph Ray Main/Andrea Luria & Zachary Feuer's house in Los Angeles designed by Studio Works, Robert Mangurian & Mary-Ann Ray; **162al** ph Ray Main/an apartment in New York designed by Laura Bohn Design Associates, Inc.; **162cl** ph Ray Main/a house in Pennsylvania designed by Jeffrey Bilhuber, light from The Light Center; **162bl** ph Ray Main/an apartment in New York designed by Lucretia Moroni; **162ar** ph Ray Main; **162br** ph Ray Main/a house in London designed by François Gilles and Dominique Lubar, IPL Interiors; **163a** ph Ray Main/an apartment in New York designed by Laura Bohn Design Associates, Inc.; **163b** ph Ray Main/Nello Renault's loft in Paris; **164l** ph Chris Everard/Gentucca Bini's apartment in Milan; **164ar** ph Chris Everard; **164cr** ph Ray Main; **164br** ph Chris Everard/an apartment in Milan designed by Daniela Micol Wajskol, interior designer; **165ar & l** ph Ray Main/Malin Iovino's apartment in London; **165b** ph Andrew Wood/Nanna Ditzel's home in Copenhagen; **166al, ac & ar** ph Ray Main; **166bl** ph Ray Main/a house in East Hampton, interior by Vicente Wolf; **165cr & bc** ph Ray Main; **166br** ph Andrew Wood; **167l** ph Andrew Wood/an apartment in The San Remo on the Upper West Side of Manhattan, designed by John L. Stewart and Michael D'Arcy of SIT; **167r** ph Andrew Wood; **168al** ph Ray Main/light from Babylon Design; **167ac** ph Chris Everard/Christina Wilson's house in London, light courtesy of SCP; **168bl** ph Chris Everard/Jonathan Wilson's apartment in London, light courtesy of SCP; **168bc** ph Chris Everard/Glenn Carwithen & Sue Miller's house in London, light courtesy of Coexistence; **168br** ph Andrew Wood/Guido Palau's house in North London, designed by Azman Owens Architects; **168–169a** ph Andrew Wood/Freddie Daniells's loft apartment in London designed by Brookes Stacey Randall; **169bl** ph Chris Everard/Reuben Barrett's apartment in London, light courtesy of Purves & Purves; **169c** ph Chris Everard/Simon Crookall's apartment in London designed by Urban Salon, light courtesy of Geofrey Drayton; **169ar & br** ph Andrew Wood/Guido Palau's house in North London, designed by Azman Owens Architects; **170al** ph Ray Main/light from Ingo Maurer for London Lighting; **170bl** ph Ray Main/light from Tsé Tsé associées, Catherine Levy & Singoléné Prébois; **170ar** ph Ray Main/Greg Yale's house in Southampton, New York; **170cr** ph Catherine Gratwicke/an apartment in Paris designed by Bruno Tanquerel; **170br** ph Andrew Wood/the Pasadena, California home of Susan D'Avignon; **170–171a** ph Chris Everard/an apartment in London designed by Littman, Goddard & Hogarth; **171al** ph Chris Everard/Reuben Barrett's apartment in London, light courtesy of Purves & Purves; **171ar** ph Ray Main/light from Mathmos; **ph** Andrew Wood/The Caroline De Forest House in Pasadena, California, home to Michael Murray & Kelly Jones; **171bcl** ph Andrew Wood/Jane Collins of Sixty 6 in Marylebone High Street, home in central London; **171bcr** ph Ray Main/Lee F. Mindel's apartment in New York, lighting designed by Johnson Schwinghammer; **171br** ph Ray Main/light by Tom Kirk from Space; **172–173** ph Ray Main; **174al** ph Andrew Wood/Roger & Fay Oates's house in Herefordshire, The Long Barn, Eastnor, Ledbury, Herefordshire HR8 1EL (+44 1531 632718); **174cl** ph Chris Everard; **174bl** ph Chris Everard/Gentucca Bini's apartment in Milan; **174br** ph Chris Everard/David Mullman's apartment in New York designed by Mullman Seidman Architects; **174–175** ph Chris Everard/an apartment in New York designed by Steven Learner; **175bl** ph Chris Everard/Eric De Queker's apartment in Antwerp; **175ar** ph Henry Bourne; **175cr** ph Chris Everard/the London apartment of the Sheppard Day Design Partnership; **175br** ph Chris Everard/an apartment in London designed by Jo Hagan of USE Architects; **176 below, top row l** ph Henry Bourne; **top row r** ph Ray Main; **middle row l** ph Simon Upton; **middle row r** ph Tom Leighton; **bottom row both** ph Catherine Gratwicke; **176–177a** ph Chris Everard/an apartment in Antwerp designed by Claire Bataille & Paul ibens; **177al** ph Chris Everard/François Muracciole's apartment in Paris; **177ar** ph James Merrell/a house in Sydney designed by Luigi Rosselli; **177bl** ph Chris Everard/a house in Paris designed by Bruno Tanquerel; **177br** ph Chris Everard/Stephan Schulte's loft apartment in London; **178a** ph Simon Upton; **178b** ph James Merrell/Frédéric Méchiche's house near Toulon; **179bl** ph James Merrell/Khai Liew & Sue Kellett; **179ac** ph Andrew Wood/Bernie de Le Cuona's house in Windsor; **179c** ph Chris Everard; **179br** ph Andrew Wood; **179ar** ph Chris Everard/

an apartment in New York designed by Gabellini Associates; **179cr** *ph* Chris Everard; **180al & bl** *ph* Chris Everard; **180cl** *ph* Andrew Wood; **180ar** *ph* Chris Everard/Eric De Queker's apartment in Antwerp; **180br** *ph* Chris Everard/François Muracciole's apartment in Paris; **181** *ph* Chris Everard/Mrs Venturini's apartment in Milan; **182a** *ph* Chris Everard/Simon Crookall's apartment in London designed by Urban Salon, light courtesy of London Lighting; **182bl** *ph* Chris Everard/an apartment in Antwerp designed by Claire Bataille & Paul ibens; **182br** *ph* Ray Main/Jonathan Leitersdorf's apartment in New York designed by Jonathan Leitersdorf/Just Design; **183a** *ph* Ray Main/the contemplative space of Greville Worthington; **183c** *ph* Ray Main; **183bl** *ph* James Merrell; **183r** *ph* James Merrell/a house in Sydney designed by Interni Interior Design Consultancy; **184** *ph* Henry Bourne/Circus Architects/floor by First Floor; **185a** *ph* Henry Bourne; **185bl** *ph* Henry Bourne/John Raab's apartment in London/floor by Sinclair Till; **185br** *ph* James Merrell/Sue & Andy's apartment in Blackheath; **186al** *ph* James Merrell/an apartment in New York designed by Marino & Giolito; **186al** *ph* Chris Everard; **186–187** *ph* Henry Bourne/Richard Mabb & Kate Green's apartment in London; **187a** *ph* Henry Bourne/a house in London designed by Charles Rutherfoord; **187b** *ph* Henry Bourne/an apartment in London designed by Emily Todhunter; **188al** *ph* Henry Bourne/a mews house in London designed by McDowell & Benedetti; **188bl** *ph* Henry Bourne/rug by Christopher Farr; **188ar** *ph* Henry Bourne/an apartment in London designed by Ash Sakula Architects; **188br** *ph* Chris Everard/an apartment in London designed by Jo Hagan of USE Architects; **189al** *ph* Andrew Wood/Jane Collins of Sixty 6 in Marylebone High Street, home in central London; **189bl** *ph* Andrew Wood/Roger & Suzy Black's apartment in London designed by Johnson Naylor; **189ar** *ph* Henry Bourne/designed by François Gilles & Dominique Lubar, IPL Interiors/floor by Helen Yardley; **189br** *ph* Polly Wreford/Louise Jackson's house in London; **190al** *ph* Henry Bourne/Roger & Fay Oates's house in Herefordshire; **190ac** *ph* James Merrell/a house in London designed by François Gilles & Dominique Lubar, IPL Interiors; **190ar** *ph* Ray Main/client's residence, East Hampton, New York, designed by ZG DESIGN; **190b** *ph* Andrew Wood/Heidi Kingstone's apartment in London; **191al & b** *ph* Andrew Wood/Roger Oates and Fay Morgan's house in Eastnor; **191ar** *ph* Andrew Wood/a house near Antwerp designed by Claire Bataille & Paul ibens; **192–193** *ph* Polly Wreford; **194al** *ph* Andrew Wood/Vanessa & Robert Fairer's studio in London designed by Woolf Architects (+44 20 7428 9500); **194cl** *ph* Andrew Wood/Roger Oates and Fay Morgan's house in Eastnor; **194bl** *ph* Jan Baldwin/a house in Cape Elizabeth designed by Stephen Blatt Architects; **194r** *ph* Andrew Wood/a house in London designed by François Gilles and Dominique Lubar, IPL Interiors; **195a** *ph* James Merrell; **195b** *ph* Chris Everard/an apartment in Milan designed by Nicoletta Marazza; **196al** *ph* Tom Leighton; **196ar** *ph* Polly Wreford/an apartment in New York designed by Belmont Freeman Architects; **196–197** *ph* Henry Bourne/Frédéric Méchiche's apartment in Paris; **197al** *ph* Chris Everard/interior designer Ann Boyd's own apartment in London; **197ac** *ph* Andrew Wood/Ian Bartlett & Christine Walsh's house in London; **197r** *ph* Verity Welstead/Lulu Guinness's house in London; **198al, ac & cl** *ph* Andrew Wood/a house in London designed by Guy Stansfeld (+44 20 7727 0133); **198bl & br** *ph* Tom Leighton; **198–199** *ph* Alan Williams/Katie Bassford King's house in London designed by Touch Interior Design; **199bl** *ph* Chris Everard/Mark Weinstein's apartment in New York designed by Lloyd Schwan; **199ar** *ph* Tam Nhu Tran/Ian Chee's apartment in London; **200al** *ph* Fritz von der Schulenburg/Frédéric Méchiche's apartment in Paris; **200ar** *ph* Andrew Wood/Paula Pryke's house in London; **200bl** *ph* Chris Everard/an apartment in Antwerp designed by Claire Bataille & Paul ibens; **201l** *ph* James Morris/a house in Wiltshire designed by Ken Shuttleworth; **201ar** *ph* Chris Everard/interior designer Ann Boyd's own apartment in London; **202a** *ph* Andrew Wood; **202bl & br** *ph* Chris Everard/Mark Weinstein's apartment in New York designed by Lloyd Schwan; **203** *ph* Andrew Wood; **204al** *ph* James Merrell/a house in London designed by stylist Baba Bolli/kitchen by Smallbone; **204bl** *ph* Andrew Wood/Dawna & Jerry Walter's house in London; **204cb** *ph* Ray Main/Thierry Watorek's house near Paris; **204br & 204–205a** *ph* Andrew Wood/a house in London designed by François Gilles and Dominique Lubar, IPL Interiors; **205b** *ph* Simon Upton; **205c** *ph* Tom Leighton/Siobhan Squire and Gavin Lyndsey's loft in London designed by Will White, 326 Portobello Road, London W10 5RU (+44 20 8964 8052); **205r** *ph* Andrew Wood/Ian Bartlett & Christine Walsh's house in London; **206a** *ph* Andrew Wood/Vanessa & Robert Fairer's studio in London designed by Woolf Architects (+44 20 7428 9500); **206b** *ph* Andrew Wood; **206–207** *ph* Chris Everard/Gentucca Bini's apartment in Milan; **207a** *ph* Andrew Wood; **207bl** *ph* Polly Wreford/Jen Harte's apartment in New York, home of 27.12 Design Ltd, Chelsea NYC; **207br** *ph* Andrew Wood/Dawna & Jerry Walter's house in London; **208–209** *ph* James Merrell; **210a** *ph* James Merrell/Interni Interior Design Consultancy; **210b** *ph* James Merrell/a house in London designed by François Gilles & Dominique Lubar, IPL Interiors; **211al** *ph*

James Merrell/designed by Charlotte Barnes; **211ar** *ph* James Merrell/an apartment in New York designed by Jacqueline Coumans, Le Décor Français with the help of Olivier Glebsmann; **211bl** *ph* James Merrell/Amy & Richard Sachs's apartment in New York designed by Vicente Wolf; **211cr** *ph* Polly Wreford/Glenn Carwithen & Sue Miller's house in London; **211br** *ph* James Merrell/Vicente Wolf's apartment in New York; **212al** *ph* Simon Upton; **212cl** *ph* James Morris/The Lew House, originally designed by Richard Neutra in 1958, architect and contractor Marmol Radziner + Associates, Architecture and Construction; **212bl** *ph* James Merrell/Nigel Greenwood's apartment in London; **212cr** *ph* James Merrell/Interni Interior Design Consultancy; **212bc & br** *ph* James Merrell; **212–213a** *ph* James Morris/a loft in London designed by Simon Conder Associates; **213cl & bl** *ph* James Merrell; **213ar** *ph* James Merrell/a house in London designed by François Gilles & Dominique Lubar, IPL Interiors; **214l & r** *ph* Polly Wreford/the Sawmills Studio; **214c** *ph* James Merrell; **215l** *ph* Ray Main/Nello Renault's loft in Paris; **215ar** *ph* James Merrell/Larcombe & Soloman; **215br** *ph* Christopher Drake/Nelly Guyot's house in Ramatuelle, France, styled by Nelly Guyot; **216al** *ph* James Merrell; **216bl** *ph* James Merrell/an apartment in New York, architect Campion A. Platt; **216ar** *ph* James Merrell/a house in London designed by François Gilles & Dominique Lubar, IPL Interiors; **217al** *ph* James Merrell/designed by Charlotte Barnes; **217bl** *ph* Polly Wreford/Daniel Jasiak's apartment in Paris; **217r** *ph* James Merrell/Frédéric Méchiche's house near Toulon; **218al & bl** *ph* James Merrell; **218–219a** *ph* James Merrell/Nigel Greenwood's apartment in London; **218–219b** *ph* James Merrell/an apartment in London designed by François Gilles & Dominique Lubar, IPL Interiors; **219cr** *ph* James Merrell/an apartment in London designed by Charles Rutherfoord; **219ar, br & bc** *ph* James Merrell; **220al** *ph* James Merrell/a house in Sydney designed by Interni Interior Design Consultancy; **220bl** *ph* James Merrell/Richard Ronald's house in London; **220ar** *ph* James Merrell/Nigel Greenwood's apartment in London; **220br** *ph* David Montgomery/Annabel Astor's house in London is full of furniture and accessories designed exclusively for her OKA Direct Mail Order Catalogue; **221a** *ph* Ray Main/a house in East Hampton, interior by Vicente Wolf; **221b** *ph* James Merrell/Amy & Richard Sachs's apartment in New York designed by Vicente Wolf; **222a** *ph* James Merrell/Andrew Parr's house in Melbourne; **222bl** *ph* James Merrell/Kelly Hoppen's apartment in London; **222br** *ph* James Merrell/William Hayes & Annie Har's house near Brisbane; **223al** *ph* James Merrell; **223bl** *ph* James Merrell/Robyn & Simon Carnachan's house in Auckland; **223ar** *ph* Ray Main/a house in London designed by Seth Stein and Sarah Delaney; **223br** *ph* Ray Main/a house in London designed by Mark Guard Architects; **224** *ph* James Merrell/Kelly Hoppen's apartment in London; **225 main** *ph* Christopher Drake/Marisa Cavalli's home in Milan; **225 all details** *ph* James Merrell **except 225bl & ac** *ph* David Montgomery; **226–227** *ph* Polly Wreford; **228bl** *ph* James Merrell; **228ar & 228–229** *ph* Polly Wreford/Ros Fairman's house in London; **229ar** *ph* Alan Williams/owner of Gloss, Pascale Bredillet's own apartment in London; **229br** *ph* Polly Wreford/Clare Nash's house in London; **230al** *ph* Andrew Wood; **230acl** *ph* Andrew Wood/Bernie de Le Cuona's home in Windsor; **230bcl** *ph* Polly Wreford; **230bl** *ph* David Montgomery/Annabel Astor's house in London is full of furniture and accessories designed exclusively for her OKA Direct Mail Order Catalogue; **230c** *ph* David Montgomery; **230ar** *ph* Polly Wreford/The Sawmills Studio; **230br** *ph* Henry Bourne; **231ar** *ph* Chris Everard; **231br** *ph* Simon Upton; **232al** *ph* Polly Wreford/Glenn Carwithen & Sue Miller's house in London; **230bl & c** *ph* Polly Wreford; **232ar** *ph* Polly Wreford/Ros Fairman's house in London; **232br** *ph* Andrew Wood/a house in London designed by Bowles & Linares; **233l** *ph* Alan Williams/Janice Kirkpatrick's apartment in Glasgow, director of design consultants Graven Images; **233ar** *ph* Catherine Gratwicke/antique mirrored bedthrow from the Gallery of Antique Costume & Textiles, striped throw from Selfridges; **233cr** *ph* Catherine Gratwicke/Agnès Emery's house in Brussels, tiles and bedding from Emery & Cie; **233br** *ph* Polly Wreford/an apartment in New York designed by Belmont Freeman Architects; **234al** *ph* Polly Wreford/Mary Foley's house in Connecticut; **234ar** *ph* Henry Bourne; **234b & 235al & ar** *ph* David Montgomery/Sasha Waddell's house in London; **235bcl** *ph* Polly Wreford/Daniel Jasiak's apartment in Paris; **235b** *ph* Polly Wreford/Adria Ellis's apartment in New York; **236al** *ph* Andrew Wood/Mary Shaw's Sequana apartment in Paris; **236bl** *ph* Andrew Wood/Bernie de Le Cuona's home in Windsor; **236ar & cr** *ph* Polly Wreford/Kimberly Watson's house in London; **236br, 237al & bl** *ph* James Merrell; **237r** *ph* Chris Everard/interior designer Ann Boyd's own apartment in London; **238l** *ph* James Merrell/Gabriele Sanders's apartment in New York; **238–239a** *ph* Tom Leighton/Roger & Fay Oates's house in Herefordshire, The Long Barn, Eastnor, Ledbury, Herefordshire HR8 1EL (+44 1531 632718); **238–239b** *ph* Alan Williams/owner of Gloss, Pascale Bredillet's own apartment in London; **239** *ph* Polly Wreford/Liz Stirling's apartment in Paris; **endpapers** *ph* Andrew Wood/Charlotte Crosland's home in London, designed by Charlotte Crosland, Wingrave Crosland Interiors.

ARCHITECTS & DESIGNERS WHOSE WORK IS FEATURED IN THIS BOOK:

Elizabeth Alford Design
60 Thomas Street
New York
NY 10013
t. 212 385 2185
f. 212 385 2186
e. esa799@banet.net
Page 125al

Anthropologie
375 West Broadway
New York
NY 10012
Pages 27br, 63br

Nicholas Arbuthnott
Arbuthnott Ladenbury
Architects
15 Gosditch Street
Cirencester GL7 2AG UK
*Architects & urban
designers.*
Pages 24b, 83ar, 147al, 150a

Vanessa Arbuthnott Fabrics
The Tallet, Calmsden
Cirencester GL7 5ET UK
www.vanessaarbuthnott.co.uk
Pages 24b, 83ar, 147al, 150a

Asfour Guzy
594 Broadway, Suite 1204
New York
NY 10012
t. 212 334 9350
f. 212 334 9009
Page 156

Ash Sakula Architects
Studio 115
38 Mount Pleasant
London WC1X 0AN UK
t. +44 20 7837 9735
Pages 58al & ar, 188ar

Susie Atkinson Design
t. +44 468 814 134
Page 126bl

Azman Owens Architects
8 St Albans Place
London NW1 0NX UK
t. +44 20 7354 2955
f. +44 20 7354 2966
Pages 168br, 169ar&br

Babylon Design Ltd
301 Fulham Road
London SW10 9QH UK
t. +44 20 7376 7233
e. info@babylon
    design.demon.co.uk
*Lighting designers. Lights
by up-and-coming
designers such as Peter
Wylly, Ross Menuez, and
Roland Simmons.*
Page 168al

Barefoot Elegance
3537 Old Conejo Road
Suite 105
Newbury Park
CA 91320
t. 805 499 5959
*Dot Spikings & Jennifer
Castle, Interior Designers.*
Pages 67a, 132br

Charlotte Barnes Interiors
26 Stanhope Gardens
London SW7 5QX UK
*An interior decorator,
Charlotte Barnes provides
elegant, beautiful, and
practical solutions, tailored
to each client and property.*
Pages 211al, 217al

**Claire Bataille & Paul ibens
Design NV, Architects**
Vekestratt 13 Bus 14
2000 Antwerpen, Belgium
t. +32 3 231 3593
f. +32 3 213 8639
*Pages 11b, 13b, 102br, 106ar,
142–143, 176–177a, 182bl,
191ar, 200bl*

**Bedmar & Shi Designers
Pte Ltd**
12a Keong Saik Road
Singapore 089119
t. +65 22 77117
f. +65 22 77695
*A Singapore-based firm
established in 1980
specializing in residential
projects and interior
design, mainly for
restaurants and offices.*
Pages 94–95b

**Michael Benevento
Orange Group**
515 Broadway
New York
NY 10012
t. 212 965 8617
Page 81a

Bruce Bierman Design, Inc.
29 West 15th Street
New York
NY 10011
t. 212 243 1935
f. 212 243 6615
www.Biermandesign.com
*Residential interior
design firm.*
Page 148b

Bilhuber Inc.
330 East 59th Street
6th Floor
New York
NY 10022
t. 212 308 4888
Pages 31al, 162cl

**Laura Bohn Design
Associates, Inc.**
30 West 26th Street
New York
NY 10010
t. 212 645 3636
f. 212 645 3639
*Pages 30al, 49al&ar,
158–159, 162al, 163a*

Felix Bonnier
7 rue St Claude
75003 Paris, France
t. +33 42 26 09 83
Pages 47al, cl & ar

Bowles & Linares
32 Hereford Road
London W2 5AJ UK
t. +44 20 7229 9886
Pages 102al, 145a, 232br

Ann Boyd Design Ltd
33 Elystan Street
London SW3 3NT UK
t. +44 20 7591 0202
Pages 33b, 197al, 201ar, 237r

Nancy Braithwaite Interiors
2300 Peachtree Road
Suite C101
Atlanta
Georgia 30309
Page 103ar & br

**Sabrina Fay Braxton
Cloth of Gold**
Grennan Watermill
Thomastown
Co Kilknenny, Ireland
t. +353 565 4383
by appointment in New York:
t. 212 535 2587
by appointment in Paris:
t. +33 1 46 57 11 62
Page 35a

**Caroline Breet
Caroline's Antiek &
Brocante**
Nieuweweg 35A
1251 LH Laren, Holland
Page 22br

Briffa Philips
19–21 Holywell Hill
St Albans
Hertfordshire AL1 1EZ UK
t. +44 1727 840 567
Pages 70a, 70–71

Brookes Stacey Randall
New Hibernia House
Winchester Walk
London SE1 9AG UK
t. +44 20 7403 0707
f. +44 20 7403 0880
e. info@bsr-architects.com
Pages 101br, 168–169a

Hugh Broughton Architects
4 Addison Bridge Place
London W14 8XP UK
t. +44 20 7602 8840
f. +44 20 7602 5254
e. hugh@hbarchitects.
    demon.co.uk
Award-winning architects.
Page 18ar

Buildburo Design & Build
Unit 4, Iliffe Yard
Crampton Street
London SE17 3QA UK
t. +44 20 7708 2538
f. +44 20 7277 2104
e. gordanamandic@
    buildburo.co.uk
e. petertyler@buildburo.co.uk
www.buildburo.co.uk
Pages 21ar, 153br

Cabot Design Ltd
1925 Seventh Avenue
Suite 71
New York
NY 10026
t. 212 222 9488
e. eocabot@aol.com
Interior design.
Pages 138–139

Milly de Cabrol Ltd
150 East 72nd Street
Suite 2–C
New York
NY 10021
Interior decorator.
Page 138a

Aude Cardinale, Designer
12 Avenue de Madrid
92000 Neuilly, France
Pages 63a, 141b

Garth Carter
t. +44 958 412953
Specialist interiors painter.
Page 97bl

Marisa Tadiotto Cavalli
via Solferino, 11
20121 Milano, Italy
t. +39 03 48 41 01 738
    +39 02 86 46 24 26
f. +39 02 29 00 18 60
e. marisscavalli@hotmail.com
Pages 148al, 225 main

**Alexandra Champalimaud &
Associates Inc.**
One Union Square West, #3
New York
NY 10003
t. 212 807 8869
f. 212 807 1742
www.acainteriordesign.com
*Interior architecture and
design.*
Page 88al

Ian Chee VX Designs
t. +44 20 7370 5496
Page 199ar

Circus Architects
Unit 1, Summer Street
London EC1r 5BD UK
t. +44 20 7833 1999
*Pages 19br, 122, 123al, 157b,
184*

Simon Conder Associates
Nile Street Studios
8 Nile Street
London N1 7RF UK
t. +44 20 7251 2144
f. +44 20 7251 2145
e. simon@simonconder.co.uk
Architects & designers.
Pages 100, 212–213a

Conner Prairie Museum
134000 Alisonville Road
Fishers
Indiana 46038
Pages 25al, 150bl

**Jaqueline Coumans
Le Décor Français**
1006 Lexington Avenue
New York
NY 10021
t. 212 734 0032
f. 212 988 0816
Page 211ar

**Charlotte Crosland
Wingrave Crosland Interiors**
t. +44 20 8960 9442
Endpapers

Carden Cunietti
83 Westbourne Park Road
London W2 5QH UK
t. +44 20 7229 8559
f. +44 20 7229 8799
www.carden-cunietti.com
Pages 20ac, 105bl

Barbara Davis
t. 607 264 36736
Interior design; antique hand-dyed linen, wool, and silk textiles by the yard; soft furnishings & clothes to order.
Pages 22ar, 24a, 26bl, 76bl, 130al, 131br

De Le Cuona Textile Home Collection
Head Office:
9–10 Osborne Mews
Windsor SL4 3DE UK
e. bernie@softech.co.uk
Please call De Le Cuona for stockists: +44 1753 830301
Pages 12–13, 15cl, 15bl, 62, 179ac, 230bcl, 236bl

Eric De Queker
DQ Design In Motion
Koninklijkelaan 44
2600 Bercham, Belgium
Pages 69al&r, 88bl, 175bl, 180ar

De Metz Architects
Unit 4, 250 Finchley Road
London NW3 6DN UK
t. +44 20 7435 1144
Page 80

Ischa van Delft
September
Vughterstraat 72
5211 GK's Hertogenbosch
Holland
Interior decorator.
Page 66a

Nanna Ditzel MDD FCSD
Nanna Ditzel Design
Klareboderne 4
DK-1115 Copenhagen K
Denmark
www.nanna.ditzel.design.dk
Industrial designer specializing in furniture, textiles, jewelry, & exhibitions.
Page 165b

Agnès Emery
Emery & Cie and Noir D'Ivorie
Rue de l'Hôpital 25–29
Brussels, Belgium
t. +32 2 513 5892
f. +32 5 513 3970
Page 233cr

Jamie Falla
MooArc
198 Blackstock Road
London N5 1EN UK
t. +44 20 7345 1729
Page 70bl, cl & br

Han Feng, Fashion Designer
333 West 39th Street
12th Floor
New York
NY 10018
t. 212 695 9509
Page 71a & b

Ken Foreman, Architect
105 Duane Street
New York
NY 10007
t./f. 212 924 4503
Page 4

Belmont Freeman Architects
Sangho Park
110 West 40th Street
New York
NY 10018
t. 212 382 3311
f. 212 730 1229
Project Team: Belmont Freeman (Principal Designer), Alane Truitt.
Pages 196ar, 233br

Full House
38 Renwick Street
New York
NY 10013
t. 646 486 4151
Page 34b

Gabellini Associates
665 Broadway, Suite 706
New York
NY 10012
t. 212 388 1700
f. 212 388 1808
Michael Gabellini A.I.A., Principal designer. Dan Garbowit A.I.A., Managing Principal. Ralph Bellandi, Sal Tranchina, Jonathan Knowles A.I.A., Project Architects. Stephanie Kim, Lisa Monteleone, Tom Vandenbout, Project Team.
Pages 63bl, 87al, 179ar

Zina Glazebrook
ZG Design
10 Wireless Road
East Hampton
NY 11937
t. 631 329 7486
f. 631 329 2087
e. dzina@ATT.net
www.zgdesign.com
Page 190ar

Gloss Ltd
274 Portobello Road
London W10 5TE UK
t. +44 20 8960 4146
f. +44 20 89604842
e. pascale@
   glossltd.u-net.com
Designers of home accessories.
Pages 229ar, 238–239b

Russell Glover, Architect
e. russellglover@earthlink.net
Pages 91bl&br

James Gorst Architects
35 Lamb's Conduit Street
London WC1N 3NG UK
t. +44 20 7831 8300
Page 30br

Hester Gray
25 Pembridge Villas
London W11 3EP UK
t. +44 20 7229 3162
Page 18bl

Mark Guard Architects
161 Whitfield Street
London W1P 5RY UK
t. +44 20 7380 1199
Page 223br

Nelly Guyot
12 rue Marthe Edouard
92190 Meudon, France
Interior designer & photographic stylist.
Pages 22al, 215br

Yves Halard Interior Decoration
27 Quai de la Tournelle
75005 Paris, France
t. +33 1 4407 14 00
f. +33 1 44 07 1030
Page 152bl

Annie Har
Sunnit Architects
10 Attunga Lane
Mount Glorious
Queensland 4520, Australia
Page 222br

William R. Hefner A.I.A.
William Hefner Architect L.L.C.
5820 Wilshire Boulevard
Suite 601
Los Angeles
CA 90036
t. 323 931 1365
f. 323 931 1368
e. wh@williamhefner.com
www.williamhefner.com
Page 112b

Alastair Hendy
f. +44 20 7739 6040
Food writer, art director, and designer.
Pages 16ar, 21b, 104al

Hirst Pacific Ltd
250 Lafayette Street
New York
NY 10012
t. 212 625 3670
f. 212 625 3673
e. hirstpacific@earthlink.net
Page 111br

HM2 Architects
33–37 Charterhouse Square
London EC1M 6EA UK
t. +44 20 7600 5151
f. +44 20 7600 1092
e. andrew.hanson@
   harper-mackay.co.uk
Architects & designers. Richard Webb, Project Director. Andrew Hanson, Director.
Pages 102bl, 149l, 151a

The Holding Company
243–245 Kings Road
London SW3 5EL UK
t. +44 20 7352 1600
Innovative storage solutions for every room in the home.
Pages 107r, 204bl, 207br

Kelly Hoppen Interiors
2 Alma Studios
32 Stratford Road
London W8 6QF UK
Pages 222bl, 224

Hotel de la Mirande
Avignon, France
Page 218

Hotel Villa Gallici
Aix-en-Provence, France
Page 218

Jack Ingham
Bookworks
34 Ansleigh Place
London W11 4BW UK
t. +44 20 7792 8310
Page 47bl & br

Interni Pty Ltd
15–19 Boundary Street
Rushcutters Bay
Sydney 2010, Australia
Interior design consultancy.
Pages 48a, 183r 210a, 212cr, 220al

Malin Iovino Design
t. +44 20 7252 3542
f. +44 20 7252 3542
e. iovino@btinternet.com
Pages 121br, 161ar, 165ar & l

IPL Interiors
François Gilles & Dominique Lubar
Unit 26C1
Thames House
140 Battersea Park Road
London SW11 4NY UK
Pages 18al, 31ar, 50b, 59br, 157c, 162br, 190ac, 194r, 204br, 204–205a, 210b, 213ar, 216ar, 218–219b

Jacomini Interior Design
1701 Brun, Suite 101
Houston
Texas 77019
Pages 27al, 152al, 212al

Daniel Jasiak, Designer
12 rue Jean Ferrandi
Paris 75006, France
t. +33 1 45 49 13 56
f. +33 1 45 49 23 66
Pages 217bl, 235bcl

Joanna Jefferson Architects
222 Oving Road
Chichester
West Sussex PO19 4EJ UK
t. +44 1243 532398
f. +44 1243 531 550
e. jjeffearch@aol.com
Page 132ar

Brian Johnson
Johnson Naylor
13 Britton Street
London EC1M 5SX UK
t. +44 20 7490 8885
f. +44 20 7490 0038
e. brian.johnson@
   johnsonnaylor.co.uk
Pages 15ar, 68l, 72, 82–83, 83al, 189bl

Just Design Ltd
80 Fifth Avenue, 18th Floor
New York
NY 10011
t. 212 243 6544
f. 212 229 1112
e. wbp@angel.net
Pages 36b, 182br

Ben Kelly Design
10 Stoney Street
London SE1 9AD UK
t. +44 20 7378 8116
f. +44 20 7378 8366
e. bkduk@dircon.co.uk
Page 89al

Khai Liew Design
166 Magill Road
Norwood
South Australia 5067
Australia
Page 179bl

Robert E. Kinnaman & Brian A. Ramaekers Inc.
2466 Montauk Highway
Bridgehampton
NY 11932
Postal address:
P.O. Box 1140
Wainscott
NY 11975
t. 516 537 0779
American folk art & early painted furniture.
Page 22cl

KRD Kitchen Rogers Design
t. +44 20 8944 7088
e. ab@krd.demon.co.uk
Pages 118c, 120al

Bruno & Hélène Lafforgue
Mas de l'Ange
Maison d'Hôte
Petite route de St. Remy-de Provence
13946 Mollégès, France
Page 178al & ar

Larcombe & Soloman Architects
Level 3, 397 Riley Street
Surry Hills 2010
New South Wales, Australia
Pages 13a, 215ar

Steven Learner Studio
307 Seventh Avenue
New York
NY 10001
t. 212 741 8583
f. 212 741 2180
www.stevenlearner
   studio.com
Pages 54r, 76ar, 87br, 107al,
174–175

Littman Goddard Hogarth Architects
12 Chelsea Wharf
15 Lots Road
London SW10 0QJ UK
t. +44 20 7351 7871
f. +44 20 7351 4110
www.lgh-architects.co.uk
Pages 82al & bl, 99al & ar,
99c, 170–171a

Dale Loth Architects
1 Cliff Road
London NW1 9AJ UK
t. +44 20 7485 4003
f. +44 20 7284 44920
e. mail@daleloth
   architects.ltd.uk
Pages 96c&br, 104bl, 153bl

Hilton McConnico
8 rue Antoine Panier
93170 Bagnolet, France
t. +33 1 43 62 53 16
f. +33 1 43 62 73 44
e. hmc@club-internet.fr
Interior home designer.
Page 95

McDowell + Benedetti
62 Rosebury Avenue
London EC1R 4RR UK
t. +44 20 7278 8810
Pages 53b, 188al

Nicoletta Marazza
via G Morone, 8
20121 Milan, Italy
t./f. +39 2 7601 4482
Pages 77b, 131ar, 185b

Marino + Giolito
161 West 16th Street
New York
NY 10011
t./f. 212 675 5737
Pages 110al, 186al

Andy Martin
Fin Architects and Designers
73 Wells Street
London W1P 3RD UK
e. finbox@globalnet.co.uk
Page 104ar

Marshall Haines & Barrow
35 Alfred Place
London WC1E 7DP UK
Page 57ar

Frédéric Méchiche
4 rue de Thorigny
75003 Paris, France
Pages 97ar, 178b, 196–197,
200al, 217r

Jean-Louis Ménard
32 Boulevard de l'Hôpital
75005 Paris, France
t. +33 43 36 31 74
Page 105br

Philippe Model
33 Place du Marché St.
   Honoré
75001 Paris, France
t. +33 1 4296 8902
Decoration, home furnishing & coverings.
Pages 174cl, 179cl, 180al

The Moderns
900 Broadway, Suite 903
New York
NY 10003
t. 212 387 8852
f. 212 387 8824
e. moderns@aol.com
Page 30bl

Belén Moneo & Jeff Brock
Moneo Brock Studio
371 Broadway, 2nd Floor
New York
NY 10013 USA
t. 212 625 0308
f. 212 625 0309
e. moneo@aol.com
Architecture & interior design.
Page 118al & b

L. A. Morgan, Interior Designer
P.O. Box 39
Hadlyme
CT 06439 USA
t. 860 434 0304
f. 860 434 3013
Page 14al

Lynn Morgan Design
19 Hilltop Road
Norwalk
CT 06854
t. 203 854 5037
Page 26c

Charles Morris Mount
300 West 108th Street/2c
New York
NY 10025
t. 212 864 2937
Page 54al & bl

Mullman Seidman Architects
443 Greenwich Street
New York
NY 10013
t. 212 431 0770
f. 212 431 8428
e. mullseid@monmouth.com
Architecture & interior design.
Pages 74b, 174br

François Muracciole, Architect
54 rue de Montreuil
75011 Paris, France
t. +33 1 43 71 33 03
e. francois.muracciole@
   libertysurf.fr
Pages 73b, 177al, 180br

Claire Nelson
Nelson Design
169 St John's Hill
London SW11 1TQ UK
t. +44 20 7924 4542
Pages 17, 33cr

Roger Oates Design
The Long Barn
Eastnor
Ledbury
Herefordshire HR8 1EL UK
t. +44 1531 631611
Pages 12l, 97br, 174al,
190al, 191al&b, 194cl,
238–239a

OKA Direct
www.okadirect.com
For a catalogue, please call
+44 870 160 6002.
A unique collection of mail-order furniture & home accessories including rattan, painted furniture, leather, and horn.
Pages 33ac, 220br, 230bl

Orefelt Associates
4 Portobello Studios
5 Haydens Place
London W11 1LY UK
t. +44 20 7243 3181
f. +44 20 7792 1126
e. orefelt@msn.com
Design Team: Gunner Orefelt, John Massey, Gianni Botsford, Jason Griffiths.
Pages 15cr, 104cl

Parnassus
Corso Porta Vittoria, 5
Milan, Italy
t. +39 02 78 11 07
Pages 26br, 56bl&ac

Andrew Parr
SJB Interior Design Pty, Ltd
Studio Southbank
5 Haig Street
South Melbourne 3205
Australia
Page 222a

Plain English Kitchen Design
The Tannery
Tannery Road
Coombs, Stowmarket
Suffolk IP14 2EN UK
Pages 133al, 138bl

Campion A. Platt
64l Fifth Avenue
New York
NY 10022
Page 216bl

Jennifer Post Design
25 East 67th Street, 8D
New York
NY 10021
t. 212 734 7994
f. 212 396 2450
e. jpostdesign@aol.com
Spatial & interior designer.
Pages 16bl, 29ar, 32b, 84bl,
143bl&ar

Géraldine Prieur, Interior Designer
7 rue Faraday
75017 Paris, France
t. +33 1 44 40 29 12
f. +33 1 44 40 29 17
Page 140b

Lena Proudlock
Denim in Style
Drews House
Leighterton
Gloucestershire GL8 8UN UK
t./f. +44 1666 890230
Pages 26a, 147bl & ar

Brian Purcell, Artist
436 Fort Washington Avenue
New York
NY 10033
Page 86

Mark Pynn A.I.A.
McMillen Pynn Architecture LLP
P.O. Box 1068
Sun Valley
Idaho 83353
t. 208 622 4656
f. 208 726 7108
e. mpynn@sunvally.net
www.sunvallyarchitect.com
Page 89bl

Reed Creative Services Ltd
151a Sydney Street
London SW3 6NT UK
t. +44 20 7565 0066
Pages 29br, 30ar, 32c, 33al

Nico Rensch Architeam
t. +44 411 412 898
Pages 67b, 90ac&ar,
118–119, 161l

Johanne Riss
35 Place du Nouveau
   Marché aux Graens
1000 Brussels, Belguim
t. +32 2 513 0900
f. +32 2 514 3284
Stylist, designer, & fashion designer.
Pages 82ar, 84ar

Frances Robinson
Detail
t. +44 20 7582 9564
f. +44 20 7587 3783
Jewelry designers & consultants.
Page 111bl

Richard Ronald
c/o Manuel Canovas
2 North Terrace
London SW3 2BA UK
Page 220bl

Luigi Rosselli
Surry Hills
2010 Sydney
New South Wales, Australia
t. +61 2 9281 1498
Page 177ar

Charles Rutherfoord
51 The Chase
London SW4 0NP UK
Pages 20al, 104br, 187a, 219cr

Sage Wimer Coombe Architects
480 Canal Street Room 1002
New York
NY 10013
t. 212 226 9600
Project Team: Jennifer Sage, Peter Coombe, Suzan Selcuk, Peggy Tan.
Pages 28a, 31cr, 113bl, 120a, 131al

Sophie Sarin
c/o The Ground Floor
201 Mitcham Lane
London SE16 6PW UK
t. +44 20 8769 4204
Page 45

Sheila Scholes, Designer
t. +44 1480 498 241
Pages 14b, 130cl

Lloyd Schwan/Design
195 Chrystie Street, # 908
New York
NY 10002
t. 212 375 0858
f. 212 375 0887
Pages 21al, 66b, 199bl, 202bl & br

Johnson Schwinghammer
339 West 38th Street # 9
New York
NY 10018
t. 212 643 1552
Pages 159ar, 171bcr

Sequana
64 Avenue de la Motte Picquet
75015 Paris, France
t. +33 1 45 66 58 40
f. +33 1 45 67 99 81
e. sequana@wandoo.fr
Page 236al

Sharland & Lewis
45 Long Street
Tetbury
Gloucestershire UK
t. +44 1666 502440
Page 22bl, 96al

Shelton, Mindel & Associates
216 West 18th Street
New York
NY 10011
t. 212 243 3939
Pages 159ar, 171bcr

Sheppard Day Design
t. +44 20 7821 2002
Pages 28br, 83b, 94–95a, 175cr

Ann Shore
t./f. +44 20 7377 6377
London-based designer & stylist, owner of Story. Personal selection of old and new furniture and accessories. Appointment only.
Pages 10, 58br

Stephen Slan A.I.A.
Variations In Architecture Inc.
2156 Hollyridge Drive
Los Angeles
CA 90068
t. 323 467 4455
f. 323 467 6655
Page 31b

Nigel Smith, Architect
t. +44 20 7278 8802
e. n-smith@dircon.co.uk
Page 103al

Henry Smith-Miller and Laurie Hawkinson, Architects
305 Canal Street
New York
NY 10013
t. 212 966 3875
f. 212 966 3877
www.smharch.com
Pages 54–55

Enrica Stabile
via della Spiga, 46
Milan, Italy
t. +39 02 76 00 84 20
e. e.stabile@enrica stabile.com
www.enricastabile.com
Antiques dealer, interior decorator, & photographic stylist.
Pages 25bl, 27ar, 56bc, 123b

Seth Stein
15 Grand Union Centre
West Row
London W10 UK
t. +44 20 8968 8581
Pages 15br, 223ar

John L. Stewart CIT, L.L.C.
113–115 Bank Street
New York
NY 10014–2176
t. 212 620 777
f. 212 620 0770
e. JLSCollection@aol.com
Pages 157a, 167l

Stickland Coombe Architecture
258 Lavender Hill
London SW11 1LJ UK
t. +44 20 7924 1699
f. +44 20 7652 1788
e. nick@scadesign. freeserve.co.uk
Pages 19bl, 20b, 147br

Studio Works
6775 Centinela Avenue, Building #3
Culver City
CA 90230
t. 301 390 5051
f. 301 390 2763
Page 161br

Stutchbury & Pape Architecture + Landscape Architecture
4/364 Barrenjoey Road
Newport
New South Wales 2106
Australia
t. +61 2 9979 5030
f. +61 2 9979 5367
e. snpala@ozemail.com.au
Have a reputation for innovative thinking and environmental sensitivity. The land, site and place are seen as directives toward the solution of formulating a building.
Pages 84–85

Tia Swan Bed & Breakfast
Crooked House
P.O. Box 13
Knighton D O
Powys LD8 2WE UK
Page 22cr

Alan Tanksley, Inc.
114 East 32nd Street
Suite 1406
New York
NY 10016
t. 212 481 8458
f. 212 481 8456
Interior design.
Page 99b

Bruno Tanquerel, Artist
2 Passage St. Sébastien
75011 Paris, France
t. +33 1 43 57 03 93
Pages 101ac & al, 170cr, 171bl

Todhunter Earle Interiors
Chelsea Reach
1st Floor, 79–89 Lots Road
London SW10 0RN UK
t. +44 20 7349 9999
Pages 33ar, 187b

Touch Interior Design
t. +44 20 7498 6409
Pages 198–199

Tsao & McKown, Architects
20 Vandam Street
10th Floor
New York
NY 10013
t. 212 337 3800
f. 212 337 0013
Pages 20ar, 107bl & c

27.12 Design Ltd
451 Greenwich Street
Suite 504
New York
NY 10013
t. 212 334 5245
Pages 90c, 207bl

Urban Research Laboratory
3 Plantain Place
Crosby Row
London SE1 1YN UK
t. +44 20 7403 2929
e. jeff@urbanresearch lab.com
Pages 19al, 98, 105al, 152–153

Urban Salon Architects
Unit D, Flat Iron Yard
Ayres Street
London SE1 1ES UK
t. +44 20 7357 8000
Pages 64–65, 105ar, 160a, 169c, 182a

USE Architects
11 Northburgh Street
London EC1V 0AH UK
t. +44 20 7251 5559
f. +44 20 7253 5558
e. use.arch@virgin.net
Pages 175br, 188br

Sasha Waddell
269 Wandsworth Bridge Road
London SW6 2TX UK
t. +44 20 7736 0766
Pages 234b, 235al, 235ar

Miv Watts
House Bait Interior Decoration
Market Place
Burnham Market
Norfolk PE31 8HV UK
t. +44 1358 730557
f. +44 1485 52 8970
e. miv.watts@virgin.net
Page 77a

Bunny Williams Inc.
306 61st Street, Fifth Floor
New York
NY 10021–8752
Page 59cr

Vicente Wolf Associates, Inc.
333 West 39th Street
New York
NY 10018
t. 212 465 0590
Pages 35b, 74–75, 158b, 166bl, 211bl, 211br, 221a, 221b

Woolf Architects
39–51 Highgate Road
London NW5 1RT UK
t. +44 20 7428 9500
Pages 133ar, br & bl, 194al, 206a

Voon Wong Architects
Unit 27, 1 Stannary Street
London SW11 4AD UK
t. +44 20 7587 0116
f. +44 20 7840 0178
e. Voon@dircon.co.uk
Pages 16al, 19ar

Greg Yale Landscape Illumination
27 Henry Road
Southampton
NY 11968
t. 516 287 2312
f. 516 287 2182
Pages 158cr, 159br, 170ar

Bonnie Young
t./f. 212 228 0832
Director of global sourcing and inspiration, Donna Karan International.
Page 85al & ac

INDEX

Page numbers in *italic* refer to the illustrations

ACKNOWLEDGMENTS

In addition to the homeowners mentioned the publishers would like
to thank the following people:

Rodney Archer, Katsuji Asada, Ann Boyd, Caroline & Michael Breet,
Conner Prairie Museum, Ischa van Delft, Sherri Donghia & Robert Eulau, Tricia Foley,
Katie Fontana & Tony Niblock, Daniel Gabay, K. Russell Glover & Angela Miller, Janie Jackson,
Beverly Jacomini, Glen Senk & Keith Johnson of Anthroplogie, Monsieur Jouve, Marie Kalt,
Bruno & Hélène Lafforgue, James Lynch & Sian Tucker, Alf & Wendy Martensson, Ellen O'Neill,
Kristin Perers, Lena Proudlock, Lars Røtterud, Gabriele Sanders, Ann Shore, Dot Spikings,
Monsieur & Madame Stein, Mark & Tia Swan.